core JAVA

GARY CORNELL • CAY S. HORSTMANN

SunSoft Press
A Prentice Hall Title

The publisher offers discounts on this book when ordered in bulk quantities.
For more information, contact Corporate Sales Department, Prentice Hall PTR ,
One Lake Street, Upper Saddle River, NJ 07458. Phone: 800-382-3419; FAX: 201- 236-7141.
E-mail: corpsales@prenhall.com.

Editorial/production supervision: *Navta Associates*
Cover design director: *Jerry Votta*
Cover designer: *Anthony Gemellaro*
Cover illustration: *Karen Streleck*
Manufacturing manager: *Alexis R. Heydt*
Acquisitions editor: *Gregory G. Doench*
SunSoft Press publisher: *Rachel Borden*

10 9 8 7 6 5 4 3 2 1

ISBN 0-13-565755-5

SunSoft Press
A Prentice Hall Title

Contents

Chapter 4
Objects and Classes, 90

Chapter 9
Data Structures, 360

Preface

To the Reader

The Java language burst onto the scene in 1995 and was given instant celebrity status. While most computer languages do not inspire the popular press to grow rhapsodic, Java did. While most computer languages do not get coverage on radio and TV, Java did. Why?

The point and promise of Java is that it hopes to be the *universal glue* connecting users and information. It doesn't matter whether information is stored on Internet Web servers, databases, information providers, or any other imaginable source, Java will eventually let you use the Web to access this information, and more.

Java is an extremely solidly-engineered language. Its syntax seems instantly familiar to most programmers. Its security features are reassuring to both programmers and users of their programs. Java makes it easier to produce bug-free code than C or C++. Java has built-in support that makes advanced programming tasks, such as network programming and multithreading, straightforward and convenient.

This book is aimed at serious programmers who want to put Java to work on real projects. We assume that you have a solid background in a programming language such as C, C++, or Visual Basic. It would help, but is not necessary, to have some experience building graphical user interfaces in Windows, Unix or the Macintosh. If you want to write real code and are willing and eager to learn about all the advanced features that Java puts at your disposal, this book is for you. Here are some of the topics we cover at length:

*   object-oriented programming

*   graphical user interfaces

*   multithreading

*   network programming.

On the other hand, we *do not* assume that you have any special background in object-oriented techniques or have ever seen topics such as network programming or multithreading. There are two detailed chapters on object-oriented programming, complete with hints for good design practices. The network programming chapter assumes nothing more than experience with a Web browser. Our focus is to get you up to speed quickly on the issues that are relevant to practical programming.

We do not spend much time on the fun, but ultimately less useful, Java programs whose sole purpose is to liven up your Web page. Our goal is to show you the techniques for making Java *do what you want*. In particular, once you master our techniques, you can easily code applets. In any case, there are already quite a few sources for "lighter" material—we recommend John Pew's book, *Instant Java*, also published by SunSoft Press/Prentice-Hall.

You will find *lots* of sample code on the CD-ROM that accompanies this book. The code demonstrates almost every language and library feature that we discuss in the book. The sample programs are purposefully kept simple to focus on the major points, but they do not cut corners. They should make good starting points for your own code.

When writing a long book at breakneck speed about a new topic, some errors and inaccuracies inevitably creep in. We want and need to know about them. Of course, we would also prefer to learn about each of them only once. We have put up a list of frequently asked questions (FAQ), fixes, and workarounds on a Web page at `http://www.mathcs.sjsu.edu/faculty/horstman/corejava.html`. Strategically-placed at the end of the FAQ, to encourage you to read through them first, is a Java applet to report bugs and problems. We also welcome posted suggestions for improvements and additions for future editions.

We hope that you find this book enjoyable and helpful in your Java programming.

Acknowledgments

It takes a team of dedicated professionals to turn the output of the authors into a useable and attractive book. We would like to thank our freelance copy editor, Margaret Broucek, for whipping Gary's colloquial chatter and Cay's Teutonic constructions into readable English; our editor Greg Doench, of Prentice-Hall, and Rachael Borden, our publisher at SunSoft press, for coordinating the gruesome details of the book and CD development with great determination and resolve under sometimes trying circumstances. Thanks to Devang Shah of Sun Microsystems for reviewing the chapter on multithreading, and to Gregory Longshore and Doug Langston for their reviews. Most of all we want to thank Nikki Wise and her whole team at Navta Associates for their superb production job under an impossible schedule.

Thanks, also, to Maurie Wilson of Wilson WindowWare and to Niko Mak for allowing us to put their WinEdit editor and WinZip programs onto the CD-ROM.

Writing a book is stressful, and without a lot of patience on the part of the author's friends and loved ones, it is impossible.

Cay's thanks go to Rick Warner and Annie Chang of San Jose State University for their help with the Solaris installation of Java, and for providing a testbed for CGI scripts. He also thanks Tina Hu for her help with manuscript preparation. His apologies go to his coauthor and colleagues who had to suffer through his testy moods when he had to find yet another workaround to a Java bug. His love and gratitude go to his wife, Hui-Chen, and his son, Tommy, whose initial enthusiasm for this project turned into patient support as the project dragged on and on.

Gary's thanks go to all his friends who put up with his stressed-out ways during these trying times—curt phone calls and no social visits were the norm. He wants to especially thank his friends Bruce, Caroline, and Kurt, without whose special friendship, hospitality, and support, writing his part of the book would have been impossible. Finally, Gary also needs to thank Cay's family. They were gracious hosts on his too-frequent visits. They were extraordinarily patient during the seemingly endless phone calls, and were, in a word, extraordinary.

About this Book

Organization

Chapter 1 gives an overview of Java's capabilities that set it apart from other programming languages. We explain what the designers of the language set out to do and to what extent they succeeded. Then we give a short history of how Java came to be.

In Chapter 2, we give instructions regarding the installation of Java and the companion software for this book from the CD-ROM. We guide you through compiling and running three typical Java programs—a console application, a graphical application and an *applet*. (An applet is Java's term for a program that runs from within a Web browser.)

Chapter 3 starts with the discussion of the Java language. This chapter covers the basics, including variables, loops and simple functions. If you are a C or C++ programmer, this will be smooth sailing because the syntax for these language features is essentially the same as in C. If you come from a Visual Basic or Pascal/Delphi background, you will want to read this chapter carefully.

Object-oriented programming (OOP) has now reached the mainstream of programming, and Java is thoroughly object-oriented. Chapter 4 introduces *encapsulation*, the first of two fundamental building blocks of object-orientation, and the Java language mechanism to implement it—that is, classes and methods. In addition to the rules imposed by the Java language, we also give what we hope is some sound advice on object-oriented design. If you are familiar with C++ or another object-oriented language, you can also browse through this chapter quickly. Other programmers should expect to spend some time mastering the OOP concepts.

Classes and encapsulation are only one part of OOP, and Chapter 5 introduces another part, namely *inheritance*. Inheritance allows an existing class to be modified according to your needs. This is a fundamental technique for programming in Java. The inheritance mechanism in Java is quite similar to that in C++. Once again, C++ programmers can focus on the differences between the languages.

In Chapter 6, we begin application programming in earnest. We show how you can make windows, how to paint on them, and how to display images. Then we show you how to *really* display images. There are quite a few subtle Java programming tasks, and displaying images is one of them. The Java library is optimized to load an image piece by piece, assuming it is transferred via a slow network connection. You can ignore the subtlety, but your image will flicker. In this book we make an effort to dig down into the details and show you how the pros do it. Feel free to skip over this section if you don't care about images.

Chapter 7 is the longest chapter in the book—almost 100 pages. It discusses AWT, the toolkit used in Java for building a graphical user interface. If you are accustomed to programming a user interface by dragging controls onto a form and writing a bit of code to glue them together, you are in for a rude awakening. Java has no form designer, and no automatic user interface builder tools. You need to write code for every button, text field, and menu item. Code controls where text will appear and how it will look. You need to write code for everything that is interface-related, and we cover all the necessary techniques. We also cover how to get user input and how to cause Java applications to respond to user events.

By the time you finish Chapter 7, you will have all the tools you need to write applets. Applets are the topic of Chapter 8. We show you a number of useful and fun applets, and what goes on behind the scenes. One of our favorite applets crawls through the World Wide Web, linking itself from one Web page to the next. Click on any URL that it finds to be transported to a specific Web page, while the applet hunts for more pages. This is possible only through the power of multithreading and Netscape frames, which Java fully supports.

In Chapter 9 we move on to a more mundane programming issue, how to use the data structures in the Java library such as vectors and hash tables, and how to write your own data structures like linked lists and queues. This material is important if your Java program needs to quickly store and retrieve a large amount of data.

Chapter 10 discusses *exception handling*, a robust mechanism that deals with the fact that bad things can happen to good programs. For example, a network connection can become unavailable in the middle of a file download, or a disk can become full. Exceptions give you an efficient way of separating the normal processing code from the error handling. Of course, even after hardening your program by handling most exceptional conditions, it still might fail to work as expected. In the second half of this chapter, we give you some debugging tips. Finally, we guide you through a sample debugging session with the JDB debugger. This debugger is very primitive; you only want to use it as a last resort.

The topic of Chapter 11 is another mundane but important issue—files. If your application reads or writes data, you need to know about input and output. Java has a whole zoo of classes for this purpose. We look at four different I/O scenarios in detail, including binary files, random access files, saving objects of mixed types, and saving and restoring objects and pointers.

Users like programs that complete slow tasks in the background, leaving them in control to perform other operations. In Java, this is achieved through *multithreading*. A *thread* is a flow of control within a program. Java programs can run multiple threads concurrently, switching between them to service both the user interface and background tasks. In Chapter 12, we show you how to set up threads, and how to make sure none of them get stuck. We put this material to practical use by giving an implementation for a timer class that you can use in your own code. Finally, we look into the inner workings of an animation class that displays a spinning globe.

The last chapter covers one of the most exciting topics of Java programming, networking. Java makes it easy to connect to a remote computer and send and receive data. The chapter starts out with an introduction to sockets. We outline a sample application, an order-taking applet that reads a price list from a server, takes ordering information from a customer, and sends the information back to the server. We then turn to the important issue of security. An applet cannot make arbitrary network connections, because it could then quietly send private data back to its server. We show how to overcome this limitation by using a proxy server, opening the door to a class of very useful applets that *harvest information* from the Internet.

Conventions

As is common in many computer books, we use `courier` type to represent computer code.

There are many C++ and Visual Basic (VB) notes that explain the difference between Java and these languages. You should skip over them if you aren't interested in either of those languages.

Notes are tagged with a "notepad" icon that looks like this.

Java comes with a large programming library or Application Programming Interface (API). When using an API call for the first time, we add a short summary description, tagged with an API icon. These descriptions are a bit more informal, but also a little more informative than those in the official on-line API documentation.

This icon denotes a *tip*.

Industrial-strength warnings are set like this, so you cannot possibly overlook them.

Programs whose source code is on the CD-ROM are tagged with this icon, which denotes a spoonful of pulverized CD-ROM. Actually, the crystals represent instant coffee. The icon was designed for use in the "Instant Java" book where it denotes an applet that you can instantly plug into your Web page.

CD-ROM

The CD-ROM on the back of the book contains the Sun Java Development Kit (JDK) and the code for this book. It also contains the code for three other books from the Sun Java series. Feel free to install the extra code if you like. These materials are available for Windows 95/NT, Solaris 2, and the Macintosh. However, Macintosh users need to be aware that the beta version of the JDK supports only applets, not applications. Unfortunately, the bulk of the code in this book is comprised of applications. If Sun is not providing full support for application development on the Macintosh by the time this book is released, we will post a workaround on our Web page.

The CD-ROM also contains shareware versions of the WinEdit and WinZip programs for Windows 95/NT. We have customized WinEdit to work smoothly with Java. Finally, there is Café Lite, a "lite" version of Symantec's Cafe Java development environment for Windows.

Chapter 2 and Appendix III contain detailed CD-ROM installation instructions.

CHAPTER 1

An Introduction to Java

It seems impossible to open a computer magazine that does not feature an article on Java. Even mainstream newspapers and magazines like the *New York Times*, the *Washington Post*, and *Business Week* have all had major articles on Java. It gets better (or worse depending on your perspective): can you remember the last time National Public Radio ran a 10-minute story on a computer language? CNN, CNBC, you name the mass medium, it seems everyone is talking about how Java will do this or Java will do that.

What we decided was that you bought this book because you are a serious programmer, so rather than immediately getting caught up in the Internet hype and trying to deal, at length, with the limited (if still interesting) truth behind the hype, we will write first, and in some detail, about Java as a programming language (including the features added for its use on the Internet). After that, we will try to separate current fact from fancy by explaining what Java can and cannot do on the Internet.

In the end, we should add, a great deal of the hype *will* be justified; it is just that it is not true *yet*: Java is still in its formative stages.

Java as a Programming Language

Regarding a computer language, Java's hype is overdone: the current version of Java is a good language. It could *potentially* have been a great programming language, but it is probably too late for that. Once a language is out in the field, the ugly reality of compatibility with existing code sets in. We expect there to be some improvements over time, but, basically, the structure of Java tomorrow will be what it is today. So what are its advantages and disadvantages?

One obvious advantage is a run time library that gives it platform independence: you can use the same code on Windows 95, Solaris, Unix, Macintosh, and so on. This is certainly necessary for Internet programming. Another advantage for many programmers is that Java has a similar syntax to C++. This means that it is economical without being absurd. Then again, Visual Basic (VB) programmers will probably find the syntax annoying and miss some of the nicer syntactic VB constructs.

> If you are coming from a language other than C++, some of the terms used in this section will be less familiar—just skip those sections. You will be comfortable with all of these terms by the end of Chapter 5.

Java is also fully object oriented—even more so than C++. Everything in Java, except for a few basic types like numbers, is an object. (Object-oriented design has replaced earlier structured techniques because it seems to have many advantages for dealing with sophisticated projects. If you are not familiar with Object-Oriented Programming (OOP), Chapters 4 and 5 provide what you need to know.)

However, having yet another, somewhat improved, dialect of C++ would not be enough. The key points are:

• It is far easier to turn out bug-free code using Java than using C++.

Why? The designers of Java thought hard about what makes C++ code so buggy. They then added features to Java that eliminate the *possibility* of creating code with the most common kinds of bugs. (Some estimates say that roughly every 50 lines of C++ code has at least one bug.) Here is some of what they did:

• They eliminated manual memory allocation and deallocation.

Memory in Java is automatically garbage collected. You *never* have to worry about memory leaks.

• They introduced true arrays and eliminated pointer arithmetic.

You never have to worry about overwriting a key area of memory because of an off-by-one error when working with a pointer.

• They eliminated the possibility of confusing an assignment with a test for equality in a conditional.

You cannot even compile if (ntries = 3). ... (VB programmers may not see the problem, but, trust us, this is a common source of confusion in C/C++ code.)

• They eliminated multiple inheritance, replacing it with a new notion of *interface* that they derived from Objective C.

Interfaces give you what you want from multiple inheritance, without the complexity that comes with managing multiple inheritance hierarchies. (If inheritance is a new concept for you, you will see a complete treatment of it in Chapter 5.)

The Java language specification is public. It may be found on the Web by going to the Java documentation index page (at `http://java.sun.com/JDK-1.0/index.html`).

The Java "White Paper" Buzzwords

The authors of Java have written an influential "White Paper" that explains their design goals and accomplishments. Their paper is organized along the following eleven buzzwords:

Simple

Object Oriented

Distributed

Robust

Secure

Architecture Neutral

Portable

Interpreted

High Performance

Multithreaded

Dynamic

We touched on some of these points in the last section. In this section, we will:

- summarize via excerpts from the "White Paper" what the Java designers say about each buzzword, and

- tell you what we think of that particular buzzword based on our experiences with the current version of Java.

The "White Paper" may be found on the `http://java.sun.com/whitePaper/` `java-whitepaper-1.html` Web page at the Sun site.

Simple

We wanted to build a system that could be programmed easily without a lot of esoteric training and which leveraged today's standard practice. ... So even though we found that C++ was unsuitable, we designed Java as closely to C++ as possible in order to make the system more comprehensible. Java

omits many rarely used, poorly understood, confusing features of C++ that in our experience, bring more grief than benefit.

The syntax for Java is, indeed, a cleaned-up version of the syntax for C++. There is no need for header files, pointer arithmetic (or even a pointer syntax), structures, unions, operator overloading, virtual base classes, and so on. (See the C++ notes interspersed throughout the text for more on the differences between Java and C++.) The designers did not, however, *improve* on some stupid features in C++, like the switch statement. If you know C++, you will find the transition to Java's syntax easy.

If you are a VB programmer, you will not find Java simple. There is much strange syntax, (though it does not take long to get the hang of it). More importantly, you need to do a lot more programming in Java. The beauty of VB is that the visual design environment provides a lot of the "glue" that needs to be programmed manually (and with a fair bit of code) in Java.

At this point, the Java language is pretty simple, as object-oriented languages go. But there are many subtle points in using Java to solve real-world problems. As time goes by, more and more of these details will be farmed off to libraries and development environments, but right now you must contend with many tedious details that having a better class library or form designer would have hidden from you.

> *Another aspect of being simple is being small. One of the goals of Java is to enable the construction of software that can run stand-alone in small machines. The size of the basic interpreter and class support is about 40K bytes; adding the basic standard libraries and thread support (essentially a self-contained microkernel) adds an additional 175K.*

This is true and is a great achievement.

Object Oriented

> *Simply stated, object-oriented design is a technique that focuses design on the data (= objects) and on the interfaces to it. To make an analogy with carpentry, an "object-oriented" carpenter would be mostly concerned with the chair he was building, and secondarily with the tools used to make it; a "non-object-oriented" carpenter would think primarily of his tools. … The object-oriented facilities of Java are essentially those of C++.*

Object orientation has proven its worth in the last 30 years, and it is inconceivable that a modern programming language would not be object oriented. Indeed, the object-oriented features of Java are comparable to C++. The major difference between Java and C++ lies in multiple inheritance, for which Java has found a better solution.

On the other hand, programmers coming from Smalltalk may be disappointed. Java has strong typing, which is a plus. But the metaclass model is very weak. As a result, persistent objects are painful to implement, a curious limitation for a language that prides itself on its network capabilities.

If you do not have any experience with OOP languages you will want to carefully read Chapters 4 and 5. These chapters explain what OOP is and why it is more useful for programming sophisticated projects than traditional, procedure-oriented languages like BASIC or C.

Distributed

Java has an extensive library of routines for coping easily with TCP/IP protocols like HTTP and FTP. Java applications can open and access objects across the Net via URLs with the same ease that programmers are used to when accessing a local file system.

We have found the networking capabilities of Java to be both strong and easy to use. Anyone who has tried to do Internet programming using another language will revel in how simple Java makes onerous tasks like opening a socket connection. Java even makes common gateway interface (CGI) scripting easier. (See Chapter 13 if you do not know what a socket or a CGI script is.)

Robust

Java is intended for writing programs that must be reliable in a variety of ways. Java puts a lot of emphasis on early checking for possible problems, later dynamic (run time) checking, and eliminating situations that are error prone. ... The single biggest difference between Java and C/C++ is that Java has a pointer model that eliminates the possibility of overwriting memory and corrupting data.

This is true and also very useful. The Java compiler detects many problems that, in other languages, would only show up at run time (or, perhaps, not even then). As for the second point, anyone who has spent hours chasing a memory leak caused by a pointer bug will be very happy with this feature of Java.

If you are coming from a language like VB that never uses pointers, you are probably wondering why this is so important. Your fellow programmers who use C are not so lucky. They need pointers to access strings, arrays, objects, even files. In Basic, you do not use pointers for any of these entities, nor do you need to worry about memory allocation. On the downside, in VB, you cannot easily implement some of the fancier data structures that require pointers.

Java gives you the best of both worlds. You do not need pointers for everyday constructs like strings and arrays. You have the power of pointers if you need it, for example, for linked lists. And you always have complete safety, since you can never access a bad pointer or make memory allocation errors.

Secure

Java is intended to be used in networked/distributed environments. Toward that end, a lot of emphasis has been placed on security. Java enables the construction of virus-free, tamper-free systems.

Well, one should "never say never again," but it does seem that Java makes it extremely difficult to outwit its security mechanisms.

A Java program cannot overrun the run time stack, like the famous Internet worm did. It cannot corrupt memory outside its process space. When invoked through a security-conscious loader, like the Netscape browser, a Java program cannot even read or write local files.

Architecture Neutral

The compiler generates an architecture neutral object file format—the compiled code is executable on many processors, given the presence of the Java run time system. ... The Java compiler does this by generating bytecode instructions which have nothing to do with a particular computer architecture. Rather, they are designed to be both easy to interpret on any machine and easily translated into native machine code on the fly.

This is not a new idea. Twenty years ago, the UCSD Pascal system did the same thing. By using byte codes, performance takes a major hit. But the designers of Java did an excellent job developing a bytecode instruction set that works well on today's most common computer architectures. And the codes have been designed to translate easily into actual machine instructions.

Portable

Unlike C and C++, there are no "implementation-dependent" aspects of the specification. The sizes of the primitive data types are specified, as is the behavior of arithmetic on them.

For example, an `int` in Java is always a 32-bit integer. In C/C++, `int` can mean a 16-bit integer, a 32-bit integer, or an integer of any other size that the compiler vendor likes. The only restriction is that it must have at least as many bytes as a `short int` and cannot have more bytes than a `long int`. Having a fixed size of number types eliminates a major porting headache. Binary data is stored in a fixed format, eliminating the "big endian/little endian" confusion. Strings are saved in a standard Unicode format.

> *The libraries that are a part of the system define portable interfaces. For example, there is an abstract* Window *class and implementations of it for Unix, Windows, and the Macintosh.*

As anyone who has ever tried knows, it is an effort of heroic proportions to write a program that looks good on Windows, the Macintosh, and 10 flavors of Unix. Despite the authors' claims, the designers of Java did not solve this problem. They give us a library that is good for writing programs that look equally mediocre on the different systems. But it is a start. There are many applications in which portability is more important than the nth degree of slickness.

Interpreted

> *The Java interpreter can execute Java bytecodes directly on any machine to which the interpreter has been ported. And since linking is a more incremental and lightweight process, the development process can be much more rapid and exploratory.*

This is, perhaps, an advantage while developing an application, but it is clearly overstated. First, you will eventually want a compiler (they are coming, of course) since interpreted code is slower than compiled code, often by at least a factor of 10. Second, Java is fairly slow at compiling your source code to the bytecodes that will, ultimately, be interpreted in the current version. If you are used to the speed of VB's or Delphi's development cycle, you will be very disappointed. (In addition, as you will see in Chapter 2, Java currently uses command line development tools that are straight out of the early days of computing.)

High Performance

> *While the performance of interpreted bytecodes is usually more than adequate, there are situations where higher performance is required. The bytecodes can be translated on the fly (at run time) into machine code for the particular CPU the application is running on.*

As Java exists today, "high performance" is not a term that we would use to describe it. It is certainly true that the speed of the interpreted bytecodes can be acceptable. (It is slightly faster than VB, according to our tests.) On the other hand, all Java programmers will be eager to have a way to compile Java bytecodes.

Multithreaded

(Multithreading is the ability for one program to do more than one thing at once, for example, printing while getting a fax.)

[The] benefits of multithreading are better interactive responsiveness and real-time behavior.

If you have ever tried to do multithreading in another language, you will be pleasantly surprised at how easy it is to manage in Java. The threads in Java also have the capacity to take advantage of multiprocessor systems if the base operating system does so. On the downside, thread implementations on the major platforms differ widely, and Java makes no effort to be platform independent in this regard. Only the code for calling multithreading remains the same across machines; Java offloads the implementation of multithreading to the underlying operating system.

Dynamic

In a number of ways, Java is a more dynamic language than C or C++. It was designed to adapt to an evolving environment. ... Libraries can freely add new methods and instance variables without any effect on their clients. ... In Java, finding out run time type information is straightforward.

This is true, and it is an important feature in those situations for which code needs to be added to a running program. On the other hand, the run time type information provided in Java is only marginally richer than that in C++.

Java and the Internet

The idea here is simple:

- Users will download Java bytecodes from the Internet and run them on their own machines.

Java programs that work on Web pages are called *applets*. (Although they are actually the bytecodes, rather than the source file, that you download and then run.) To use an applet, you need a Java-enabled Web browser. It is the Java-enabled browser that will interpret the bytecodes for you. Netscape 2.0 is Java-enabled, and most companies have announced (or included) Java support in their browsers. Because Sun is licensing the Java source code and insisting that there be no changes in the language and basic library structure, you can be sure that a Java applet will run on any browser that is advertised as Java enabled.

We suspect that, ultimately, most of the hype stems from the lure of making money from special-purpose software. You have a nifty "Will Writer" program. Convert it to an applet, and charge people per use—presumably, most people would be using this kind of program infrequently. Once commerce on the Net is widespread, this seems to us to be inevitable—and desirable. (Some people are taking this too far. They predict a time when everyone downloads software from the Net on a per-use basis. This might be great for software companies, but we think it is absurd, for example, to expect people to download and pay for a spell-checker applet each time they send an e-mail message.)

Here are some of the advantages of applets for users of the World-Wide Web that we see as realistic now and in the immediate future:

1. Since Java is a true programming language, it is much easier to make an applet responsive than to do the same with a Web page. For example, we wrote a simple retirement calculator applet (see Chapter 8). Since this is a program, we could write it to allow people to see the effects of changes immediately—there is no need to go back to a Web page for updates after each change. (Without Java, making a Web page responsive involves sending data to a CGI script on the server. The CGI script then needs to process the data and send the results back in a form the browser can use. Often, this requires creating a whole new Web page on the fly—which can be painful, or even impossible, to program. It will almost always be slow.)

2. Applets can use a modern graphical user interface (GUI). This includes text boxes, buttons, list boxes, and so on. Java applets can also trap user events like keystrokes, mouse movements, and the like.

3. Processing is off-loaded to the user's system, which, presumably, is going to do it much faster than some host that is dealing with a few thousand hits at that moment. Moreover, if a great deal of data needs to be computed, you do not have to worry about the speed of transmission from the host machine since the data is computed locally. By the way, this relates to one area in which Java is way overhyped: adding animation to Web pages. Sure, this is easy to do (see Chapter 12), but if the animation involves the user's downloading 1 megabyte of GIF files with a 28.8k modem, you will not have a happy user. What people should do, instead (if possible), is think of fast ways to compute the special effects. This lets the applet generate the data using the local processor instead of downloading it.

4. Special purpose Java applets (usually called content and protocol handlers) allow a Java-enabled Web browser to deal with new types of information dynamically. Suppose you invent a nifty fractal compression algorithm for dealing with humongous graphics files and want to let someone sample how great your technology is before you charge them big bucks for it. Write a Java content handler that does the decompression and send it along with the compressed files. The HotJava browser by Sun Microsystems (which has, at the time of this writing, not been updated to work with Java 1.0) supports this feature. Netscape 2.0 does not.

Applets at Work

This book includes a few sample applets; the JDK that is also on the CD supplies many more. Ultimately, the best source for applets is the Web itself. Some applets on the Web can only be seen at work; many others include the source code. When you become more familiar with Java, these applets can be a great way to learn more about Java. A good Web site to check for Java applets is Gamelan—http://www.gamelan.com. (By the way, *gamelan* also stands for a special type of Javanese musical orchestra. Attend a gamelan performance if you have a chance—it is gorgeous music.)

To place an applet onto a Web page, you need to know or be working with someone who knows hypertext markup language (HTML). The number of HTML tags needed for a Java applet are few and not difficult to master. (See Chapter 8.) Using general HTML tags to design a Web page is a design issue—it is not a programming problem.

As you can see in Figure 1-1, when the user downloads an applet, it works much like embedding an image in a Web page. (For those who know HTML, we mean one set with an IMG tag.) The applet becomes a part of the page, and the text flows around the space used for the applet. The point is, the image is *alive*. It reacts to user commands, changes its appearance, and sends data between the computer viewing the applet and the computer serving it.

Figure 1-1 shows a good example of a dynamic Web page. This is a part of the virtual laboratory at the physics department of the University of Oregon. You can see some HTML text on top and the running applet on the bottom. (The lightbulb breaks if you add power without sufficient resistors. It glows if you add the right number of resistors, thus teaching students about Ohm's law.)

A Short History of Java

This section gives a short history of Java's evolution. It is based on various published sources (most importantly, on an interview with Java's creators in the July 1995 issue of *SunWorld's* on-line magazine).

Java goes back to 1991, when a group of Sun engineers, led by Sun Fellow (and all-around computer wizard) James Gosling, wanted to design a small computer language that could be used for consumer devices like cable TV switchboxes. Since these devices do not have a lot of power nor a lot of memory, the language had to be small and generate very tight code. Also, because different manufacturers may choose different central processing units (CPUs), it was important not to be tied down to any single architecture. The project got the code name "Green."

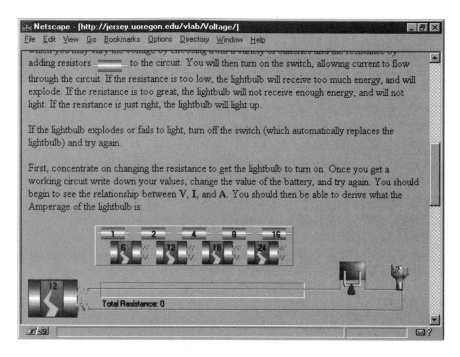

Figure 1.1 *Courtesy of Sean Russell*

The requirements for small, tight code led them to resurrect the model that a language called UCSD Pascal tried in the early days of PCs. What UCSD Pascal did, and the Green project engineers did as well, was design a portable language that generated intermediate code. This intermediate code could then be used on any machine that had the correct interpreter. Intermediate code generated with this model is always small, and the interpreters for intermediate code can also be quite small, so this solved their main problem.

The Sun people, however, come from a Unix background so they based their language on C++, rather than Pascal. In particular, they made the language object oriented rather than procedure oriented. But, as Gosling says in the interview, "All along, the language was a tool, not the end." Gosling decided to call his language "Oak." (Presumably because he liked the look of an Oak tree that was right outside his window at Sun.) The people at Sun later realized that Oak was the name of an existing computer language, so they changed the name to Java.

In 1992, the Green project delivered its first product, called "*7." It was an extremely intelligent remote control. Unfortunately, no one was interested in producing this, and the Green people had to find other ways to market their technology. They bid on a project to design a cable TV box that could deal with new cable services such as pay-per-view. They did not get the contract. (Amusingly, the company that did was led by the same Jim Clark who started Netscape—a program that did much to make Java successful.)

The Green Project (under the new name "First Person Inc.") spent all of 1993 and half of 1994 looking for people to buy its technology—no one was found. (Patrick Naughton, who did the marketing, claims to have accumulated 300,000 air miles in trying to sell the technology.) First Person was dissolved in 1994.

While all of this was going on at Sun, the World Wide Web part of the Internet was growing bigger and bigger. The key to the Web is the browser that takes the hypertext page and translates it to the screen. In 1994, most people were using Mosaic, a noncommercial Web browser that came out of the supercomputing center at the University of Illinois in 1993. (Mosaic was partially written by Marc Andreessen for $6.85 an hour as an undergraduate student on a work-study project. He moved on to fame and fortune as one of the cofounders and the chief of technology at Netscape.)

In the *SunWorld* interview, Gosling says that in mid-1994, the language developers realized that "We could build a real cool browser. It was one of the few things in the client/server mainstream that needed some of the weird things we'd done: architecture neutral, real-time, reliable, secure—issues that weren't terribly important in the workstation world. So we built a browser."

The actual browser was built by Patrick Naughton and Jonathan Payne and evolved into the HotJava browser that we have today. The HotJava browser was written in Java to show off the power of Java. But the builders also had in mind the power of what are now called applets, so they made the browser capable of interpreting the intermediate bytecodes. This "proof of technology" was shown at SunWorld '95 on May 23, 1995, and inspired the Java craze that continues unabated today.

The big breakthrough for widespread use of Java came in the fall of 1995, when Netscape decided to make the next release of Netscape (Netscape 2.0) Java enabled. Netscape 2.0 came out in January of 1996, and it is, indeed, Java 1.0 enabled. Other licensees include IBM, Symantec, Borland, and many others. Even Microsoft plans to license and support Java in its browser.

Common Misconceptions about Java

In summary, following is a list of some common misconceptions about Java, along with commentary.

Java is an extension of HTML.

Java is a programming language; HTML is a page-description language. They have nothing in common except that there are HTML extensions for placing Java applets on a Web page.

Java is an easy programming language to learn.

No programming language as powerful as Java is easy. You always have to distinguish how easy it is to write toy programs and how hard it is to do serious work. Also, consider that only four chapters in this book discuss the Java *language*. The remaining chapters show how to put the language to work, using the Java *library*. The library contains over 150 classes and interfaces. You do not need to know all of them for many programming tasks, but you need to use some of them for every project.

Java is an easy environment in which to program.

Some people enjoy writing a program using nothing more than the vi editor and the dbx debugger. But PC and Mac programmers, who are used to VB-style drag-and-drop form designers or an integrated development platform like modern C++ compilers, are in for a shock. However, once products like Symantec's Cafe (a sample version of this product is on the CD) or Borland's Latte come out, Java development time will be cut substantially.

Java will become a universal programming language for all platforms.

This is possible, in theory, but we wonder if you would then get a lowest-common-denominator approach to the design. Java applications do not yet look (and, perhaps, can never look) as good as, say, Windows applications developed with VB or MFC. In any case, the graphics toolkit supplied with Java 1.0 is far too primitive to make the design task pleasant. Of course, we expect the libraries to get better quickly. (There will soon be many third-party libraries that, while based on the Sun toolkits, go far beyond it.)

Java is interpreted, so it is too slow for serious applications on a specific platform.

Many programs spend most of their time on things like user-interface interactions. All programs, no matter what language they are written in, will detect a mouse click in adequate time. It is true that we would not do CPU-intensive tasks with the current version of Java unless we had to. However, it is relatively simple to make a compiler that will convert Java bytecodes into native code. These should be out by summer of 1996.

All Java programs run inside a Web page.

All Java *applets* run inside a Web browser. That is the definition of an applet—a Java program running inside a browser. But it is entirely possible, and quite useful, to write stand-alone Java programs that run independent of a Web browser. These programs (usually called *applications*) are completely portable. Just take the code and run them on another machine! And because Java is more convenient and less error-prone than raw C++, it is a good choice for writing programs. It will be an even more compelling choice once it is combined with user-interface builders and database access tools. It is certainly the obvious choice for a first language in which to learn programming.

Most of the programs in this book are stand-alone programs. Sure, applets are interesting, and right now most useful Java programs are applets. But we believe that stand-alone Java programs will become extremely important, very quickly.

Java eliminates the need for CGI scripting.

Absolutely not. With today's technology, CGI is still the easiest communication path between applet and server. The server will still need a CGI script to deal with the information sent by the applet. (Of course, we feel you can *write* the CGI scripts in Java much more easily than in Perl or C, but that is a separate issue.)

Java will revolutionize client-server computing.

This is possible. Sun has announced plans for various database class libraries that will make using Java for client-server development as easy as the Net library included in the current version of Java makes network programming.

With Java, I can replace my computer with a $500 "Internet Appliance."

Some people are betting big that this is going to happen. We believe it is pretty absurd to think that people are going to give up a powerful and convenient desktop for a limited machine with no local storage. But we can envision an Internet appliance as a portable *adjunct* to a desktop. Provided the price is right, wouldn't you rather have an Internet browsing machine to read the news at breakfast instead of watching television? Such an appliance could well be Java powered.

Java will allow the component-based model of computing to take off.

No two people mean the same thing when they talk about components. Regarding visual controls, like OCX components that can be dropped into a graphical user interface (GUI) program, Java has set no standards (which is too bad, in our opinion). Regarding the ability to work with distributed computing models that use common object request broker (CORBA) interfaces and OpenDoc, this will happen soon. There already exist beta versions of the needed interfaces for CORBA communication on the Net.

CHAPTER

2

- Installing the Java Compiler and Tools

- Navigating the Java Directories

- Windows 95/NT as a Programming Environment

- Compiling and Running Java Programs

- Using WinEdit

- Graphical Applications

- Applets

- Troubleshooting

The Java
Programming
Environment

This chapter is about getting Java to work in various environments, concentrating on Windows 95 since that seems to be the most common platform. It is somewhat unusual for a book at this level to provide so many tips for various platforms; experienced programmers do not usually need to be told how to work with most software. Trust us, Java is different. The current version of Java is so rustic that "gotchas" abound.

A good, general source of information on Java may be found via the links on the Java frequently asked questions (FAQ) page: www.www-net.com/java/faq/.

Installing the Java Compiler and Tools

The most complete versions of Java are available for Sun's Solaris 2.x, Windows NT, or Windows 95 (Java is identical for both versions of Windows). Versions in various states of development exist for Linux, OS/2 or Macintosh, and a few other platforms. Java is not currently available for Windows 3.1, and, perhaps, never will be. In particular, if you use a PC, you must have Windows 95, NT (or Linux) to run Java. Realistically, you also need either a fast 486 or a Pentium, a minimum of 16 MB of memory, and at least 50 MB of free hard disk space.

For one of the big three—Solaris, Windows, or the Mac—you will want to periodically visit the Java home page to see if a more recent release is available for your platform. Point your browser to java.sun.com. For other platforms, you will need to cruise the Web. A good place to turn to is the comp.lang.java newsgroup.

The CD that accompanies this book contains the 1.0 version of the Java Development Kit (JDK) for Windows NT/Windows 95. The installation instructions in this chapter assume that you have Windows 95, and the CD-ROM comes with an installation program that unpacks the files needed for automatic installation of the Windows version. The CD-ROM also includes Solaris and Macintosh files. The Solaris files are in tar format, and the Macintosh files are self-extracting archives. You will need to unpack these archives manually and modify the installation instructions for those platforms.

Only the installation instructions for Java are system dependent. If a full version of Java 1.0 exists for your operating system, then, once you get Java up and running, everything else in this book will apply to you. System independence is a major benefit of Java. (Unfortunately, as we write this, the version of Java for the Macintosh is incomplete; much of the code in this book will run *only* when the Macintosh gets a version of Java that can handle application programs.)

Development Environments for Windows Users

If your programming experience comes from VB, Delphi, or a modern PC or Macintosh version of C or C++, you are used to a development environment with a built-in text editor and menus to compile and launch a program. The basic JDK contains nothing even remotely similar. *Everything* is done from the command line. Integrated design environments (IDEs) are just beginning to appear for Java. For example, the CD-ROM contains a limited version of Symantec's IDE, called Café. The full version of Café should be out at about the same time as this book. The limited version is called Café Lite and contains only an editor and a project manager. (The full version of Café adds a debugger, a browser for the objects in Java, and a form designer.)

We used an excellent shareware programming editor for Windows called WinEdit for developing and testing the programs in this book. WinEdit, like most good programming editors, can be configured to recognize (and color code) keywords in a language. It can also compile and execute source code. We created the necessary configuration and batch files for this and have included them on the CD. Our customized version of WinEdit became our de facto IDE for writing this book.

In sum, you have at this time four choices for a development environment under Windows:

1.   our Java-enhanced version of WinEdit,

2.   Café Lite,

3.   the raw JDK and your favorite ASCII editor (it must support long file names),

4. a full-fledged IDE from a third-party vendor. By the time you read this, we expect that both Symantec and Borland will have released such products. (Symantec's Café is for Java alone; Borland's will first be part of Version 5.0 of their C++ compiler. They will not have a stand-alone Java environment until later.)

Let's look at these choices in detail. (If you hate choices, just pick the first option. It will work fine.)

Our Java-enhanced version of WinEdit is probably the easiest to use (see below for more details). You simply write the source code for your program in the editor. When you are happy with it, you can use various WinEdit menu items to compile, execute, or see the frequent syntax-error message you will encounter for the first few weeks of working with Java.

Café Lite, on the other hand, is more cumbersome to use for a simple project, since you have to set up a separate project for each program you write. The Café Lite environment has the edge if you write larger Java programs, consisting of many source files. We do not discuss Café Lite in this book—it comes with the usual Windows Help system that you can study at your leisure.

> Keep in mind that WinEdit is shareware; you are expected to pay its author if you use the program. (We have no connection whatsoever with the author of WinEdit. We simply found it a capable program, easy to customize.) You can freely use Café Lite. Symantec hopes that you will buy the full product to take advantage of the debugger, browser, and other nifty features included in the full version, but you are under no obligation to do so.

If you are the satisfied or fanatical user of another editor (such as vi), and you are comfortable with compiling programs from the command line, you need not install either WinEdit or Café Lite to work with our files. However, your editor must support *long file names*, which rules out such venerable programs as the Brief editor. The EDIT program (or, for that matter, Notepad) that comes with Windows 95 works just fine, as would any other Windows 95-compatible program editor.

> If you have an integrated Java development environment, you can use it with our files. Just make sure that it can find our classes in its class path. (See the section "Checking Your Configuration" for more on the CLASSPATH environment variable.)

Installation Tips

If you choose WinEdit, install the following components in any order:

> WinEdit

> Core Java files and the JDK

If you use Café Lite, install the following components in order:

> Café Lite
>
> Core Java files

If you use your own editor, install the following components in any order:

> Core Java files
>
> The JDK

If you have an integrated Java environment, install Core Java files only.

(By now, you may be feeling as one would who buys a gas grill, only to find that it is actually a gas grill assembly kit, not a ready-to-use grill. There is a reason, after all, why this is called the Java Development *Kit*. Undoubtedly, all this confusion will end once integrated development environments become widely available.)

CD-ROM Installation

Here are more detailed instructions for the various development environments.

WinEdit

Go to the `\Win95NT\WINEDIT` directory on the CD-ROM and run `SETUP`. This installs the WinEdit program. Next, run our patch file that customizes WinEdit for Java programming. Go to the `\Win95NT\WINEDITA` directory on the CD-ROM. Then run the `WEPATCH` batch file. This batch file requires two arguments:

- the name of the directory into which you installed WinEdit and

- the name of the directory that contains your Windows files.

For example,

```
WEPATCH    C:\WinEdit    C:\Windows
```

If the directory name contains spaces, enclose it in quotation marks.

```
WEPATCH    "C:\Program Files\WinEdit"    C:\Windows
```

Café Lite

Run the file `CAFELITE.EXE` from the CD-ROM to install Café Lite on your computer.

Core Java Files and the JDK

On the CD-ROM, go to the `\Win95NT\BOOKSJDK` directory. Run the `SETUP` program.

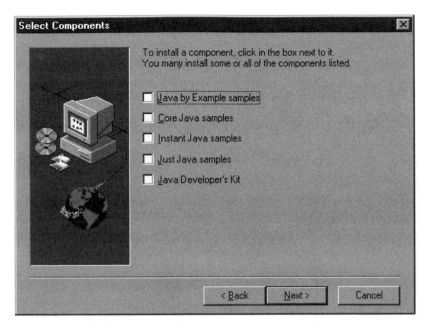

Figure 2-1

Select the option "Core Java". If you need the JDK, also select "JDK". (The CD-ROM includes version 1.0 of the JDK.)

When the SETUP program prompts you for the installation directories, you should accept the defaults \CoreJavaBook and \java. (You can change the disk drive letters if you do not have enough room on drive C and have a disk D or E. But if you tinker with the directory names, you are on your own.)

Checking Your Configuration

When the installation is complete, check your AUTOEXEC.BAT file. There should be two modifications:

The PATH should contain the Java compiler directory (such as \java\bin or \Cafe\bin). For example,

```
SET PATH=. . .;C:\JAVA\BIN; . . .
```

There must also be an environment variable called CLASSPATH that contains at least the following directories:

\java\lib (or the library directory of your development environment, such as \Cafe\lib)

. (the current directory)

\CoreJavaBook.

The directories are separated by semicolons on Windows, colons on Unix. For example,

```
SET CLASSPATH=C:\java\lib;C:\CoreJavaBook
```

The exact order of the directories in the path and class path does not matter, nor does the case. On Unix, you must use an absolute path for each directory in the class path, for example

```
setenv CLASSPATH /java/lib:.:/home/me/CoreJavaBook
```

A path ~/CoreJavaBook does not work.

(With Café Lite, you will also see an environment variable called JAVA_HOME. It must point to the directory that contains the Java files, such as c:\cafe\java.)

Finally, as always, you need to reboot your computer to make the changes to the path and class path effective.

Table 2-1

```
\java
     bin      the compiler and tools are here
     lib      classes.zip is here—do not unzip
     demo     (lots of subdirectories) look here for demos
     include
              win32
     .hotjava
     src      look in the various subdirectories for the library source
              java
                  lang
                  util
                  io
                  net
                  awt
                      peer
                      image
                  applet
              sun
                  tools
                      ttydebug
     api      library documentation in HTML format is here
              images
```

Navigating the Java Directories

In your explorations of Java, you will occasionally want to peek inside the Java system files. And, of course, you will need to work extensively with our `"Core Java"` files. Table 2-1 shows the Java directory tree (the layout will be different if you have installed Café Lite).

The two most important subdirectories in this tree are `\java\api` and `\java\src`. The `\java\api` directory contains the Java library documentation in HTML format. You can view it with any Web browser, such as Netscape.

Set a bookmark to `\java\api\tree.html` in your browser. You will want to refer to that page as a starting point for the library documentation.

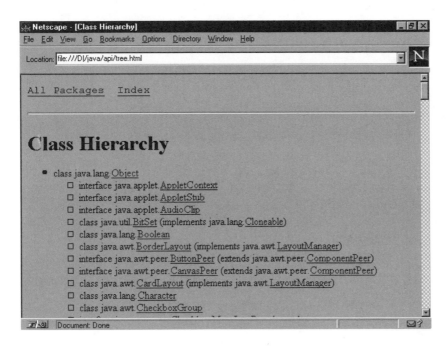

Figure 2-2

The `\java\src` directory contains the source code for the Java libraries. As you become more comfortable with Java, you may find yourself in situations for which this book and the on-line information do not provide what you need to know. At this point, the source code for Java is a good place to begin digging. It is occasionally reassuring to know that you can always dig into the source to find out what a library function really does. For example, if you are curious about the inner workings of the `Hashtable` class, you can look inside `\java\src\java\util\Hashtable.java`.

Here is how the program files in this book are organized:

```
\CoreJavaBook
    WinEdit
    corejava
        api
    ch2
        Welcome
        WelcomeApplet
        ImageViewer
    ch3
        FirstSample
        LotteryOdds
        LotteryDrawing
        Mortgage
        MortgageLoop
        Retirement
        SquareRoot
```

  . . .

(The WinEdit directory has the files needed to patch WinEdit, just in case you need to do it by hand.)

 The `corejava` directory is very important. It contains a number of useful Java routines that we wrote to supplement missing features in the standard Java library. These files are needed for a number of examples in the book. It is crucial that your CLASSPATH environment variable is set to include the `\CoreJavaBook` directory so that the programs can find our files, such as `\CoreJavaBook\corejava\Format.class` and `\CoreJavaBook\corejava\Console.class`.

There is a separate directory for each chapter of this book. Each of these directories has separate subdirectories for sample files. For example, `\CoreJavaBook\ch2\ImageViewer` contains the source code and compiled code for the image-viewer application that you will encounter later in this chapter. (There is no source code for Chapter 1.)

Windows 95/NT as a Programming Environment

If you have done all your programming in Windows, using a comfortable programming environment such as VB, Delphi or one of the C++-integrated environments, you may find the JDK primitive. ("Quaint" may be a more charitable word for it.) At this point there is not much you can do but keep your ears attuned to releases of new software.

Long File Names

Even if you are an experienced programmer under previous versions of DOS or Windows 3.1, Windows 95 has one major new feature—*long file names*. In this section, we give a few tips for working with Windows 95/NT. If you are a seasoned veteran, or if you do not use Windows 95/NT, just skip this section.

If you are coming from DOS or Windows 3.1, you know that a DOS file can have, at most, eight characters in the name and three characters in the extension, such as `WLCMAPPL.HTM`. These are the so-called 8.3 file names. With Windows 95 or NT, you can use as many characters as you like. For example, you can call a file `WelcomeApplet.html`. This is very welcome news, indeed.

- Actually, you do not have a choice when dealing with Java; *all* Java source files use long file names. They *must* have the four-letter extension `.java`.

Luckily, most of the new versions of the traditional DOS utility functions included in Windows NT or Windows 95 understand long file names. For example, you can type

```
del WelcomeApplet.html
```

or

```
copy *.java a:
```

Of course, if you prefer, you can delete and copy the files through the Explorer, but many programmers type faster than they mouse, and, therefore, prefer the command line.

To let you use programs that were written before long file names were invented, Microsoft gives each long file name an 8.3 file name *alias*. These aliases contain a ~ character, for example `WELCOM~1.HTM`. If there are two files in the same directory whose names start with `WELCOM` and have HTM in the extension, then their aliases are `WELCOM~1.HTM` and `WELCOM~2.HTM`.

In the event that there are *two* names for the same file, be careful when deleting files, especially when you use wild cards. For example, the command

```
del *.HTM
```

will delete all files with the extension HTM and all files whose extension *starts with* HTM. In particular, all `*.html` files will also be deleted.

Windows Explorer gives you access to the long file names. But if you are working with a DOS shell, how do you find the long file name?

- The DIR command shows the 8.3 alias on the left and the long file name
  on the right.

Figure 2-3

After a few weeks, you will get into the habit of looking at the right-hand side
and ignoring the left-hand side.

> **CAUTION**
>
> One of the programs that has not yet been adapted to long
> file names is PKZIP. If you use the venerable PKZIP 2.04g to
> bundle and compress files, you will find that it only packs
> and unpacks the 8.3 file names.

You can make a real hash out of a collection of Java files by using the DOS version of PKZIP. Instead, you should use a modern zipping tool like WinZip. We
include a shareware copy of WinZip on the CD-ROM. For example, you can use
WinZip to peek inside the CLASSES.ZIP file in the \java\lib directory. (But do
not actually unzip that file. The Java compiler expects it to be zipped.)

Long file names can even contain spaces. You may have noticed that some programs are installed in a directory with the name `Program Files`. As you can imagine, this can be confusing for some DOS commands that traditionally expect spaces to separate the file names and command options. You need to enclose any file or directory name that contains spaces in quotation marks, for example

```
del "The first applet in the Core Java book.java"
```

Don't worry. We will not use file names like that in our examples.

Long file names are not case sensitive *for DOS commands*. For example,

```
del WelcomeApplet.java
```

and

```
del welcomeapplet.JAVA
```

both have the same effect. But Windows 95 *retains the case* that you used when you first created the file. For example, if you named the file `WelcomeApplet.java`, then Windows will use the uppercase `W` and `A` in the directory display and all directory dialog boxes.

Java, on the other hand, *is* case sensitive. As you will soon see, a file like `WelcomeApplet.java` contains a class with the same name, `WelcomeApplet`. If you compile this file with the command

```
java welcomeapplet.java
```

then the compiler will ask DOS to open the file. DOS has no problem opening the `WelcomeApplet.java` file, but the compiler will insist that it cannot find a `welcomeapplet` class. You will get some strange error message that relates to the file not being found. The moral is that anytime you cannot compile a file that you know is there, check the case of the file name with the DIR command or with Explorer.

If you notice the problem and regret your decision, you can use the `ren` command to change the look of the file name.

```
ren welcomeapplet.java WelcomeApplet.java
```

Multiple Windows

When using JDK, multiple DOS windows are a way of life. You run the editor in one DOS window and the compiler in another. Graphical applications, applets, and the browser run in other windows. Windows 95 has a nifty *task bar* at the bottom of the screen that lets you easily switch between windows.

Figure 2-4

If you use a computer with a small screen (such as a laptop computer), you may find that the task bar takes up valuable screen real estate. You can *hide* the task bar. (Click on an empty area of the task bar with the right mouse button, then select Properties and Auto Hide.) This tells Windows to display the task bar only when you move the mouse towards the bottom of the screen. (You can also drag the task bar to another place on your screen if you like.)

Keyboard Shortcuts

As you probably know, the mouse was originally designed by researchers in the prestigious Xerox PARC lab. One of their unstated goals seems to have been to slow you down so the computer can keep up with you. Programmers do not like to be slowed down, and their programmer comrades at Microsoft have fought the mouse maniacs and kept a number of *keyboard shortcuts* in the operating system. Here are a few of these keystroke combinations that we have found helpful.

ALT+TAB: This key combination displays a small window with icons, one for each running task.

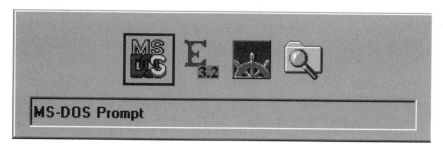

Figure 2-5

Keep your thumb on the ALT key and hold down TAB. Different icons will be selected. Let go of both keys, and you switch to the selected window.

CTRL+ESC: This key combination pops up the start menu in the task bar. If you arrange your most-used program icons into the first level of the start menu, then you can run them with a couple of keystrokes.

Put the MS-DOS prompt, WinEdit, and Netscape into the first level of the start menu. (To edit the start menu, right-click on an empty area of the task bar, then select Properties and Start Menu Programs.)

Under Windows 95, the CTRL+ALT+DEL key combination does not reboot the computer. Instead, it pops up a window of all active applications, like this:

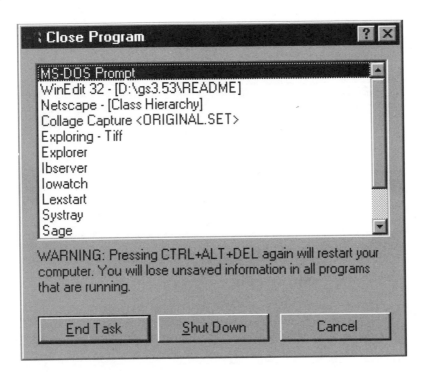

Figure 2-6

If you have a non-responsive program

1.   pop up this box,

2.   select the program from the given list,

3.   click on the End Task button.

Hitting CTRL+ALT+DEL *twice* does reboot the computer, so you want to have a steady hand when using this key combination.

More on DOS Shells

The humble MS-DOS shell has come a long way from that in earlier versions of Windows. In fact, the DOS shell in Windows 95 is, in many ways, better than ever. For starters, as you have seen, you can run multiple DOS shells and toggle between them. You can also launch Windows applications directly from the DOS shell. For example, if you type

```
notepad
```

into a DOS prompt and hit ENTER, the Notepad program starts up. This is at least 10 times faster than clicking on Start Menu | Programs | Accessories | Notepad.

If you use the DOS shell, you should use the DOSKEY program. The DOSKEY utility keeps a *command history*. Type the up and down arrow keys to cycle through the previously typed commands. Use the left and right arrow keys to edit the current command. Type the beginning of a command and hit F8 to complete it. For example, if you have typed

```
appletviewer WelcomeApplet.html
```

once, then you just type

```
apF8
```

to instantly retype the command. You get a chance to edit it, in case you want to issue a slightly different command.

To install DOSKEY into your AUTOEXEC.BAT file, simply add the line

```
DOSKEY /INSERT
```

and reboot.

The EDIT Program

If you need to do a quick edit, and you do not want to wait for your regular editor to start, try the EDIT program that comes with Windows 95. You will be pleasantly surprised. This is not the QuickBasic editor that came with DOS 5 and 6, but a completely different program. In particular, this editor handles long file names, *and* it can edit up to 10 files at a time. You switch between the files by hitting ALT+1, ALT+2, and so on. You can even launch the editor with a wild card:

```
edit *.java
```

Unfortunately, EDIT is still a DOS program, which means that it is difficult to cut and paste between it and other Windows programs. (It can be done, but you need to use the Mark, Copy, and Paste icons on the top of the DOS shell window, not the usual editor commands.) Of course, you can cut and paste between different files that are loaded into the editor. (You can use Notepad if you want a more efficient way to cut and paste between Windows programs.)

Compiling and Running Java Programs

There are two methods for compiling and launching a Java program: from the command line and from an editor. Let us do it the hard way first: from the command line. Go to the \CoreJavaBook\ch2\Welcome directory. Then enter the following commands:

```
javac Welcome.java
java Welcome
```

You should see this message on the screen:

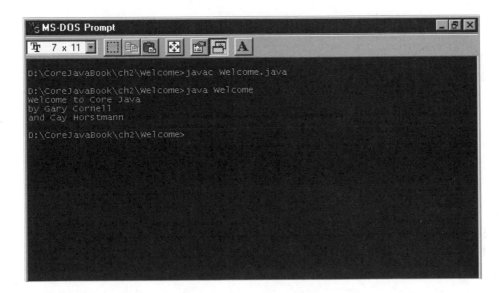

Figure 2-7

Congratulations! You have just compiled and run your first Java program.

What happened? The javac program is the Java compiler. It compiles the file Welcome.java into the file Welcome.class. The java program is the Java interpreter. It interprets the so-called bytecodes that the compiler placed in the class file.

The Welcome program is extremely simple. It simply prints a message to the console. You may enjoy looking inside the program—we will explain how it works in the next chapter.

```
public class Welcome
{   public static void main(String[] args)
    {   String greeting[] = new String[3];
        greeting[0] = "Welcome to Core Java";
        greeting[1] = "by Gary Cornell";
        greeting[2] = "and Cay Horstmann";

        int i;
        for (i = 0; i < greeting.length; i++)
            System.out.println(greeting[i]);
    }
}
```

Every integrated environment has commands for compiling and running programs. If you do not use WinEdit, read your documentation to find out how to compile and run programs. If you want to use WinEdit, read the next section.

Using WinEdit

Compiling and Running Programs

Of course, we grew quite comfortable with our customized version of WinEdit in the course of writing this book. WinEdit defaults to using the normal editing commands that most Windows programs expect. (The keystrokes for most tasks are customizable as well.) WinEdit comes with a complete help system, so we will not go into the details of using it as an editor. (It should take an experienced programmer maybe 15 minutes to master it.)

In this section, we will show you the steps needed to run the Welcome program from inside the WinEdit environment. *Then* we will explain the advantages of using WinEdit when you make a typo or three.

To compile and run the Welcome program from our customized version of WinEdit,

1. start up WinEdit,

2. choose File | Open and work with the dialog box to find and then load the Welcome.java source code,

3. select Project | Compile from the menu. This runs the Java compiler and captures any error messages. (We hope there are none.) While Java is compiling the file, you see a screen like this:

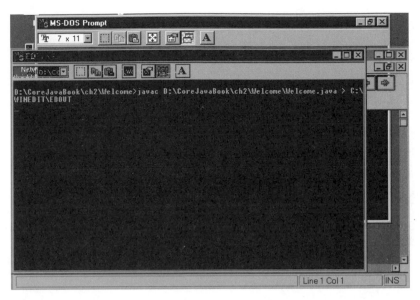

Figure 2-8

WinEdit has automatically opened a temporary DOS shell to run the Java compiler. When the compiler has finished, you will see a dialog box that looks like this:

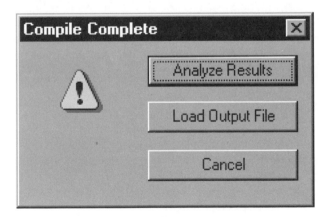

Figure 2-9

Hit the Analyze Results button. There should be a message "No errors or warnings" in the status bar. Then select Project | Execute to see the compiled code at work. This pops up another DOS window, shown here, for the output.

Figure 2-10

We customized WinEdit so that this window remains open until you hit a key to continue.

Locating Compilation Errors

Presumably, our program did not have typos or bugs. (It was only a few lines of code, after all.) Let us suppose, for the sake of argument, that you occasionally have a typo (perhaps even a bug) in your code. Try it out—ruin our file, for example, by changing the capitalization in the first few lines like this:

```
Public class Welcome
{  Public Static Void Main(String[] args)
   {  String Greeting[] = new String[3];
      greeting[0] = "Welcome to Core Java";
      greeting[1] = "by Gary Cornell";
      greeting[2] = "and Cay Horstmann";

      int i;
      for (i = 0; i < greeting.length; i++)
         System.out.println(greeting[i]);
   }
}
```

Now run the Java compiler again by choosing Project | Compile. You will see the dialog box that contains the Analyze Results button. Click on this button. Now WinEdit will put the cursor onto the offending line and display an error message in the status bar like this:

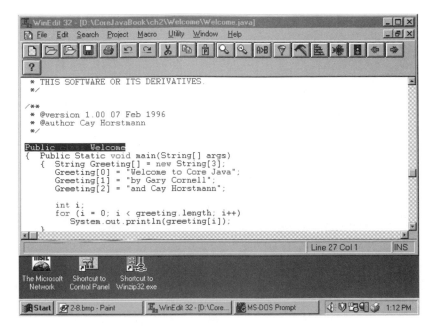

Figure 2-11

Use the Search | Next error command to walk through any error messages.

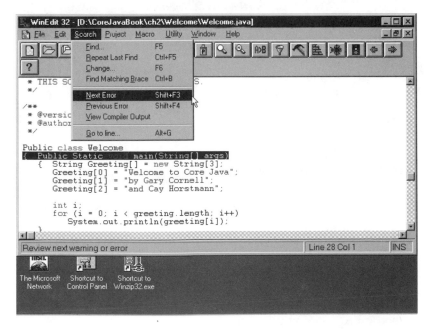

Figure 2-12

Again, once your program compiles without errors, you can try to run it by selecting Project | Run from the menu.

Graphical Applications

The Welcome program was not terribly exciting. Next, let us run a graphical application. This program is a very simple GIF file-viewer. It simply loads and displays a GIF file. Again, let us first compile and run it from the command line.

1. Open a DOS shell window.

2. Change to the directory \CoreJavaBook\ch2\ImageViewer.

3. Enter

   ```
   javac ImageViewer.java
   java ImageViewer
   ```

A new program window pops up with our ImageViewer application.

Now select File | Open and look for a GIF file to open. (We supplied a couple of sample files in the directory.)

Figure 2-13

To close the program, click on the Close box in the title bar or pull down the system menu and close the program. (To compile and run this program inside WinEdit or a development environment, do the same as before. For example, for WinEdit, choose Project | Compile, then choose Project | Run.)

We hope that you find this program interesting and useful. Have a quick look at the source code. The program is substantially longer than the first program, but it is not terribly complex if you consider how much code it would take in C or C++ to write a similar application. In VB, of course, it is easy to write, or, rather, drag and drop, such a program—you need only add about two lines of code to make it functional. At this time, Java does not have a visual interface builder, so you need to write code for everything. We will learn how to write graphical programs like this in Chapter 6.

```java
import java.awt.*;
import java.awt.image.*;
import java.net.*;
import java.io.*;

public class ImageViewer extends Frame
{   public ImageViewer()
    {   setTitle("ImageViewer");
        MenuBar mbar = new MenuBar();
        Menu m = new Menu("File");
        m.add(new MenuItem("Open"));
        m.add(new MenuItem("Exit"));
        mbar.add(m);
        setMenuBar(mbar);
    }

    public boolean handleEvent(Event evt)
    {   if (evt.id == Event.WINDOW_DESTROY) System.exit(0);
        return super.handleEvent(evt);
    }

    public boolean action(Event evt, Object arg)
    {   if (arg.equals("Open"))
        {   FileDialog d = new FileDialog(this,
                "Open image file", FileDialog.LOAD);
            d.setFile("*.gif");
            d.show();
            String f = d.getFile();
            if (f != null)
                image = Toolkit.getDefaultToolkit().getImage(f);
            repaint();
        }
        else if(arg.equals("Exit")) System.exit(0);
        else return false;
        return true;
    }

    public void paint(Graphics g)
    {   if (image != null)
```

```
        g.drawImage(image, 0, 0, this);
   }

   public static void main(String args[])
   {  Frame f = new ImageViewer();
      f.resize(300, 200);
      f.show();
   }

   private Image image = null;
}
```

Applets

The first two programs presented in this book are Java *applications*, stand-alone programs like any native programs. On the other hand, as we mentioned in the last chapter, most of the hype about Java comes from its ability to run *applets* inside a Web browser. We want to show you how to build and run an applet, first from the command line, then from WinEdit. Finally, we will load the applet into a Web browser (Netscape, in our case).

First, go to the directory \CoreJavaBook\ch2\WelcomeApplet then enter the following commands:

```
javac WelcomeApplet.java
appletviewer WelcomeApplet.html
```

Here is what you see in the applet viewer window.

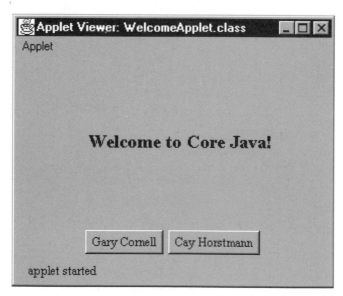

Figure 2-14

The first command is the now-familiar command to invoke the Java compiler. This compiles the `WelcomeApplet.java` source into the bytecode file `WelcomeApplet.class`. This time, however, we do not run the Java interpreter; we use the applet-viewer program instead. This program is a special tool included with the JDK that lets you quickly test an applet. You need to give it an HTML file, rather than the name of a `Java.class` file. Here are the contents of the `WelcomeApplet.html` file:

```
<HTML>
<TITLE>WelcomeApplet</TITLE>
<HR>
This applet is from the book
<A
HREF="http://www.sun.com/smi/ssoftpress/catalog/java_series.html">
Core Java</A> by Gary Cornell and
<A HREF="http://www.mathcs.sjsu.edu/faculty/horstman">
Cay Horstmann</A>, published by SunSoft Press/Prentice-Hall

<APPLET CODE=WelcomeApplet.class WIDTH=200 HEIGHT=200>
<PARAM NAME=greeting VALUE="Welcome to Core Java!">
</APPLET>

<HR>
<A href="WelcomeApplet.java">The source.</A>
```

If you are familiar with HTML, you will notice some standard HTML instructions and the new APPLET tag, telling the applet-viewer to load the applet whose code is stored in `WelcomeApplet.class`. The applet-viewer ignores all other codes in this file. But a Java-aware browser, such as Netscape version 2.0 or later, will display both the traditional HTML text and the applet on the same Web page. (See Chapter 8 for more on these tags.)

Try it out. You need Netscape 2.0 (or later) or another Java-enabled browser. (We do not include Netscape on the CD-ROM; you can always download a trial version from `www.netscape.com`.)

1. Start Netscape.

2. Select File | Open File.

3. Go to the `\CoreJavaBook\ch2\WelcomeApplet` directory.

You should see the `WelcomeApplet.html` file in the file dialog. Load that file. Netscape now loads the applet, including the surrounding text.

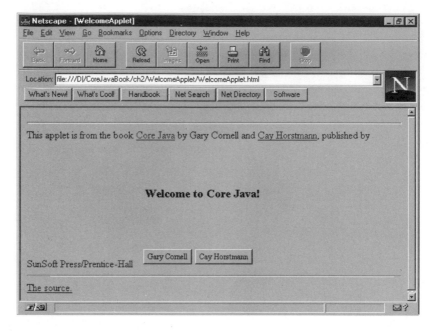

Figure 2-15

You can see that this application is actually alive and willing to interact with the Internet. Click on the Gary Cornell button. The applet directs Netscape to pop up a mail window, with Gary's address already filled in. Click on the Cay Horstmann button. The applet directs Netscape to display Cay's Web page.

Notice that neither of these two buttons work in the applet viewer. The applet viewer has no capabilities to send mail or display a Web page, so it ignores your requests. The applet viewer is good for testing applets in isolation, but you need to put it inside Netscape or another Java-enabled browser to see how applets interact with the browser and the Internet.

You can also compile and run applets from inside WinEdit. As always, select Project I Compile, then Project I Run. This time, what happens is that WinEdit launches a batch file that realizes you are running an applet, not an application. It builds an HTML file on the fly and launches the applet-viewer. If you use an integrated environment such as Café, it has its own commands to launch an applet.

Finally, here is the code for the `Welcome` applet. At this point, do not give it more than a glance. We will come back to writing applets in Chapter 8.

```java
import java.applet.*;
import java.awt.*;
import java.net.*;

public class WelcomeApplet extends Applet
{   public void start()
    {   setLayout(new BorderLayout());
        Label l = new Label(getParameter("greeting"),
            Label.CENTER);
        l.setFont(new Font("Times", Font.BOLD, 18));
        add("Center", l);
        Panel p = new Panel();
        p.add(new Button("Gary Cornell"));
        p.add(new Button("Cay Horstmann"));
        add("South", p);
    }

    public boolean action(Event evt, Object arg)
    {   String uName;
        URL u;
        if (arg.equals("Gary Cornell"))
            uName = "mailto:75720.1524@compuserve.com";
        else if (arg.equals("Cay Horstmann"))
            uName =
"http://www.mathcs.sjsu.edu/faculty/horstman/cay.html";
        else return false;
        try
        {   u = new URL(uName);
            getAppletContext().showDocument(u);
        }
        catch(Exception e)
        {   showStatus("Error " + e);
        }
        return true;
    }
}
```

Troubleshooting

We want to end this section with a few tips whose discovery caused us some grief; we hope you can learn from our pain.

PATH, CLASSPATH, and Other Environment Variables

The single most common problem we encountered with Java is an incorrect PATH or CLASSPATH environment variable.

1. The `\java\bin directory` (or the directory containing your integrated environment's executables) must be on the *PATH*.

2. The `\java\lib` and the current directory (that is, the . directory) must be on the *CLASSPATH*.

3. The `CoreJavaBook` directory must also be on the *CLASSPATH*.

4. Some environments (like Café) also use a *JAVA_HOME* environment variable.

Double-check these settings and reboot your computer if you run into trouble.

Memory Problems

If you have only 16 MB of memory, you may get "insufficient memory" errors from the Java compiler. In that case, close memory hogs like Netscape and Microsoft Exchange. If you have less than 16 MB of memory, you will probably be unable to compile large programs.

Only the compiler and applet viewer pig out on memory. Once you compile an application, you should have no trouble running it with the Java interpreter or Netscape, even with less than 16 MB of memory.

Case Sensitivity

Java is case sensitive. HTML is sometimes case sensitive. DOS is not case sensitive. This caused us no end of grief, especially since Java can give very bizarre error messages when it messes up because of a spelling error. Always check file names, parameter names, class names, keywords, and so on for capitalization.

About Other Platforms

Watch the Web for information on other platforms. For starters, keep track of the discussions on `comp.lang.java`. This will often be the place that first reports information on updates or on versions for new platforms. This also seems to be the place where (after you filter out some noise) you will see reports on problems with current versions.

For example, as we write this, the Mac version of Java cannot handle stand-alone applications. Unfortunately, we use these to teach the Java language in Chapters 3–7. You will need to wait until this capability is added in order to run these applications on the Mac. To get the latest information on the Mac, go to the Sun site `java.sun.com`.

IBM has an OS/2 site (`ncc.hursley.ibm.com/javainfo/faq.html`). The latest information about Linux can usually be found from the FAQ page (`www.www-net.com/java/faq/`), and one site that will have the current version is `ftp://java.blackdown.org/pub/Java/linux`.

Updates and Bug Fixes

The CD-ROM contains almost 400 files, and some of them are bound
to have minor glitches and inconsistencies. We will keep a list of frequently
asked questions, bug reports, and bug fixes on the Web page
`http://www.mathcs.sjsu.edu/faculty/horstman/corejava.html`.
Please read the FAQ before sending in a complaint or bug report. We also welcome any suggestions for improvements.

CHAPTER

3

Fundamental Programming Structures in Java

At this point, we are assuming that you successfully installed Java and were able to run the sample programs in Chapter 2. It is time to show how to program in Java. This chapter shows you how the basic programming concepts such as data types, loops, and user-defined functions (actually, they are usually called *methods* in Java) are implemented in Java. If you are an experienced C++ programmer, you can get away with just skimming this chapter: concentrate on the C/C++ notes that are interspersed throughout the text. Programmers coming from another background, such as Visual Basic (VB), will find most of the concepts familiar and all of the syntax maddening—you will want to read this chapter very carefully.

Unfortunately, getting output from Java is cumbersome. For this reason, almost all the sample programs in this chapter will be "toy" programs, designed to illustrate a concept. In all cases they will simply send or receive information to or from the console. (For example, if you are using Windows 95, the console is an MS-DOS window.) In particular, we will be writing *applications* rather than *applets* in this chapter.

If output in Java is cumbersome, input is even worse. Since it is hard to write even toy programs without a decent method of getting input from the user, the CD contains sufficient code for doing simple (prompted) input. We suggest not worrying too much about how input works at first. We will explain some of the details later in this chapter and finish it off in the next chapter.

A Very Simple Java Program

Let's return to the very simple Java program that you saw in the last chapter:

```
public class FirstSample
  {   public static void main(String[] args)
      {   System.out.println("We will not use 'Hello world!'");
      }
  }
```

After you compiled this *source code*, you obtained a byte code. After running the byte code through the Java interpreter, you saw that this code simply displays the quoted string on the console (an MS-DOS window for users of Windows 95).

It is worth spending all the time you need in order to understand the framework of this sample; the pieces will reoccur in all applications. First and foremost, *Java is case sensitive*. If you made any mistakes in capitalization (such as typing `Main` instead of `main`), the program will not compile.

Having said this, let's look at this source code from the top. The keyword `class` is there because everything in a Java program lives inside a class. Although we will spend a lot more time on classes in the next chapter, for now think of a class as a container for the data and methods (functions) that make up part or all of an application. As mentioned in Chapter 1, classes are the building blocks with which all Java applications and applets are built. *Everything* in a Java program must be inside a class.

Following, the keyword `class` is the name of the class. You need to make the file name for the source code the same as the name of the class with the word *java* appended. Thus, we would store this code in a file called `FirstSample.java` (notice that long file names are needed). The compiled byte code is then automatically called `FirstSample.class` and stored in the same directory.

The Java compiler looks at the name of the class and not at the name of the file where source code is stored to determine the file name for the compiled byte code.

(The CD stores the code for each sample. For example, the first sample program is stored in the `\CoreJavaBook\ch2\FirstSample` directory.)

Applets have a different structure—see Chapter 8 for information on applets.

When you use

```
java NameOfClass
```

to run a compiled program, the Java interpreter always starts execution with the code in the main method in the named class. Thus you *must* have a main method (function) for your code to compile. You can, of course, add your own methods to a class and call them from the main function. (We cover writing your own methods later in this chapter.)

Next, notice the braces in the source code. In Java, as in C/C++ (but not in Pascal or VB), braces are used to delineate the parts (usually called *blocks*) in your program. A VB programmer can think of the outermost pair of braces as corresponding to a Sub/End Sub pair; a Pascal programmer can relate them to the first begin/end pair. In Java, the code for any method must be started by an open brace and so ended by a close brace. (We will have more to say about braces later in this chapter.)

Brace styles have inspired an inordinate amount of useless controversy. We use a style that lines up the braces that delineate each block. Since white space is irrelevant to the Java compiler, you can use whatever brace style you like. We will have more to say about the use of braces when we talk about the various kinds of loops.

If you are not a C++ programmer, don't worry about the keywords static void. For now, just think of them as part of the incantation needed to get a Java program to compile. By the end of Chapter 4, you will understand this incantation completely. The point to remember for now is that every Java application must have a main method (function) whose header is identical to the one shown here.

You know what a class is. Java classes are similar to C++ classes, but there are a few differences that can trap you. For example, in Java *all* functions are member functions of some class, and the standard terminology refers to them as *methods* rather than member functions. Thus, in Java you must have a shell class for the main method. You may also be familiar with the idea of *static member functions*. These are functions defined inside a class that do not operate on objects. The main method (function) in Java is always static. Finally, as in C/C++, the void keyword indicates that this method (function) does not return a value.

The closest analogy in VB would be a program that uses a Sub Main rather than a startup form. Recall that if you choose to have a Sub Main, *everything* has to be explicitly called from Sub Main.

Next, turn your attention to this fragment.

```
{   System.out.println("We will not use 'Hello world!'");
}
```

Braces mark the beginning and end of the *body* of the method. This method only has one statement in it. As in most programming languages, you can think of Java statements as being the sentences of the language. In Java *every statement must end with a semicolon*. (For those coming from a Pascal background, the semicolon in Java is not the statement separator, but rather the statement terminator.)

In particular, neither white space nor carriage returns mark the end of a statement, so statements can span lines if need be. There are essentially no limits on the length of a statement. Here we are using a statement that outputs a single line of text to the console.

Here we are using the `System.out` object and asking it to use its `println` method. The `println` method works with a string and displays it on the standard console. It then adds a line feed. C/C++ and VB (but not Pascal), use double quotes. (See the section on strings later in this chapter for more information.)

Methods in Java, like functions in any programming languages, can use zero, one, or more *arguments* (some languages call them *parameters*). Even the `main` method (function) in Java accepts what the user types on the command line as its argument. You will see how to use this information later in this chapter. (Even if a method takes zero arguments, you must still use empty parentheses.)

You also have a `print` method in `System.out` that doesn't add a carriage return/line feed combination to the string.

Although in Java, as in C/C++, the `main` function receives an array of command line arguments, the array syntax in Java is different. A `String[]` is an array of strings. The name of the program is not stored in the `args` array. For example, when you start up the program `Bjarne.java` as

```
java Bjarne Stroustrup
```

from the command line, then `args[0]` will be `Stroustrup` and not `Bjarne`.

Comments

Comments in Java, like comments in most programming languages, do not show up in the executable program. Thus, you can add as many comments as needed without fear of bloating the code. Java has three ways of showing comments. The most common method is a //, to be used for a comment that will run only the length of a line:

```
System.out.println("We will not use 'Hello world!'");
// is this too cute?
```

In the case of // comments, the end of a line is marked by a carriage return, a line feed, or both.

When larger comments are needed, you can mark each line with a //, but it is more common to use the /* and */ that let you block off a larger comment:

```
/*
This is the first sample program in Core Java
Copyright (C) 1996 Gary Cornell and Cay Horstmann
*/
class FirstSample
{  public static void main(String[] args)
   {  System.out.println("We will not use 'Hello world!'");
   }
}
```

The // comment style is painful to modify when you need to extend comments over multiple lines, so we suggest using it only when you are sure the comment will never grow.

Finally, there is a third kind of comment that can be used to generate documentation automatically. This comment uses a /** to start and a */ to end. For more on this type of comment and on automatic documentation generation, please see Appendix II.

Comments do not nest in Java.

Data Types

Java is an example of a *strongly typed language*. This means that every variable must have a declared type. There are eight *primitive types* in Java. Six of them are number types (four integer and two floating-point types); one is the character type char, used for characters in Unicode encoding (see the section on the char type), and one is a boolean type for truth values.

Java hasn't any type analogous to the Variant data type, in which you can store all possible types. It does have a way of converting all types to strings for display purposes that you will see later in this chapter.

Integers

The integer types are for numbers without fractional parts. Negative values are allowed. Java provides four integer types:

Type	Storage Requirement	Range (inclusive)
int	4 bytes	–2,147,483,648 to 2,147,483,647 (just over 2 billion)
short	2 bytes	–32,768 to 32,767
long	8 bytes	–9,223,372,036,854,775,808L to 9,223,372,036,854,775,807L
byte	1 byte	–128 to 127

In most situations, the int type is the most practical. If you want to represent the national debt in pennies, you'll need to resort to long. The byte and short types are mainly intended for specialized applications such as low-level file handling, or for large arrays when storage space is at a premium. The point is that, under Java, the integer types do not depend on the machine on which you will be running the Java code. This alleviates a major pain for the programmer who wants to move software from one platform to another, or even between operating systems on the same platform. A C program that runs well on a Sparc may exhibit integer overflow under Windows 3.1. Since Java programs must run with the same results on all machines by its design, the ranges for the various types are fixed. Of course having platform-independent integer types brings a small performance penalty, but in the case of Java this is not a particular bottleneck. (There are worse bottlenecks....)

Long integer literals have a suffix L (for example, 4000000000L). Hexadecimal numbers have a prefix 0x, for example 0xCAFE.

In C and C++, int denotes the integer type that depends on the target machine. On a 16-bit processor, like the 8086, integers are 2 bytes. On a 32-bit processor like the Sun Sparc, they are 4-byte quantities. On an Intel Pentium, the integer type depends on the operating system: for DOS and Windows 3.1, integers are 2 bytes. When using 32-bit mode for Windows 95 or Windows NT programs, integers are 4 bytes. In Java, the sizes of all numeric types are platform independent.

The ranges for the integer types are quite different in Java. An integer in VB corresponds to a short in Java. The int type in Java corresponds to the Longint type in VB, and so on.

Floating-Point Types

The floating-point types denote numbers with fractional parts. There are two floating-point types:

Type	Storage Requirement	Range
float	4 bytes	range roughly ±3.40282347E+38F (7 significant decimal digits)
double	8 bytes	range roughly ±1.79769313486231570E+308 (15 significant digits)

The name double refers to the fact that these numbers have twice the precision of the float type. (Some people call these *double-precision* variables.) Here, the type of choice in most applications is double. The limited precision of float is simply not sufficient for many situations. Seven significant (decimal) digits may be enough to precisely express your annual salary in dollars and cents, but it won't be enough for your company president's salary. The only reason to use float is in the rare situations in which the slightly faster processing of single-precision numbers is important, or when you need to store a large number of them.

Literals of type float have a suffix F, for example 3.402F.

> All the floating-point types follow the IEEE 754 specification. They will overflow on range errors and underflow on operations like a divide by zero.

The Character Type (char)

First, the char type, unlike the string type, uses single quotes to denote a char. Second, the char type denotes characters in the Unicode encoding scheme. You may not be familiar with Unicode, and, fortunately, you don't need to worry much about it if you don't program international applications. (Even if you do, you still won't have to worry about it too much because Unicode was designed to make the use of non-Roman characters easy to handle.) Because Unicode was designed to handle essentially all characters in all written languages in the world, it is a 2-byte code. This allows 65,536 characters, unlike ASCII/ANSI, which is a 1-byte code allowing only 255 characters. The familiar ASCII/ANSI code that you use in Windows programming is a subset of Unicode. More precisely, it is the first 255 characters in the Unicode coding scheme. Thus, character codes like 'a', '1', and '[' are valid Unicode characters. Unicode characters are most often expressed in terms of a hexadecimal encoding scheme that runs from '\u0000' to '\uFFFF' (with '\u0000' to '\u00FF' being the ordinary ASCII/ANSI characters). The \u prefix indicates a Unicode value.

Besides the \u escape character that denotes a Unicode character, Java allows you to use the following escape sequences for special characters

\b	backspace	\u0008
\t	tab	\u0009
\n	linefeed	\u000a
\r	carriage return	\u000d
\"	double quote	\u0022
\'	single quote	\u0027
\\	a backslash	\u005c

In C and C++, char denotes an *integral* type, namely 1-byte integers. The standard is coy about the exact range. It can be either 0...255 or –128...127. In Java, char data are not numbers. Converting from numbers to characters requires an explicit cast in Java.

Boolean

The boolean type has two values, false and true. It is used for logical testing using the relational operators that Java, like any programming language, supports.

In C, there is no Boolean type. Instead, the convention is that any non-zero value denotes true, and zero denotes false. In C++, a Boolean type (called bool, not boolean) has recently been added to the language standard. It, too, has values false and true, but for historical reasons conversions between Boolean values and integers are allowed, and you can still use numbers or pointers in test conditions. In Java, you cannot convert between numbers and Boolean values, not even with a cast.

In VB any non-zero value is regarded as true and zero is regarded as false. This simply will not work in Java—you cannot use a number where a Boolean value is needed.

Variables

Java, like C++ and Pascal-based languages, requires you to declare the type of a variable. (Of course, good programming practice in VB would require this as well.) You declare a variable by placing the type first, followed by the name of the variable. Here are some examples:

```
byte b; // for space sensitive considerations
int anIntegerVariable;
long aLongVariable; // for the national debt in pennies
char ch;
```

Notice the semicolon at the end of each declaration (and the comment in the first line). The semicolon is necessary because a declaration is a complete Java expression.

You cannot use a Java reserved word for a variable name. (See Appendix I for a list of reserved words.) The rules for a variable name are as follows:

A name must begin with a letter and be a sequence of letters or digits. A letter is defined as 'A'–'Z', 'a'–'z', '_', '$', or any Unicode character that denotes a letter in a language. For example, German users can use umlauts such as 'ä' in variable names. Digits are '0'–'9' and any Unicode characters that denote a digit in a language. Symbols like '+' or '©' cannot be used inside variable names. *All characters in the name of a variable are significant and case is also significant.* The length of a variable name is essentially unlimited.

You can include multiple declarations on a single line

```
int i, j; //both are integers unlike in VB!
```

but we generally comment and initialize each variable separately and so prefer declarations on separate lines.

Assignments and Initializations

After you declare a variable, you should assign it a value: explicitly initialize a variable by means of an assignment statement—you should never have uninitialized variables. (And the compiler will usually prevent you from having them anyway.) You assign to a previously declared variable using the variable name on the left, an equal sign (=), and then some Java expression that has an appropriate value on the right.

```
int foo; // this is a declaration
foo = 37; // this is an assignment
```

Here's an example of an assignment to a character variable:

```
char yesChar;
yesChar = 'Y';
```

Notice that chars (unlike strings) use single quotes to identify the character. It is also possible to use a direct hexadecimal representation of a Unicode char. To do this, you must translate the Unicode character number into a four digit hexadecimal code—and you must use the two leading zeros. For example, a capital "A" has Unicode (and ASCII/ANSI, of course) code decimal 65 = hex 41. If you wanted to use the code for the character, you could use:

```
char capitalA;
capitalA = '\u0041'; // decimal 65
```

Finally, in Java you can put declarations anywhere in your code, but you can only declare a variable once in any block in a method. (See the section on Control Flow in this chapter for more on blocks.)

One nice feature of Java that it inherited from C/C++ is the ability to both declare and initialize a variable on the same line. (This is usually called a definition of a variable and is not technically an assignment.) This is also done with an = sign. For example:

```
int i = 10; // we will countdown with this
```

Conversions between Numeric Types

Java does not have any trouble multiplying, say, an integer by a double—it will treat the result as a double. More generally, any binary operations on numeric variables of different types will be acceptable and be treated in the following fashion:

- If any of the operands is of type `double`, the other one will be treated as a `double` for the scope of the operation.

- Otherwise, if any of the operands is of type `float`, the other one will be treated as a `float`.

- Otherwise, if any of the operands is of type `long`, the other one will be treated as a `long`.

This works similarly down the line of the integer types: int, short and byte.

On the other hand, there are obviously times when you want to consider a `double` as an integer. All numeric conversions are possible in Java but, of course, information may be lost. These conversions are usually done by means of *casts*. The syntax for casting is to give the target type in parentheses, followed by the variable name. For example:

```
double x = 9.997;
int nx = (int) x;
```

Then the variable nx has the value 9, as casting a floating-point value to an integer discards the fractional part.

Java does not complain ("throw an exception" in Java-speak—see Chapter 10) if you try to cast a number of one type to another that is out of the range for the target type. The result will be a truncated number that has a different value. It is, therefore, a good idea to explicitly test that the value is in the correct range before you perform the cast.

You cannot cast between Boolean values and any numeric type.

Finally, Java allows you to make certain assignment conversions by assigning the value of a variable of one type to another without an explicit cast. Those that are permitted are

```
byte →short →int →long →float →double
```

where you can always assign a variable of a type that is to the left to the type on its right in the list above.

Constants

Java has only very limited ways for defining constants. In particular, you cannot define local constants for an individual method like `main`. Instead, you can only have constants that are available to all the methods in the class. These are usually called *class constants*. The keywords used in this incantation will be explained in Chapter 4, but here is an example of using a class constant:

```
class UsesConstants
{   static final double g = 32;
      // gravitation in feet/second squared;
   public static void main(String[] args)
   {   System.out.println(g + "feet per second squared");
   }
}
```

Note that the definition appears before the function header that defines the `main` function and must use the keywords `static final`.

`const` is a reserved Java keyword, but it is not currently used for anything. You must use `static final` to declare constants in the scope of a file (or `public static final` for a global constant). For a local constant, just pretend it is a variable.

Operators

The usual arithmetic operators `+ - * /` are used in Java for addition, subtraction, multiplication, and division. The `/` operator denotes integer division if both arguments are integers, and floating-point division otherwise. Integer remainder (i.e., the mod function) is denoted by `%`. For example, `15 / 4` is 3, `15 % 2` is 1, and `11.0 / 4` is 2.75. You can use the arithmetic operators in your variable initializations:

```
int n = 5;
int a = 2 * n; // a is 10
```

There is actually a shortcut for using binary arithmetic operators in an assignment. For example,

```
x += 4;
```

is equivalent to

```
x = x + 4;
```

(In general, place the operator to the left of the = sign.)

Exponentiation

Unlike languages like VB, Java has no operator for raising a quantity to a power: you must use the pow function. The pow function is part of the Math class in Java.lang so one way of using it is via the incantation

```
y = Math.pow(x, a);
```

which gives you x raised to the a'th power. The pow function takes arguments that are both of type double.

Increment and Decrement Operators

Programmers, of course, know that one of the most common operations with a numeric variable is to add or subtract one. Java, following in the footsteps of C and C++, has both increment and decrement operators: x++ adds one to the current value of the variable x, and x-- subtracts one from it. For example, the code

```
int n = 12;
n++;
```

changes n to 13. Because these operators change the value of a variable, they cannot be applied to numbers themselves. For example, 4++ is not a legal statement.

There are actually two forms of these operators; you have seen the "postfix", i.e., after the variable form. There is also a prefix form, ++n. Both change the value of the variable by one. The difference between the two only appears when they are used inside expressions. The prefix form does the addition first, the postfix form evaluates to the old value of the variable.

```
int m = 7;
int n = 7;
int a = 2 * ++m; // now a is 16, m is 8
int b = 2 * n++; // now b is 14, n is 8
```

We recommend against using ++ inside other expressions as this often leads to annoying bugs that are hard to track down.

> Of course, while it is the ++ operator that gives the C++ language its name, it also led to the first joke made by anti-C++ programmers who have long complained about the bug-ridden code that is too often produced by sloppy C++ coding. This joke points out that even the name of the language contains a bug: "After all, it should really be called ++C, since we only want to use a language after it has been improved." Java programmers, on the other hand, really are dealing with a ++C. This is because Java really does make it easier to produce bug-free code. It does this by eliminating many of C++ more bug-prone features such as pointer arithmetic, memory allocation, and null-terminated arrays of chars. (Of course, it does retain the murky side effects of prefix and postfix ++.)

Relational and Boolean Operators

The value of a variable or expression is compared with a double equals sign, ==. For example, the value of

```
(3==7)
```

is `false`

> It is important to remember that Java uses different symbols for assignment and equality.

> Java eliminates the possibility of bugs resulting from the use of the = sign when you meant the ==. A line that begins if (k=0) won't even compile since this evaluates to the integer 0, which doesn't convert to a Boolean value in Java.

```
Use a !=    for inequality
(3 !==7)
```

is `true`.

Finally, you have the usual < (less than), > (greater than), <= (less than or equal), and >= (greater than or equal) operators.

Java, following C++, uses && for the *and* operator and || for the *or* operator. As you can easily remember from the != operator, the exclamation point is the negation operator. The && and || operators are evaluated in "short-circuit" fashion. This means that when you have something like:

```
A && B
```

once the truth value of the expression A has been determined to be false, the value for the expression B is *not* calculated. (See the sections on conditionals for an example of where this is useful.)

Bitwise Operators

When working with any of the integer types, you have operators that can work directly with the bits that make up the integers. This means that you can use masking techniques to get at individual bits. The bitwise operators are

    & ("and")

    | ("or"),

    ^ ("xor"),

    ~ ("not")

Remember that ^ is the xor operator and not the power operator.

These operators work on bit patterns. For example, if `foo` is an integer variable, then

```
int thirdBit = (foo&8)/8:
```

gives you a one if the third bit in the binary representation of foo is on, and a zero if not. This technique lets you mask out all but a single bit when need be.

There are also >> and << operators, which shift a bit pattern to the right or left. There is no need to use these operators to divide and multiply by powers of two, though. Compilers are almost certainly smart enough to change multiplication by powers of two into the appropriate shift operators. There is even a >>> operator that fills the top bits with zero, whereas >> extends the sign bit into the top bits. There is no <<< operator.

In C/C++, there is no guarantee as to whether >> performs an arithmetic shift (extending the sign bit) or a logical shift (filling in with zeroes). Implementors are free to choose whatever is more efficient. That means, the C/C++ >> operator is really only defined for non-negative numbers. Java removes that ambiguity.

Parentheses and Operator Hierarchy

As in all programming languages, you are best off using parentheses to indicate the order in which you want operations to be carried out. However, in Java the hierarchy of operations is as follows:

[] . () (function call)	left to right
! ~ ++ -- + (unary) – (unary) () (cast) new	right to left
* / %	left to right
+ -	left to right
<< >> >>>	left to right
< <= > >= instanceof	left to right
== !=	left to right
&	left to right
^	left to right
|	left to right
&&	left to right
||	left to right
?:	left to right
= += -= *= /= %= &= |= ^= <<= >>= >>>=	right to left

If no parentheses are used, operations are performed in the hierarchical order indicated. Operators on the same level are processed from left to right, except for those that are right associative, as indicated in the table above.

Unlike C or C++, Java does not have a comma operator.

Strings

Strings are sequences of characters, such as `"hello"`. Java does not have a built-in string type. Instead, the standard Java library contains a predefined class called, naturally enough, `String` that contains most of what you want.

```
String e = ""; // an empty string
String greeting = "Hello";
```

Concatenation

Java, like most programming languages, allows you to use the + sign to join (concatenate) two strings together.

```
String expletive = "Expletive":
String PG13 = "deleted";
String message = expletive + PG13;
```

The above code makes the value of the string variable message `"Expletivedeleted"`. (Note the lack of a space between the words: the + sign joins two strings together in the order received, *exactly* as they are given.)

When you concatenate a string with a value that is not a string, the latter is converted to a string. (As we will see.in Chapter 5, every Java object can be converted to a string.) For example,

```
String rating = "PG" + 13;
```

sets `rating` to the string `"PG13"`.

This feature is commonly used in output statements.

```
System.out.println("The answer is " + answer);
```

is perfectly acceptable and will print what one would want (and with the correct spacing because of the space after `is`).

Although Java will convert a number to a string when concatenating with another string, it does not add a space in front of a positive value.

Substrings

You extract a substring from a larger string with the `substring` method of the `String` class. For example,

```
string greeting = "Hello";
string s = greeting.substring(0, 4)
```

creates a string consisting of the characters `"Hell"`. Java counts strings in a peculiar fashion: the first character in a string has position 0, just like in C and C++. (In C, there was a technical reason for counting positions starting at 0, but that reason has long gone away, and only the nuisance remains.)

For example, the character `'H'` has position 0 in the string `"Hello"`, and the character `'o'` has position 4. The second argument of `substring` is the first position that you *do not* want to copy. In our case, we want to copy the characters in positions 0, 1, 2, and 3 (from position 0 to position 3 inclusive). As `substring` counts it, this means from position 0 inclusive to position 4 *exclusive*.

There is one advantage to the way `substring` works: It is easy to compute the length of the substring. The string `s.substring(a, b)` always has `b - a` characters. For example, the substring `"Hell"` has length 4 − 0 = 4.

String Editing

To find out the length of a string, use the `length` method. For example,

```
String greeting = "Hello";
int n = greeting.length() // is 5.
```

Just as `char` denotes a Unicode character, `String` denotes a sequence of Unicode characters. It is possible to get at individual characters of a string. For example, `s.charAt(n)` returns the Unicode character at position n, where n is between 0 and `s.length()` − 1.

However, you can't *change* a character in the string. If you want to turn `greeting` into `"Help!"`, you cannot change the third position of `greeting` into a `'p'` and the fourth position into a `'!'`. If you are a C programmer, this will make you feel pretty helpless. How are you going to modify the string? In Java, it is quite easy: take the substring that you want to keep and concatenate it with the characters that you want to replace.

```
greeting = greeting.substring(0, 3) + "p!";
```

This changes the current value of the `greeting` variable to `"Help!"`.

Since you cannot change the individual characters in a Java string, the documentation refers to the objects of the `String` class as being *immutable*. You should think of them as first-class objects just like the number 3 is always 3, and the string `"Hello"` will always contain the character sequence `'H'`, `'e'`, `'l'`, `'l'`, `'o'`. You cannot change these values. You can, however, change the contents of the string *variable* `greeting`, and make it refer to a different string. (Just as you can make a numeric variable currently holding the value 3 hold the value 4.)

Isn't that a lot less efficient? It would seem simpler to change the characters than to build up a whole new string from scratch. Well, yes and no. Indeed it isn't efficient to generate a new string that holds the concatenation of `"Hel"` and `"p!"`. But immutable strings have one great advantage: The compiler can arrange that strings are *shared*.

To understand how this works, think of the various strings as sitting on the heap. (For non C/C++ programmers, think of them as just being located in memory somewhere.) String variables then point to locations on the heap. For example, the substring `greeting.substring(0, 3)` is just a pointer to the existing `"Hello"` string, together with the range of characters that are used in the substring. Overall, the designers of Java decided that the efficiency of string-sharing outweighs the inefficiency of immutability.

Look at your own programs; we suspect that most of the time, you don't change strings—you just compare them. Of course, there are some cases in which direct manipulation of strings is more efficient. (One example is when assembling strings from individual characters that come from a file or the keyboard.) For these situations, Java provides a separate `StringBuffer` class that we describe in Chapter 11. If you are not concerned with the efficiency of string handling (which is not a bottleneck in many Java applications anyway), you can ignore `StringBuffer` and just use `String`.

C programmers generally are bewildered when they see Java strings for the first time, because they think of strings as arrays of characters:

```
char greeting[] = "Hello";
```

That is the wrong analogy: a Java string is roughly analogous to a char* pointer,

```
char* greeting = "Hello";
```

When you replace greeting with another string, the Java code does roughly the following:

```
char* temp = malloc(6);
strncpy(temp, greeting, 3);
strcpy(temp + 3, "p!");
greeting = temp;
```

Sure, now greeting points to the string "Help!". And even the most hardened C programmer must admit that the Java syntax is more pleasant than a sequence of strncpy calls. But what if we make another assignment to greeting?

```
greeting = "Howdy";
```

Don't we have a memory leak? After all, the "Help!" string was allocated on the heap. C and C++ programmers *must* change their way of thinking because Java does automatic garbage collection. Java automatically reclaims any unused memory. If the string "Help!" is no longer needed, its memory will eventually be recycled.

If you are a C++ programmer and use the string class defined by ANSI C++, you will be much more comfortable with the Java String type. C++ string objects also perform automatic allocation and deallocation of memory. The memory management is performed explicitly by constructors, assignment operators, and destructors. However, C++ strings are mutable—you can modify individual characters in a string.

Testing Strings for Equality

To test whether or not two strings are equal, use the `equals` method,

```
s.equals(t)
```

returns `true` if the strings s and t are equal, `false` otherwise. For the `equals` method, s and t can be string variables or string constants. For example,

```
"Hello".equals(command)
```

is perfectly legal.

> Do *not* use the == operator to find out if two strings are equal! It only determines whether or not the strings are stored in the same location.

Sure, if the strings are in the same location, they must be equal. But it is entirely possible to store multiple copies of identical strings in different places.

```
String greeting = "Hello"; //initialize greeting to a string
if (greeting == "Hello") . . . // probably true
if (greeting.substring(0, 4) == "Hell") . . . // probably false
```

If the compiler would always arrange for equal strings to be shared, then you could use == for testing equality, but it doesn't and you can't. (The trouble is that string storage is implementation dependent. The standard implementation only shares string constants, not strings that are the result of operations like + or `substring`.) Therefore, *never* use == to compare strings.

If you are used to the C++ `string` class, you have to be particularly careful about equality testing. That class does overload the == operator to test for equality of the string contents. It is pretty silly that Java goes out of its way to give strings the same "look and feel" as numeric values, but then makes strings behave like pointers for equality testing. The language designers could have redefined == for strings, just as they made a special arrangement for +. Oh well, every language has its share of inconsistencies.

C programmers never use == to compare strings, but use `strcmp` instead. The Java function `compareTo` Is the exact analog to `strcmp`. You can use

```
if (greeting.compareTo("Help") == 0) . . .
```

but it seems clearer to use `equals` instead.

Directions for Using the Console Class

Before we go on (so that we can give you some examples that are at least somewhat non-trivial!) this sidebar shows you the incantations needed in order to use the Console class to get various kinds of prompted input from the keyboard. The Console class has three methods. These methods let you:

- capture an integer by a prompted input,
- capture a floating-point number with a prompted input,
- capture a string or word by a prompted input.

The Console class may be found in the \corejava directory on the CD. To use the Console class, it is important that you set up your CLASSPATH environment variable as described in Chapter 2.

Once you have done this, you can use the class as in the following example:

```
class StringPromptSample
{   public static void main(String[] args)
    {   String yourName;
        yourName = Console.readString
           ("Please enter your name.");
        System.out.println("Hello " + yourName);
    }
}
```

If you compile and run this program you will see that the readString method displays the string prompt and grabs the text the user enters before he or she hits the ENTER key.

More generally you will have the following methods available to you (all use a string prompt):

readWord () reads the string until the first space is entered.

readInt (String prompt) reads an integer. If you do not enter an integer, it reprompts you to enter the integer correctly.

readDouble (String prompt) reads a floating-point number in the double range. If you do not enter a float it reprompts you to do so.

All these functions can be "broken out of" by hitting the CTRL+C combination, which kills any Java application under Windows or Unix.

A Mortgage Calculator

As our first semi-serious application for Java, let's write a program that calculates the cost of a mortgage. We will use our `Console` class to prompt the user to enter the principal amount, the term in years, and the interest rate. The program will then output the mortgage amount per month.

We use the following standard formula to calculate the mortgage payment

$$\frac{\text{Principal} \times \text{MonthlyInterest}}{(1 - (1/(1 + \text{MonthlyInterest})^{\text{Years} \times 12}))}$$

Here's the code:

```java
class Mortgage
{   public static void main(String[] args)
    {   double principal;
        double yearlyInterest;
        int years;

        principal = Console.readDouble
            ("Loan amount (no commas):");
        yearlyInterest = Console.readDouble
            ("Interest rate in % (ex: use 7.5 for 7.5%):")/100;
        years = Console.readInt("The number of years:");

        double monthlyInterest = yearlyInterest / 12;
        double payment = principal * monthlyInterest
            / (1 - (Math.pow(1/(1 + monthlyInterest), years * 12)));
        System.out.println("Your payment is" + payment);
    }
}
```

Control Flow

Java, like any programming language, supports both conditional statements and loops to determine control flow. We start with the conditional statements and then move on to loops. We end with the somewhat cumbersome switch statement that can be used when you have many values of a single expression to test for. Before we get into the actual controls structures, you need to know more about *blocks*.

A block is any number of simple Java statements that are surrounded by a pair of braces. Blocks define the scope of your variables. However, it is not possible to declare identically named variables in two different blocks in the same method.

Since the scope of a variable starts at the place it was declared and goes to the end of the block in which it was declared, if you want to have a variable accessible to all the code in a method like `main`, you must declare it before you start a new block.

The Java control flow constructs are identical to those in C and C++, with one exception. There is no `goto`, but there is a "labelled" version of `break` that you can use to break out of a nested loop (where you perhaps would have used a `goto` in C).

Conditional Statements

The simplest conditional statement in Java has the form

```
if (condition) statement;
```

but in Java, as in most programming languages, you will often want to execute multiple statements when a single condition is true. In this case, the conditional takes the form:

```
if (condition) { block }
```

The condition must be surrounded by parentheses, and here the "block" is, as indicated before, any number of statements that are surrounded by a pair of braces. For example:

```
if (yourSales >= target)
{   performance = "Satisfactory";
    bonus = 100;
}
```

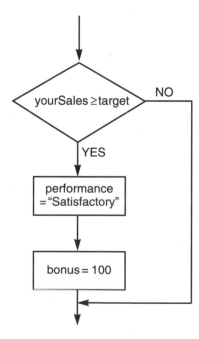

Here all the statements surrounded by the braces will be executed when yourSales is greater than or equal to target.)

A block (sometimes called a *compound statement*) allows you to have more than one (simple) statement in any Java programming structure that might otherwise have a single (simple) statement.

The more general conditional in Java looks like this:

```
if (condition) statement else statement;
```

or, more likely,

```
if (condition) {block₁} else {block₂}
```

For example:

```
if (yourSales >= target)
{   performance = "Satisfactory";
    bonus = 100 + 0.01 *(yourSales - target);
}
else
{   performance = "Unsatisfactory";
    bonus = 0;
}
```

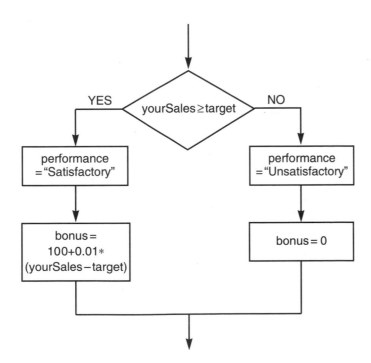

The `else` part is always optional. An `else` groups with the closest `if`. For example:

```
if {yourSales >= 2*target)
{   performance = "Excellent";
    bonus = 1000;}}

else if {yourSales >= 1.5*target)
{   performance = "Fine";
    bonus = 500;
}
else if (yourSales >= target)
{   performance = "Satisfactory";
    bonus = 100;
else
{   System.out.println("You're fired");
}
```

Because of the short circuit evaluation built into Java,

```
if (x != 0 && 1 / x > 0) // no problems ever
```

does not evaluate `1 / x` if x is zero, and so cannot lead to a divide-by-zero error.

Java does support the ternary ?: operator for simple conditionals. But we tend to think this leads to hard-to-read code, so we won't use it in this book.

Indeterminate Loops

In Java, as in all programming languages, there are control structures that let you repeat statements. There are two forms for repeating loops that are best when you do not know how many times a loop should be processed (these are "indeterminate loops").

First, there is the *while* loop that only executes the body of the loop while a condition is true. The general form is:

```
while (condition) { block };
```

The `while` loop may never execute it if the condition is `false` at the outset. For example, let's use our `Console` class to determine how long it will take to save a specific amount of money, assuming you get a specified interest rate per year and deposit the same amount of money per year:

```java
class Retirement
{   public static void main(String[] args)
    {   double goal;
        double interest;
        double payment;
        int years = 0;
        double balance = 0;

        goal = Console.readDouble
            ("How much money do you need to retire?");
        payment = Console.readDouble
            ("How much money will you contribute every year?");
        interest = Console.readDouble
            ("Interest rate in % (ex: use 7.5 for 7.5%):") / 100;
        while (balance < goal)
        {   balance = (balance + payment) * (1 + interest);
            years++;
        }

        System.out.println("You can retire in " + years
            + " years.");
    }
}
```

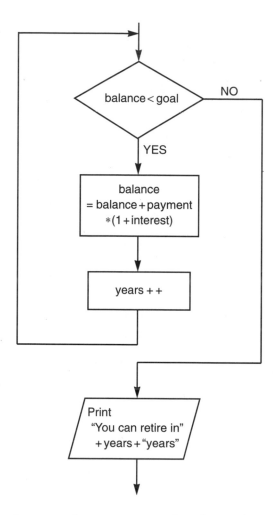

In this case, we are incrementing a counter and updating the amount currently accumulated in the body of the loop until the total exceeds the targeted amount. (Don't rely on this program to plan for your retirement. We left out a few niceties such as inflation and your life expectancy.)

A while loop tests at the top. Therefore, the code in the block may never be executed. If you want to make sure a block is executed at least once, you will need to move the test to the bottom. This is done with the do version of a while loop. Its syntax looks like this:

```
do { block } while (condition);
```

This executes the block and only then tests the condition. It then repeats the block and retests the condition, and so on. For example, the following code computes an approximation to the square root of any positive number, using an iterative process.

```java
class SquareRoot
{   public static void main(String[] args)
    {   double a = Console.readDouble("Please enter a number:");

        double xnew = a / 2;
        double xold;

        do
        {   xold = xnew;
            xnew = (xold + a / xold) / 2;
            System.out.println(xnew);
        }
        while (Math.abs(xnew - xold) > 1E-4);
    }
}
```

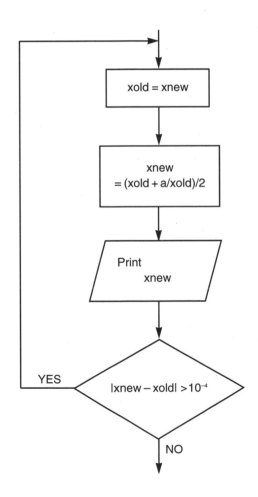

Finally, since a block may contain *any* Java statements, you can nest loops as deeply as you want.

Determinate Loops

Java, like C++, has a very general construct to support iteration. For example, the following prints the numbers from 1 to 10 on the screen.

```
for (int i = 1; i <= 10; i++)
    System.out.println(i);
```

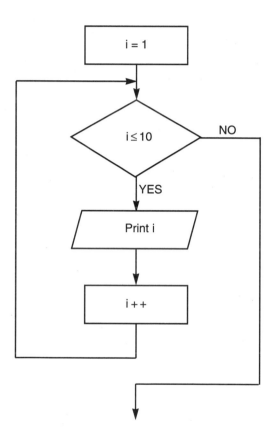

The idea is that the first slot of the `for` statement will (usually) hold the counter initialization. (The first slot is occasionally declared and initialized there as in this example). The second slot gives the condition for which to test the loop, and the third slot explains how to change the state of the counter. What follows the initialization can be a simple Java statement or a block. (Thus, nested `for` loops are possible in Java.)

Although Java, like C++, allows almost any expression in the various slots of a `for` loop, it is an unwritten rule of good taste that the three slots of a `for` statement should only initialize, test, and update a counter variable. One can write very obscure loops by disregarding this rule.

Even within the bounds of good taste, much is possible. This is because you can have variables of any type and use any method of updating them, so you can have loops that count down:

```
for (int i = 10; i > 0; i--)
    System.out.println("Counting down " + i);
System.out.println("Blastoff!")
;
```

Or you can have loops in which the variables and increments are of one of the floating-point types.

Again, be careful about testing for equality of floating-point numbers. A `for` loop that looks like this

```
for (x = 0; x != 10; x += 0.01)
```

may never end.

As an example of a reasonable use of floating-point numbers in a loop, let's extend the mortgage program to print out the monthly payments for a range of interest rates around the entered value that go up and down by ⅛%.

```
class MortgageLoop
{   public static void main(String[] args)
    {   double principal;
        double yearlyInterest;
        int years;

        principal = Console.readDouble("Loan amount (no commas):");
        yearlyInterest = Console.readDouble
            ("Interest rate in % (ex: use 7.5 for 7.5%):") / 100;
        years = Console.readInt("The number of years:");

        double y;
        for (y = yearlyInterest - 0.01; y <= yearlyInterest +
            0.01; y += 0.00125)
        {   double monthlyInterest = y / 12;
            double payment = principal * monthlyInterest
                / (1 - (Math.pow(1/(1 + monthlyInterest), years *
                    12)));
            Format.print(System.out, "With rate %6.3f", 100 * y);
            Format.print(System.out, "%%, your monthly payment is
                $%10.2f\n", payment);
        }
    }
}
```

When you declare a variable in the first slot of the `for` statement, the scope of such a variable extends until the end of the body of the `for` loop. In particular, if you do this, you cannot use that value of this variable outside the loop. Therefore, if you wish to use the end value of a loop counter outside the `for` loop, be sure to declare it outside the header for the loop!

Of course, a `for` loop is equivalent to a `while` loop; choose the one that fits your picture of the situation. More precisely,

```
for (statement₁; expression₁; expression₂) { block };
```

is completely equivalent to:

```
{statement₁;
while (expression₁)
  {block;
    expression₂;
}}
```

Multiple Selections—the Switch Statement

The `if/else` construct can be cumbersome when you have to deal with multiple selections with many alternatives. Unfortunately, the only alternative available in Java is almost just as cumbersome—it is not nearly as neat as VB's Select Case statement, which allows you to test for ranges or for values in any type. Java, following the lead of C/C++, calls the device for multiple selection a `switch` statement. Unfortunately, the designers didn't improve on C/C++'s switch statement. You still can select only against all the integer types but `long` or against a `char`. You still cannot use a range of values.

For example, if you set up a menuing system with four alternatives, you could use code that looks like this:

```
System.out.println("Select an option (1 to 4)");
int choice = Console.readInt() // reads one keypress
switch(choice)
{   case 1:
      . . .
      break;
    case 2:
      . . .
      break;
    case 3:
      . . .
      break;
    case 4:
      . . .
      break;
    default:
      // bad input
      break;
}
```

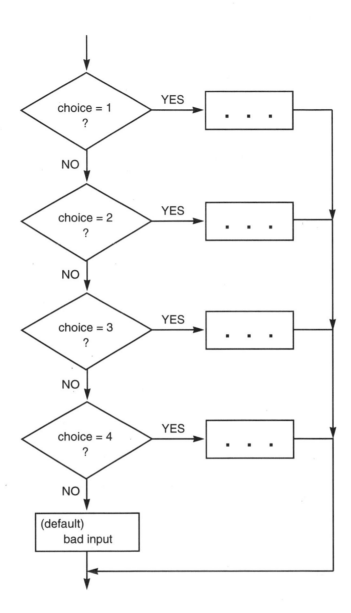

Unlike in languages like VB, it is possible for multiple switches to be triggered because execution falls through to another case unless a `break` keyword gets you out of the whole switch statement. (It is extremely unusual to use a `switch` statement without a `break` keyword in every case. In the extremely rare situation where you want the "fall through" behavior, you ought to clearly comment it.)

In general, execution starts at the `case` label, matching the value on which the selection is performed, and continues until the next `break`, or the end of the switch. The `default` clause is optional.

Labeled Breaks

Although the designers of Java kept the `goto` as a reserved word, they decided not to include it in the language. In general, `goto` statements are considered poor style. Some programmers feel the anti-goto forces have gone too far (see for example the famous article of Donald Knuth called "Structured Programming with goto's"). They agree that unrestricted use of `goto` is error-prone, but that an occasional jump *out of a loop* is beneficial. The Java designers agreed and even added a new statement to support this programming style, the labeled break.

Let us first look at the unlabeled break statement. The same `break` statement that you use to exit a `switch` can also be used to break out of a loop. For example,

```
while (years <= 100)
{   balance = (balance + payment) * (1 + interest);
    if (balance > goal) break;
    years++;
}
```

Now the loop is exited if either `years > 100` on the top of the loop or `balance > goal` in the middle of the loop. Of course, you could have achieved the same effect without a break. You would need an `if/else` inside the loop and another termination condition in the loop header.

Unlike C/C++, Java also offers a *labeled break* statement that lets you break out of multiple nested loops. The reason for this is simple: occasionally something weird happens inside a deeply nested loop. In that case, you may want to break completely out of all the nested loops. It is inconvenient to program that simply by adding extra conditions.

Here's an example that shows this at work. (Notice that the label must preceed the outermost loop out of which you want to break. It also must be followed by a colon (:))

```
int n;
read_data:
while(. . .)
{   . . .
    for (. . .)
    {   n = Console.readInt(. . .);
        if (n < 0) // should never happen—can't continue
            break read_data;
```

```
            // break out of read_data loop
         . . .
    }
}
// check for sucess or failure here
if (n < 0)
{    // deal with bad situation
}
else
{    // got here normally
}
```

If there was a bad input, the labeled break moves past the end of the labeled block. As with any use of the break statement, you then need to test if the loop exited normally or as a result of a break.

Directions for Using the Format Class

Not only did we give you a console class to read characters from the screen, we also supply you with a class that can format output nicely. Java's idea of floating-point output is "no trailing zeroes, up to six digits of precision". That makes it tough to format dollars and cents like 1141.30. Rather than reinvent the wheel, we simply reimplemented the C `printf` function that has a good set of formatting options and is, for the most part, easy to use. For example, to format a floating-point number with a field width of 10 and two digits after the decimal point, you use

```
Format.print(System.out, "Your monthly payment is %10.2f\n",
    payment);
```

That sends a string like

```
"Your monthly payment is    1141.30\n"
```

to `System.out`. If you'd rather capture that string in a string variable, use

```
String s = new Format("Your monthly payment is %10.2f\n")
    .form(payment);
```

The output string contains all characters of the format string, except that the format specification (starting with a %) is replaced by the formatted value. However, a %% denotes a percent sign.

Unlike the `printf` statement in C, you can only have one formatted value at a time. If you need to print two values, use two calls.

```
Format.print(System.out, "With rate %6.3f", 100 * y);
Format.print(System.out, "%%, your monthly payment is
    %10.2f\n", payment);
```

Apart from the `%m.nf` format, the most common format is `%nd`, to print an integer in a field with width n. Those two will get you a long way, and you may never need to learn more about the formatting codes.

Here are the rules for the formatting specifiers. The code starts with % and ends with one of the letters c, d, e, E, f, g, G, i, o, s, x, X. They have the following meanings:

f	floating-point number in fixed format
e, E	floating-point number in exponential notation (scientific format). The E format results in an uppercase E for the exponent (1.14130E+003), the e format in a lowercase e.
g, G	floating-point number in general format (fixed format for small numbers, exponential format for large numbers). Trailing zeroes are suppressed. The G format results in an uppercase E for the exponent (if any), the g format in a lowercase e.
d, i	integer in decimal
x	integer in hexadecimal
o	integer in octal
s	string
c	character

In between the % and the format code are the following fields. They are all optional.

+	forces display of + for positive numbers
0	show leading zeroes
–	align left in the field
space	prepend a space in front of positive numbers
#	use "alternate" format. Add 0 or 0x for octal or hexadecimal numbers. Don't suppress trailing zeroes in general floating point format.

Class Methods (User-Defined Functions)

Like any programming language, Java has a way of breaking down complex tasks into simpler tasks via user-defined gadgets (traditionally called *functions*). Every modern programming language takes pride in introducing a new terminology for these gadgets. As mentioned previously, in Java the terminology *method* is used instead of functions. (Well, it is used most of the time; the designers and documenters are somewhat inconsistent. They occasionally slip and use the C/C++ function terminology.) We will follow in the footsteps of the designers of Java and use the term *method* with an occasional slip when it seems appropriate. (In the next chapter, we will try to survey the ideas behind Object-Oriented Programming that lead to the multitude of possible terminologies.)

A method definition must occur inside a class. It can occur anywhere inside the class, although custom places all the other methods of a class before the `main` method. There are many types of methods, but in this chapter we will only use those that, like `main`, are `public static`. For now, don't worry about what this means—it has to do with which other methods can use a method—we will explain the terminology in the next chapter.

> Java does not have "global" functions. All functions must be defined inside a class. The functions we study in this chapter don't yet operate on objects and are, therefore, defined as `static`. Except for visibility issues, there is no difference between a C function and a `static` Java method.

For example, suppose we want to write a program that computes the odds on winning any lottery that requires bettors to choose a certain number of numbers from the range 1 to n. For example, if you must match six numbers from the numbers 1 to 50, then there are $(50\cdot49\cdot48\cdot47\cdot46\cdot45)/(1\cdot2\cdot3\cdot4\cdot5\cdot6)$ possible outcomes, so your chance is 1 in 15,890,700. Good luck!

Just in case someone asks you to participate in a "pick 7 out of 38" lottery, you will want a method that computes the odds. Later we'll put it together with a `main` function that asks you for how many numbers you need to choose and then asks for the highest number from which to draw.

Here's the method:

```
public static long lotteryOdds(int high, int number)
{   long r = 1;
    int i;
    for (i = 1; i <= number; i++)
    {   r = r * high / i;
    high--;
    }
    return r;
}
```

Notice the header for the LotteryOdds:

```
public static long lotteryOdds(int high, int number)
```

In general, the header for a method starts with keywords—in our case, `public static`—that explain the scope of the method. Next, the method header lists the type of the returned value. In our case, a `long`. Next comes the name of the method, and finally the types and names of its arguments.

After the header comes the code that implements the method. Notice the brace structure in the example above: the outermost braces (that start after the function header) mark off what is traditionally called the *body*. Variables declared inside a method (like the `int i` for the loop counter in our `lotteryOdds`) are *local* to the method. They can neither be accessed nor contaminate any similarly named variables in the other methods of the class. More precisely, when a method is called, the local variables for all function arguments are initialized as indicated in the body of the method, and the memory for them will automatically be reclaimed.

Within a method, of course, the scope of a variable is determined by the block in which it is declared.

The `return` statement causes an immediate exit from the method. The expression following the `return` keyword is the method result. Methods in Java can return values of any Java type. On the other hand, methods need not return any value. In this case, the return type is `void`. (Functions that do this are commonly referred to as procedures.)

Here's an application that actually calls the `lotteryOdds` method as needed from the `main` method.

```java
class LotteryOdds
{   public static long lotteryOdds(int high, int number)
    {   long r = 1;
        int i;
        for (i = 1; i <= number; i++)
        {   r = r * high / i;
            high--;
        }
        return r;
    }

    public static void main(String[] args)
    {   int numbers = Console.readInt
          ("How many numbers do you need to draw?");
        int topNumber = Console.readInt
            ("What is the highest number you can draw?");
        long oddsAre = lotteryOdds(topNumber, numbers);

        System.out.println("Your odds are 1 in " + oddsAre +
          ". Good luck!");
    }
}
```

Notice how the `lotteryOdds` method is called from the `main` method in our application:

```
long oddsAre = lotteryOdds(topNumber, numbers);
```

As you can see, method calls for user-defined methods occur (return types permitting) in any expression for which a value is required. In our case, since the method belongs to the `lotteryOdds` class, we can call the method simply by giving its name followed by the argument. (As opposed to something like `System.out.println` for which we need to give the object on which the method operates.)

When this line of code is processed, Java uses the current values of the `topNumber` and `numbers` variables and passes this information to the `lotteryOdds` method. *All arguments to methods in Java are passed by value and not by reference.* It is, therefore, *impossible* to change variables by means of method calls. In particular, you cannot write a "swap" method in Java. (On the other hand, if you are familiar with pointers, since arrays and objects in Java are actually pointers, functions can modify the contents of arrays and objects. They just can't modify numbers.)

Methods in Java are similar but not identical to functions in C++. For example, there is no analogue to function prototypes in Java. They are not required, because functions can be defined after they are used—the compiler makes multiple passes through the code. More significantly, pointer and reference arguments do not exist in Java: you cannot pass the location of a variable. Overloading function names is always possible, just like in C++.

In general, `public` methods can be called from other classes. (An example of this is our use of the `println` method, which is a public method in `PrintableStream`.)

Arguments and return values in methods can be of any type. In particular, they can be arrays (see the next section) or classes (see the next chapter).

Class Variables

Occasionally, you need to declare a variable that will be accessible by all the methods in the class. (It is possible but not recommended to declare a variable that can be seen outside its class—i.e., a true global variable.) Usually these are called *class variables* because the scope of such a variable is potentially the whole class. The syntax is similar to the *class constants* that you saw earlier, and class variables are declared above the `main` method using the following syntax.

```
class Employee
{
    private static double socialSecurityRate = 7.62;
    public static void main(String[] args)
    { . . .}
}
```

Class variables can be shadowed by variables of the same name declared in a block inside a method of the class. (Although this is a rather strange way to program.)

It is also possible to call a method that has a `void` return type simply for its side effects—for example, the change in the state of the class variables. This is done simply by giving the method's name with the appropriate arguments as a stand-alone statement.

Finally, although it completely defeats the premises behind Object-Oriented Programming, by replacing the keyword `private` with the keyword `public` one can have true global variables accessible by all methods in an application.

Except for visibility issues, there is no difference between a global variable in C/C++ and a `static` variable in Java.

Recursion

Recursion is a general method of solving problems by reducing them to simpler problems of a similar type. The general framework for a recursive solution to a problem looks like this:

> Solve recursively (problem)
>
>> If the problem is trivial, do the obvious
>>
>> Simplify the problem
>>
>> Solve recursively (simpler problem)
>>
>> Turn (if possible) the solution to the simpler problem(s) into a solution to the original problem

A recursive subprogram constantly calls itself, each time in a simpler situation, until it gets to the trivial case, at which point it stops. For the experienced programmer, thinking recursively presents a unique perspective on certain problems, often leading to particularly elegant solutions and, therefore, equally elegant programs. (For example, most of the very fast sorts, such as QuickSort, are recursive.)

For a Web-oriented example of recursion, consider the problem of designing a "Web crawler" that will search *every* hyperlink that is accessible from the page that you are currently on. (We show you a simplified example of this in Chapter 8.) The pseudo-code for this kind of application is:

Recursive URL search(link)

Do

find next link

Recursive URL search(next link)

Until No more links

There are actually two types of recursion possible. The first is where the subprogram only calls itself. This is called *direct recursion*. The second type is called, naturally enough, *indirect recursion*. This occurs, for example, when a method calls another method that, in turn, calls the first one. Both types of recursion are possible in Java and (unlike Pascal, say) no special incantations are needed for the indirect situation.

Let's look at a recursive way to compute the lottery odds. If you draw one number out of 50, your chances are plainly one in 50. In general, we can write

```
public static long lotteryOdds(int high, int number)
{   if (number == 1) return high;
    . . .
}
```

That wasn't too bad. Now let's look at the number of possible ways of drawing 6 numbers out of 50. Let's just grab one number. There are 50 chances. That leaves us with 5 numbers out of 49. Aha! A simpler problem. There are lotteryOdds(49, 5) ways to pick those five numbers. That gives a total of 50 * lotteryOdds(49, 5) possibilities to pick the six numbers. Actually, we have to fudge a little and divide that result by six because our process counts each combination six times, depending which number we choose first.

Replacing the 50 and 6 with the general parameters high and number, we get the recursive solution

```
public static long lotteryOdds(int high, int number)
{   if (number <= 0) return 0; // just in case
    else if (number == 1) return high;
    else return high * lotteryOdds
      (high - 1, number - 1) / number;
}
```

Note that the number argument gets decremented in each recursive call and, therefore, must eventually reach 1.

In this case, the recursive solution is actually somewhat less efficient than the loop that we used previously, but it clearly shows the syntax (or rather the absence of any special syntax) of the recursive call.

Arrays

In Java, arrays are first-class objects. You are better off not thinking about how arrays are implemented in Java—accept them as objects that exist in and by themselves. For example, you can assign one array of integers to another, just as you can assign one integer variable to another.

Once you create an array, you cannot change its size (although you can, of course, change an individual array element). If you need to expand the size of an array while a program is running, you need to use a different Java object called a *vector*. (See Chapter 9 for more on vectors and how to handle multi-dimensional arrays.)

You have already seen some examples of Java arrays. The `String[] args` argument in the `main` method says the only parameter in the `main` method is an array of strings. In this case, the first ("zeroth" = `args[0]`) entry is the first command line argument; `args[1]` is the second command line argument, and so on.

Arrays are the first example of objects whose creation the programmer must explicitly handle. This is done through the `new` operator. For example:

```
int[] arrayOfInt = new int[100];
```

sets up an array that can hold 100 integers. The array entries are *numbered from 0 to 99* (and not 1 to 100). Once created, the entries in an array can be filled, for example, by using a loop:

```
int[] arrayOfInt = new int[100];
for(int i =0; i< 100; i++)
   arrayOfInt[i] = i;   // fills the array with 0 to 99
```

Entries from an array can be used anywhere a value of that type can be used.

If you try to access, say, the 101st element of an array declared as having 100 elements, Java will compile and you will be able to run your program. It will, however, stop the program when this statement is encountered.

If you assign one array to another, then both refer to the same set of values. Any change to one will affect the other.

You can define an array variable either as `int[] arrayOfInt` or as `int arrayOfInt[]`. Most Java programmers prefer the former style because it neatly separates the type `int[]` (integer array) from the variable name.

A Java array is quite different from a C/C++ array on the stack. It is, however, essentially the same as a pointer to an array allocated on the *heap*. The `[]` operator is predefined to perform *bounds checking*. There is no pointer arithmetic—you can't increment `arrayOfInt` to point to the second element in the array.

You can tell that arrays are pointers, because their contents can be modified when you pass an array to a function and because arrays can be assigned.

There is no convenient way to use index ranges in a Java array.

Arrays can be used in a user-defined method exactly as any other type. However, since arrays in Java are actually hidden pointers, the method can change the elements. For example, here is a shell sort that sorts whatever integer array is passed to it.

```java
class ShellSort
{   public static void sort(int[] a)
    {   int n = a.length;
        int incr = n / 2;
        while (incr >= 1)
        {   for (int i = incr; i < n; i++)
            {   int temp = a[i];
                int j = i;
                while (j >= incr && temp < a[j - incr])
                {   a[j] = a[j - incr];
                    j -= incr;
                }
                a[j] = temp;
            }
            incr /= 2;
        }
    }

    public static void main(String[] args)
    {   // make an array of ten integers
        int[] a = new int[10];
        int i;
        // fill the array with random values
        for (i = 0; i < a.length; i++)
            a[i] = (int)(Math.random() * 100);
        // sort the array
        sort(a);
        // print the sorted array
        for (i = 0; i < a.length; i++)
            System.out.println(a[i]);
    }
}
```

The return type of a method can also be an array. This is really useful when a method computes a sequence of values. For example, let us write a method that draws a sequence of numbers in a simulated lottery and then returns the sequence. The header of the function is

```
public static int[] drawing(int high, int number)
```

The method makes two arrays, one that holds the numbers 1, 2, 3, ..., high from which the lucky combination is drawn, and one to hold the numbers that are drawn. The first array is abandoned when the method exits and will eventually be garbage collected. The second array is returned as the computed result.

```
class LotteryDrawing
{   public static int[] drawing(int high, int number)
    {   int i;
        int numbers[] = new int[high];
        int result[] = new int[number];
        // fill an array with numbers 1 2 3 . . . high
        for (i = 0; i < high; i++) numbers[i] = i + 1;
        for (i = 0; i < number; i++)
        {   int j = (int)(Math.random() * (high - i));
            result[i] = numbers[j];
            numbers[j] = numbers[high - 1 - i];
        }
        return result;
    }

    public static void main(String[] args)
    {   int numbers = Console.readInt
          ("How many numbers do you need to draw?");
        int topNumber = Console.readInt
            ("What is the highest number you can draw?");

        int[] a = drawing(topNumber, numbers);
        ShellSort.sort(a);
        System.out.println
            ("Bet the following combination. It'll make you rich!");
        int i;
        for (i = 0; i < a.length; i++)
            System.out.println(a[i]);
    }
}
```

CHAPTER
4

Objects and Classes

T his chapter will:

- introduce you to Object-Oriented Programming (OOP);

- show you how Java implements OOP by going further into its notion of a *class* and how you can use existing classes supplied by Java or by third parties;

- show you how to write your own *reuseable* classes that can perform nontrivial tasks.

If you are coming from a procedure-oriented language like VB (especially versions prior to VB4), C, or COBOL, you will want to read this chapter carefully. You may also need to spend a fair amount of time on the introductory sections. OOP requires a different way of thinking than procedure-oriented languages (or even object-based languages like VB). The transition is not always easy, but you do need some familiarity with OOP to go further with Java. (We are, however, assuming you are comfortable with a procedure-oriented language.)

For experienced C++ programmers, this chapter, like the previous chapter, will present familiar information; however, there are enough differences between how OOP is implemented in Java and how it is done in C++ to warrant your reading the later sections of this chapter (concentrating on the C++ notes).

Because you need to understand a fair amount of terminology in order to make sense of OOP, we'll start with some concepts and definitions. Then, we'll show you the basics of how Java implements OOP. We should note, however, that it is possible to write endlessly about the ideas behind OOP. A quick survey of *Books in Print* shows that there are more than 150 books with "Object-Oriented Programming" in the title, and more seem to appear each week. (We do make references to the literature, if you need more information on the ideas behind OOP and object-oriented design.)

Introduction to OOP

OOP is the dominant programming paradigm these days, having replaced the "structured," procedure-based programming techniques that were developed in the early '70s. Java is totally object-oriented, and it is not possible to program it in the procedural style that you may be most comfortable with. We hope this section—especially when combined with the example code supplied in the text and on the CD—will give you enough information about OOP to become productive with Java.

Let's begin with a question that, on the surface, seems to have nothing to do with programming: How did companies like Dell, Gateway, Micron Technologies, and the other major personal computer manufacturers get so big, so fast? Most people would probably say they made generally good computers and sold them at rock-bottom prices in an era when computer demand was skyrocketing. But go further—how were they able to manufacture so many models so fast and respond to the changes that were happening so quickly?

Well, a big part of the answer is that these companies farmed out a lot of the work. They bought components from reputable vendors and then assembled them. They often didn't invest time and money in designing and building power supplies, disk drives, motherboards, and other components. This made it possible for the companies to produce a product and make changes quickly for less money than if they had done the engineering themselves.

What the personal computer manufacturers were buying was "prepackaged functionality." For example, when they bought a power supply, they were buying something with certain properties (size, shape, and so on) and a certain functionality (smooth power output, amount of power available, and so on). Compaq provides a good example of how effective this operating procedure is. When Compaq moved from engineering all of the parts in their machines to buying many of the parts, they dramatically improved their bottom line.

OOP springs from the same idea. Your program is made of objects, with certain properties and operations that the objects can perform. The current state may change over time, but you always depend on objects not interacting with each other in undocumented ways. Whether you build an object or buy it might depend on your budget or on time. But, basically, as long as objects satisfy your specifications, you don't much care how the functionality was implemented. In OOP, you only care about what the objects *expose*. So, just as clone manufacturers don't care about the internals of a power supply as long as it does what they want, most Java programmers don't care how the audio clip component is implemented as long as it does what *they* want.

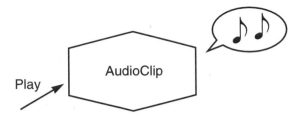

Figure 4-1

Traditional structured programming consists of designing the data structures and then manipulating them with functions in specific ways that are theoretically sure to terminate. (These functions are usually called *algorithms*.) This is why the designer of the original Pascal, Niklaus Wirth, called his famous book on programming *Algorithms + Data Structures = Programs* (Prentice Hall, 1975). Notice that in Wirth's title, algorithms come first, and data structures come second. This mimics the way programmers worked at that time. First, you decided how to manipulate the data; then you decided what structure to impose on the data in order to make the manipulations easier. OOP reverses the order and puts data structures first, then looks at the algorithms that operate on the data.

The key to being most productive in OOP is to make each object responsible for carrying out a set of related tasks. If an object relies on a task that isn't its responsibility, it needs to have access to an object whose responsibilities include that task. The first object then asks the second object to carry out the task by means of a more generalized version of the function call that you are familar with in procedural programming. (Recall that in Java these function calls are usually called *method calls*.) In OOP jargon, you *have clients send messages to server objects*.

In particular, an object should never directly manipulate the internal data of another object. All communication should be via messages, that is, function calls. By designing your objects to handle all appropriate messages and manipulate their data internally, you maximize reusability and minimize debugging time.

Of course, just as with modules in a procedure-oriented language, you will not want an individual object to do *too* much. Both design and debugging are simplified when you build small objects that perform a few tasks, rather than humongous objects with internal data that are extremely complex, with hundreds of functions to manipulate the data.

The Vocabulary of OOP

You need to understand some of the terminology of OOP to go further. The most important term is *class,* which you have already seen in the code in Chapter 3. A class is usually described as the template or blueprint from which the object is actually made. This leads to the standard way of thinking about classes: as cookie cutters. Objects are the cookies themselves. The "dough," in the form of memory, will need to be allocated as well. Java is pretty good about hiding this "dough preparation" step from you. You simply use the new keyword to obtain memory, and the built-in garbage collector will eat the cookies when nobody uses them any more. (Oh well, no analogy is perfect.) When you create an object from a class, you are said to have *created an instance* of the class. When you have a line like

```
AudioClip meow = new AudioClip();
```

you are using the new operator to create a *new instance* of the AudioClip class.

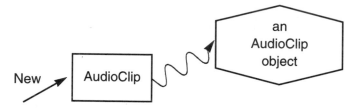

Figure 4-2

As you have seen, everything you write in Java is inside a class, and Java is composed of many classes. Unfortunately, as you will see in this and the following chapters, the built-in classes in Java do not supply as rich a toolkit as languages like VB, Delphi, or Microsoft Foundation *Classes* (MFC) do. Thus, you must create your own classes for many basic tasks that, in other languages, are taken for granted.

However, when you do write your own classes, another tenet of OOP makes this easier: Classes can be (and in Java always are) built on other classes. Java, in fact, comes with a "cosmic base class," that is, a class from which all other classes are built. We say that a class that builds on another class *extends* it. In Java, all classes extend the cosmic base class called, naturally enough, Object. You will see more about the Object base class in the next chapter.

When you extend a base class, the new class initially has all the properties and functions of its parent. You can choose whether you want to modify or get rid of any function of the parent, and you can also supply new functions that apply to the child class only. The general concept of extending a base class is called *inheritance.* (See the next chapter for more on *inheritance.*)

Encapsulation is another key concept in working with objects. Formally, encapsulation is nothing more than combining data and behavior in one package and hiding the implementation of the data from the user of the object. The data in an object are usually called its *instance variables* or *fields*, and the functions and procedures in a Java class are called its *methods*. A specific object that is an instance of a class will have specific values for its fields that define its current *state*.

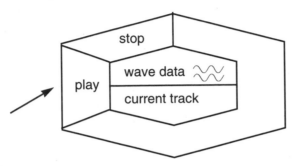

Figure 4-3

It cannot be stressed enough that the key to making encapsulation work is to have programs that *never* access instance variables (fields) in a class. Programs should interact with this data *only* through the object's methods. Encapsulation is the way to give the object its "black box" behavior, which is the key to reuse and reliability.

Objects

To work with OOP, you should be able to identify three key characteristics of objects. (For those who can remember back to high school, think of them as analogous to the "Who, What, and Where" that teachers told you characterize an event.) The three key questions are:

- What is the object's behavior?

- What is the object's state?

- What is the object's identity?

All objects that are instances of the same class share a family resemblance by supporting similar *behavior*. The behavior of an object is defined by the messages it accepts.

Next, each object stores information about what it currently looks like and how it got to be the way it currently is. This is what is usually called the object's *state*. An object's state may change over time, but not spontaneously. A change in the state of an object must be a consequence of messages sent to the object. However, the state of an object does not completely describe it.

Finally, each object has a distinct *identity*. For example, in an order-processing system, two orders are distinct even if they request identical items. Notice that the individual objects that are instances of a class *always* differ in their identity and *usually* differ in their state.

These key characteristics can influence each other. For example, the state of an object can influence its behavior. (If an order is "shipped" or "paid," it may reject a message that asks it to add or remove items. Conversely, if an order is "empty," that is, no items have yet been ordered, it should not allow itself to be shipped.)

In a traditional procedure-oriented program, you start the process at the top, with the main program. When designing an object-oriented system, there is no "top," and newcomers to OOP often wonder where to begin. The answer is: You first find classes and then you add methods to each class.

A simple rule of thumb in identifying classes is to look for nouns in the problem analysis. Methods, on the other hand, correspond to verbs.

For example, in an order-processing system, some of these nouns are:

- item
- order
- shipping address
- payment
- account

These nouns may lead to the classes `Item`, `Order`, and so on.

Next, one looks for verbs. Items are *added* to orders. Orders are *shipped* or *canceled*. Payments are *applied* to orders. With each verb, such as "add," "ship," "cancel," and "apply," you have to identify the one object that has the major responsibility for carrying it out. For example, when adding a new item to an order, the order object should be the one in charge since it knows how it stores and sorts items. That is, `add` should be a method of the `Order` class that takes an `Item` object as a parameter.

Of course, the "noun and verb" rule is only a rule of thumb, and only experience can help you decide which nouns and verbs are the important ones when building your classes.

Relationships between Classes

The most common relationships between classes are:

- *use*
- *containment* ("has–a")
- *inheritance* ("is–a")

The *use* relationship is the most obvious and also the most general. For example, the `Order` class uses the `Account` class, since `Order` objects need to access account objects to check for credit status. But the `Item` class does not use the `Account` class, since `Item` objects never need to worry about customer accounts. Thus, a class uses another class if it manipulates objects of that class.

In general, a class `A` uses a class `B` if:

- a method of `A` sends a message to an object of class `B`, or
- a method of `A` creates, receives, or returns objects of class `B`.

Try to minimize the number of classes that use each other. The point is, if a class A is unaware of the existence of a class B, it is also unconcerned about any changes to B! (And this means that revisions to B do not introduce bugs into A.)

The *containment* relationship is easy to understand because it is concrete; for example, an `Order` object contains `Item` objects. Containment means that objects of class `A` contain objects of class `B`. Of course, containment is a special case of use; if an `A` object contains a `B` object, then at least one method of the class `A` will make use of that object of class `B`.

The *inheritance* relationship denotes specialization. For example, a `RushOrder` class inherits from an `Order` class. The specialized `RushOrder` class has special methods for priority handling and a different method for computing shipping charges, but its other methods, such as adding items and billing, are inherited from the `Order` class. In general, if class `A` extends class `B`, class `A` inherits methods from (or extends) class `B`, but has more capabilities. (Inheritance will be more fully described in the next chapter, in which we discuss this important notion at some length.)

These three essential relationships between classes form the foundation of object-oriented design. *Class diagrams* show the classes (usually denoted with boxes or clouds) and their relationships (denoted with lines with various decorations that are maddeningly different from one methodologist to the next). Figure 4-4 shows an example, using the "unified Booch/Rumbaugh notation."

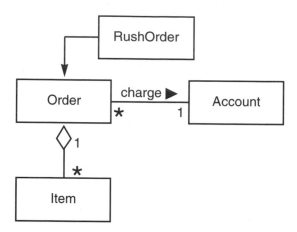

Figure 4-4

Contrasting OOP with Traditional Procedural Programming Techniques

We want to end this short introduction to OOP by contrasting OOP with the procedural model that you may be more familiar with. In procedure-oriented programming, you identify the tasks to be performed and then:

* by a stepwise refinement process, break the task to be performed into sub-tasks, and these into smaller subtasks, until the subtasks are simple enough to be implemented directly (this is the top-down approach); or

* write procedures to solve simple tasks and combine them into more sophisticated procedures, until you have the functionality you want (this is the bottom-up approach).

Most programmers, of course, use a mixture of the top-down and bottom-up strategies to solve a programming problem. The rule of thumb for discovering procedures is the same as the rule for finding methods in OOP: Look for verbs, or actions, in the problem description. The important difference is that in OOP, you *first* isolate the classes in the project. Only then do you look for the methods of the class. And there is another important difference between traditional procedures and OOP methods: Each method is associated with the class that is responsible for carrying out the operation.

For small problems, the breakdown into procedures works very well. But for larger problems, classes and methods have two advantages. Classes provide a convenient clustering mechanism for methods. A simple Web browser may require 2,000 functions for its implementation, or it may require 100 classes with an average of 20 methods per class. The latter structure is much easier to grasp by the programmer or to handle by teams of programmers. The encapsulation built into classes helps you here as well: classes hide their data representations from all code except their own methods. This means that if a programming bug messes up data, it is easier to search for the culprit among the 20 methods that had access to that data item than among 2,000 procedures.

Procedural Programming

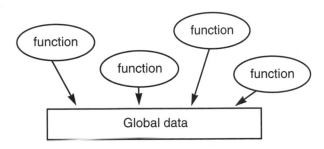

Object-Oriented Programming

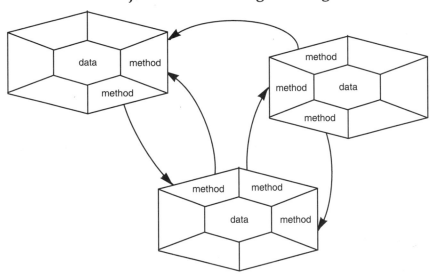

Figure 4-5

You may say that this doesn't sound much different than *modularization*. You have certainly written programs by breaking the program up into modules that communicate with each other through procedure calls only, not by sharing data. This (if well done) goes far in accomplishing encapsulation. However, in many programming languages (such as C and VB), the slightest sloppiness in programming allows you to get at the data in another module—encapsulation is easy to defeat.

There is a more serious problem: while classes are factories for multiple objects with the same behavior, you cannot get multiple copies of a useful module. Suppose you have a module encapsulating a collection of orders, together with a spiffy balanced binary tree module to access them quickly. Now it turns out that you actually need *two* such collections, one for the pending orders and one for the completed orders. You cannot simply link the order tree module twice. And you don't really want to make a copy and rename all procedures in order for the linker to work!

Classes do not have this limitation. Once a class has been defined, it is easy to construct any number of instances of that class type (whereas a module can have only one instance).

We have only scratched a very large surface. The end of this chapter has a short section on "Class Design Hints," but for more information on understanding the OOP design process, here are some book recommendations.

The definitive book on object-oriented design with the Booch methodology is

> *Object-Oriented Analysis and Design,* 2nd Edition, by Grady Booch, (Benjamin Cumming, 1994).

You can find a lighter version of the methodology in

> *Mastering Object-Oriented Design with C++,* by Cay S. Horstmann, (John Wiley & Sons, 1995).

If you are used to VB4, the best book to read to get a sense of object-oriented design is *Doing Objects in Microsoft Visual Basic 4.0,* by Deborah Kurota (Ziff-Davis Press, 1995).

Using Existing Classes

Since you can't do anything in Java without classes, we have shown you many classes at work. Unfortunately, many of these are quite anomalous in the Java scheme of things. A good example of this is our `Console` class. You have seen that you can use our `Console` class without needing to know how it is implemented—all you need to know is the syntax for its methods. That is the point of encapsulation and will certainly be true of all classes. Unfortunately, the `Console` class *only* encapsulates functionality; it neither needs nor hides data. Since there is no data, you do not need to worry about making objects and initializing their instance fields—there aren't any!

Object Variables

For most classes in Java, you create objects, specify their initial state and then work with the objects.

To access objects, you define object variables. For example, the statement

```
AudioClip meow; // meow doesn't refer to any object
```

defines an object variable, meow, that can refer to objects of type AudioClip. It is important to realize that the variable meow *is not an object*, and in fact, does not yet even refer to an object . You cannot use any methods on the variable at this time.

```
meow.play(); // not yet.
```

Use the new operator to create an object.

```
meow = new AudioClip();
    // does create an instance of AudioClip
```

Now you can start applying AudioClip methods to meow.

Most of the time, you will need to create multiple instances of a single class.

```
AudioClip chirp = new AudioClip();
```

Now there are two objects of type AudioClip, one attached to the object variable meow and one to the object variable chirp.

If you assign one variable to another variable using the equals sign,

```
AudioClip wakeUp = meow;
```

then both variables refer to the *same* object. This can lead to surprising behavior in your programs if you are not careful. For example, if you call

```
meow.play();
wakeUp.stop();
```

the audio clip object will play and then stop, since the *same* audio clip is referred to by the wakeUp and meow variables.

But suppose you want meow and wakeUp to refer to different objects, so you can change one of them without changing the other. As it turns out, there is no method available to change audio clips, and there isn't a method available to make a copy of one.

Many classes do have a method called clone that makes a true copy. When you clone an existing object, you get a copy that reflects the current state of the object. Now, however (unlike when you use the equals sign), the two objects exist independently, so they can diverge over time. We will discuss the clone method further in the next chapter.

You can explicitly set an object variable to `null` to indicate that it currently refers to no objects.

```
wakeUp = null;
. . .
if (wakeUp != null) wakeUp.play();
```

If you call a method through a `null` variable, then a run time error occurs.

Local object variables are not automatically initialized to `null`. You must initialize them, either by calling `new` or by setting them to `null`.

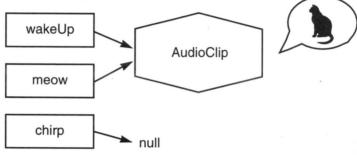

Figure 4-6

You should think of Java object variables as analogous to *object pointers* in C++. For example,

```
AudioClip meow; // Java
```

is really the same as

```
AudioClip* meow; // C++
```

Once you make this association, everything falls into place. Of course, an `AudioClip*` pointer isn't initialized until you initialize it with a call to `new`. The syntax is almost the same in C++ and Java.

```
AudioClip* meow = new AudioClip(); // C++
```

If you copy one variable to another, then both variables refer to the same audio clip—they are pointers to the same object. The equivalent of the Java `null` object is the C++ `NULL` pointer.

All Java objects live on the heap. When an object contains another object variable, that variable still contains just a pointer to yet another heap object.

In C++, pointers make you nervous because they are so error-prone. It is easy to create bad pointers or to mess up memory management. In Java, these problems simply go away. If you use an uninitialized pointer, the run time system will reliably generate a run time error, instead of producing random results. You don't worry about memory management because the garbage collector takes care of it.

C++ makes quite an effort, with its support for copy constructors and assignment operators, to allow the implementation of objects that copy themselves automatically. For example, a copy of a linked list is a new linked list with the same contents but with an independent set of links. This makes it possible to design classes with the same copy behavior as the built-in types. In Java, you must use the `clone` method to get a complete copy of an object.

Object variables in VB are actually quite close to object variables in Java—both have the capacity to point to objects; you even have an analogous use of `new`. The difference, of course, is that, in VB you use `set` rather than the equals sign to make one object variable point to another object.

The Supplied `Date` Class

It is time to go further into the ways of working with Java and third-party classes that are more typical than our `Console` class. Let's start with the `Date` class that comes with Java. An instance of the `Date` class has a state, namely its current settings for its date and time. For example,

```
Date todaysDate = new Date();
```

does the following:

1. It creates a new instance of the `Date` class called `todaysDate`.

2. At the same time, it initializes the state of the `todaysDate` object to be the current date (as maintained by the host operating system).

You can also create an instance of the `Date` class with a specific date:

```
Date preMillenium = new Date(1999,12,31);
```

This creates a `Date` instance called `preMillenium`, with the initial state of December 31, 1999.

Note that the `Date` class is actually a Date/Time class, so you can also set the time. (If you don't set it, it defaults to midnight.) For example:

```
Date preMillenium = new Date(1999,12,31,23,59,59);
```

would give you a `Date` object whose instance fields are set at one second to midnight on December 31, 1999. (When you use `Date()`, you get a date instance with the time set at the one maintained in the operating system.)

Now you may be wondering: Why is `Date` a class in Java rather than (as in some languages) a built-in type, like `int`? The reason is simple: language developers are reluctant to add too many basic types. For example, suppose Java had a notation like #6/1/95#, which is used in VB to denote an example of `Date` type. Since the ordering for year, month, and day is different in different locales, the *language designers* would need to foresee all the issues of internationalization. If they do a poor job, the language becomes an unpleasant muddle, but unhappy programmers are powerless to do anything about it. By making `Date` into a class, the design task is off-loaded to a library designer. If the class is not perfect, other programmers can easily write their own `Date` class. (In fact, we will do just this in the next section.)

Unlike our `Console` class, the `Date` class must have encapsulated data (instance fields) to maintain the date to which it is set. Without looking at the source code, *it is impossible to know the representation used internally by the* `Date` *class*. But, of course, the whole point is that this doesn't matter, and this is what makes it possible to use the `Date` class in a system-independent way.

What *matters* are the methods that the `Date` class exposes. If you look at the documentation for the `Date` class, you will find that it has 25 methods.

In this book, we present a method in the following format, which is essentially the same as the on-line documentation.

`java.util.Date`←name of class
• `void parse(String s)`←name of method

Given a string representing a date and time, this method parses it and converts it to a time value

Parameters (omitting those that are self-explanatory):

  s   the string to parse

Here are some of the most basic methods of the `Date` class. (For more of the methods of the date class, see the section that follows.)

`java.util.Date`
• `void parse(String s)`

Given a string representing a date and time, this method parses it and converts it to a time value.

• `boolean before(Date when)`

This method returns true if the `Date` whose method you are calling comes before the date `when`.

• `boolean after(Date when)`

This method returns true if the `Date` whose method you are calling comes after the date `when`.

- `String toString()`

This method (which exists in many classes) converts the date held in the `Date` object to a string representing the date (using Unix date/time conventions).

- `String toLocaleString()`

This method converts the date held in the `Date` object to a string representing the date using the local ordering convention for the day, month, and year.

For example, here's all it takes in a Java application to print out the current date using the local order conventions. For example, if you configure your computer for the German "locale," then dates should be printed like 31.12.1999.

```
class WhatIstoday
{   public static void main(String arg[])
    {   Date today = new Date();
        System.out.println(today.toLocaleString());
    }
}
```

Notice that, to use the `toLocaleString` method of the `Date` class, we needed to use the dot notation in order to access a method of the `today` instance of the `Date` class.

Mutator and Accessor Methods

At this point, you are probably asking yourself: How do I change the current state of the `Date` class? Similarly, are there methods that let you get at the current day or month or year for the date encapsulated in a specific `Date` object?

Here is a list of the most important methods for getting at or changing the state of a `Date` instance:

`java.util.Date`

- `int getDate()`

gets the day of the month of this date instance, a number between 1 and 31.

- `int getMonth()`

returns the month of this date, an integer between 0 and 11.

- `int getYear()`

gets the year, with 0 denoting 1900, and so on.

- `int getDay()`

gets the weekday, an integer between 0 and 6 (with 0 being Sunday).

- int getHours(), int getMinutes(), int getSeconds()

returns the hours, minutes, or seconds encapsulated in the current instance.

- void setDate(int), void setMonth(int), void setYear(int)

In this method, setDate sets the current day of the month. The other functions set the month and year.

- void setHours(int), void setMinutes(int), void setSeconds(int)

sets the hours, minutes, or seconds encapsulated in the current instance.

None of the set methods error-check the arguments you use. Some of them try to compensate for meaningless parameters. For example, d.setDate(32) moves into the next month. Other set functions produce invalid dates. This is not a good feature, as we will discuss later.

The convention is to call methods that change instance fields' *mutator methods* and those that access instance fields' *accessor methods*.

As you may have suspected from looking at the above list, the convention in Java is to use the lowercase prefix get for accessor methods and set for mutator methods.

In C++, it is important to make a formal distinction between mutator operations that change an object and accessor operations that merely read its data fields. The latter need to be declared as const operations. This is not needed in Java.

The analogous situation (in VB4) is that mutator methods correspond to a Property Let procedure, and accessor methods correspond to a Property Get procedure.

Using Our Day Class

Unfortunately, even if you look at *all* the methods in the Date class to see if your idea of what is important corresponds to ours, you will quickly discover that this class is missing certain types of functionality. (The lack of error-checking for the mutator methods is also annoying.) In any case, as we mentioned previously, Java's Date class is really more a Time class than a Date class.

There are instances in which you want to find the difference between two dates. For example, a retirement calculator certainly needs to compute the difference between today's date and the user's retirement date. The question then arises,

What is the best way to add this functionality to the Date class? Could we build on the Date class (*i.e.,* use *inheritance*—to be described in the next chapter)?

When we tried this, we discovered that the Date class did not let us access the information we needed to do date calculations. There is a method for finding out if the current date comes before the retirement date, but that doesn't do us a lot of good—we know we aren't retired yet. The method won't tell us how many days will elapse until our well-deserved retirement. Just out of curiousity, we examined the source code for the Date class and discovered how the Date class stores its data. But that did not solve our problem because, of course, that information is encapsulated in the class and not accessible to our programs.

The CD includes the source code for all of the publicly available parts of Java. As you become more experienced with Java, you will find the source code extremely useful for getting ideas about and (occasional) insights into Java programming.

We, therefore, decided to write our own Day class to give you a better example of a class with cleanly designed accessor and mutator functions. The source code (it's around 150 lines of code) has been installed in the corejava package inside the \CoreJavaBook directory of your hard disk during the installation described in Chapter 2. (When you finish this chapter, you may want to glance through the source code to see the basic ideas. Fair warning: some of the code is fairly obscure because of the algorithms needed to work with a year that is, in reality, slightly more than 365 days long.)

We allow two ways to create an instance of our Day class that are similar to the two methods for Java's Date class:

```
Day todaysDate = new Day();
Day preMillenium = new Day(1999,12, 31);
```

Unlike Java's Date class, our class does not do anything with the time of day and will also prevent you from creating an illegal date.

To create an object of our Day class, you need to make sure that Java knows where the Day class is. (This can be done by setting the CLASSPATH variable appropriately to include the CoreJava directory and using import corejava.* or copying the Day class to the directory in which you are working.) What we want to stress here is that once you know how to create an instance of the Day class, then all you need to use our class is the following list that tells you how our methods affect the current state of an instance of the Day class:

corejava.Date

- void advance(int n)

advances the date currently set by a specified number of days. For example, d.advance(100) changes d to a date 100 days later.

- int getDay(), int getMonth(), int getYear()

returns the day, month, or year of this date object. Days are between 1 and 31, months between 1 and 12, and years can be any year (such as 1996 or –333). The class knows about the switch from the Julian to the Gregorian calendar in 1582.

- int weekday()

returns an integer between 0 and 6, corresponding to the day of the week (0 = Sunday).

- int daysBetween(Day b)

This method is one of the main reasons we created the Day class. It calculates the number of days between the current instance of the Day class and instance b of the Day class.

Notice that our Day class has no method for changing the date other than to use the advance method.

Here's a little example program that combines the Console class with our Day class in order to calculate how many days you have been alive.

```
class DaysAlive
{   public static void main(String[] args)
    {   int year;
        int month;
        int day;

        month = Console.readInt
            ("Please enter the month, 1 for January and so on");
        day = Console.readInt
            ("Please enter the day you were born.");

        year = Console.readInt
("Please enter the year you were born (starting with 19..)");

        Day birthday = new Day(year, month, day);
        Day today = new Day();
        System.out.println("You have been alive "
            + today.daysBetween(birthday) + " days.");
    }
}
```

If you try to enter invalid data, the program will terminate with an exception. See Chapter 10 for more on exceptions.

A Calendar Program

As a more serious example of putting it all together, here is the code for an application that prints out a calendar for the month and year specified in the command line argument. For example, if you compile this class (make sure our Day class is available of course) and then say

```
java Calendar 12 1999
```

you will see the calendar for December 1999. (December 31 is rather conveniently on a Friday that year, by the way.)

```
12    1999
Sun   Mon   Tue   Wed   Thu   Fri   Sat
                    1     2     3     4
  5     6     7     8     9    10    11
 12    13    14    15    16    17    18
 19    20    21    22    23    24    25
 26    27    28    29    30    31
```

There are two issues in writing a calendar program like this: you have to know the weekday of the first day of the month, and you have to know how many days the month has. We sidestep the latter problem with the following trick: we make a Date object that starts out with the first of the month.

```
Day d = new Day(y, m, 1); // start date of the month
```

After printing each day, we advance d by one day:

```
d.advance(1);
```

Then we check the month (d.month()) and see if it is still the same as m. If not, we are done.

```
import corejava.*;

public class Calendar
{  public static void main(String[] args)
   {  int m;
      int y;
      if (args.length == 2)
      {  m = Format.atoi(args[0]);
         y = Format.atoi(args[1]);
      }
```

```
else
{   Day today = new Day(); // today's date
    m = today.getMonth();
    y = today.getYear();
}

Day d = new Day(y, m, 1); // start date of the month

System.out.println(m + " " + y);
System.out.println("Sun Mon Tue Wed Thu Fri Sat");
for( int i = 0; i < d.weekday(); i++ )
    System.out.print("      ");
while (d.getMonth() == m)
{   if (d.getDay() < 10) System.out.print(" ");
    System.out.print(d.getDay());
    if (d.weekday() == 6)
        System.out.println("");
    else
        System.out.print("   ");
    d.advance(1);
}
if (d.weekday() != 0) System.out.println("");
    }
}
```

Starting to Build Your Own Classes

You saw how to write simple classes in Chapter 3. In that chapter, the classes
were all designed to run as stand-alone programs and depended only on the
classes built into Java and our little `Console` class. When you said

```
java Mortgage
```

for example, the Java interpreter looked for the `main` method in the `Mortgage`
class and ran it. The `main` method, in turn, called other methods of the class as
needed. Although you will see more about methods like `main` later in this chapter, this kind of class is not what we are concerned with in this chapter. In more
sophisticated Java programs, the class you choose to run from the interpreter
will usually have very little functionality other than starting up the various
objects that do the actual work of your program.

What we want to do in the rest of this chapter (and in the next chapter) is show
you how to write the kind of "workhorse classes" that are needed for more
sophisticated applications. These classes do not (and often cannot) stand alone:
they are the building blocks for *constructing* stand-alone programs.

The syntax for a class in Java:

```
class NameOfClass
{   // definitions of the class's features
    // includes methods and instance fields
}
```

The outermost pair of braces (block) defines the code that will make up the class. Our convention is to use initial caps for class names. Just as with the classes from Chapter 3, individual method definitions define the operations of the class. The difference is that we want to allow other classes to use our classes while still maintaining encapsulation of the data. This means that we now want to allow for (encapsulated) instance fields that will hold the private data for these classes.

We adopt the policy that the methods for the class come first and the instance fields come at the end. (Perhaps this, in a small way, encourages the notion of leaving instance fields alone.)

An Employee *Class*

Consider the following, very simplified version of an Employee class that might be used by a business in writing a payroll system.

```
class Employee
{    public Employee(String n, double s, Day d)
     {    name = n;
          salary = s;
          hireDay = d;
     }
     public void raiseSalary(double byPercent)
     {    salary *= 1 + byPercent / 100;
     }
     public int hireYear()
     {    return hireDay.getYear();
     }
     public void print()
     {    System.out.println(name + " " + salary + " " + hireYear());
     }
      public String getName()
     { return name
     }
     private String name;
     private double salary;
     private Day hireDay;
}
```

We will break down the code in this class in some detail in the sections that follow. First, though, here's some code that lets you see how to use the Employee class.

```
import java.util.*;
import corejava.*;

public class EmployeeTest
{   public static void main(String[] args)
    {   Employee[] staff = new Employee[3];

        staff[0] = new Employee("Harry Hacker", 35000,
            new Day(1989,10,1));
        staff[1] = new Employee("Carl Cracker", 75000,
            new Day(1987,12,15));
        staff[2] = new Employee("Tony Tester", 38000,
            new Day(1990,3,15));
        int i;
        for (i = 0; i < 3; i++) staff[i].raiseSalary(5);
        for (i = 0; i < 3; i++) staff[i].print();
    }
}
```

To run the sample code, first make sure that both the `Employee` and `EmployeeTest` classes are in the same directory. Then, compile this `EmployeeTest` class and run it with the Java interpreter. This will create an instance of the `Employee` class with some sample data and then print out the state of the class in order for us to see whether or not our class appears well constructed.

In Java, all functions are defined inside the class itself. This does not automatically make them inline functions. There is no analog to the C++ syntax:

```
class Employee
{//...
};
void Employee::raiseSalary(double byPercent) // C++, not Java
{   salary *= 1 + byPercent / 100;
}
```

Analyzing the **Employee** Class

In the sections that follow, we want to dissect the `Employee` class. Let's start with the methods in this class. As you can see by examining the source code, this class has five methods, whose headers look like this:

```
public Employee(String n, double s, Day d)
```

```
public String getName()
```

```
public void raiseSalary(double byPercent)
```

```
public int hireYear()
```

```
public void print()
```

The keyword `public` is usually called an *access modifier*. In Java, these access modifiers describe who can use the method. The keyword `public` means that any method in any class that has access to an instance of the `Employee` class can call the method. (There are actually five possible access levels; they are covered in this and the next chapter.)

Next, notice that there are three instance fields that will hold the data we will manipulate inside an instance of the `Employee` class.

```
private String name;
private double salary;
private Day hireDay;
```

The `private` keyword makes sure that no outside agency can access the instance fields *except* through the methods of our class. In this book, instance fields will almost always be private. (Exceptions occur only when we have to implement very closely collaborating classes, for example a `List` and a `Link` class in a linked list data structure.)

It is possible to use the `public` keyword with your instance variables, but it would be a very bad idea. Having `public` data fields would allow any part of the program to read and modify the instance variables. That completely ruins encapsulation and, at the risk of repeating ourselves too often, we strongly urge against using public instance fields.

Finally, notice that we use an instance field that is itself an instance of our `Day` class. This is quite usual: classes will often contain instance fields that are themselves class instances.

For the `Employee` class to compile, either the `Day` class must be in the same directory as the `Employee` class, or your `CLASSPATH` variable must point to the `CoreJavaBook` directory.

Please see the section *Packages* if you want to use all of our classes in the simplest fashion, without worrying about the location of the source files.

First Step with Constructors

Let's look at the first method listed in our `Employee` class.

```
public Employee(String n, double s, Day d)
{   name = n;
    salary = s;
    hireDay = d;
}
```

This is an example of a *constructor method*. It is used to initialize objects of a class—giving the instance variables the initial state you want them to have. You didn't see any methods like this in Chapter 3 because we didn't initialize any objects in that chapter.

For example, when you create an instance of the `Employee` class with code like this

```
hireDate = new Day(1950, 1, 1);
Employee number007 = new Employee
    ("James Bond", 100000, hireDate);
```

you have set the instance fields as follows:

```
name = "James Bond";
salary = 100000;
hireDay = January 1, 1950 //actually a Day class with this
                          //data encapsulated
```

The new method is always used together with a constructor to create the class. This forces you to set the initial state of your objects. In Java, you cannot create an instance of a class without initializing the instance variables (either explictly or implicitly). The reason for this design decision is simple: an object created without a correct initialization is always useless and occasionally dangerous. In many languages, like Delphi, you can create uninitialized objects; the result is almost always the platform equivalent of a general protection fault (GPF) or segmentation fault, which means memory is being corrupted.

While we will have more to say about constructor methods later in this chapter, for now, always keep the following in mind:

1.   A constructor has the same name as the class.

2.   A constructor may (as in this example) take one or more (or even no) parameters.

3.   A constructor is always called with the new keyword.

Remember, too, the following important difference between constructors and other methods:

•   A constructor can only be called with new. You can't apply a constructor to an existing object to reset the instance fields. For example, `d.Date(1950, 1, 1)` is an error.

Of course, if resetting all fields of a class is an important and recurring operation, the designers of the class can provide a mutator method such as `empty` or `reset` for that purpose. We want to stress that only the supplied mutator methods will let you revise the state of the instance variables in an already constructed class (assuming, of course, that all data are private).

It is possible to have more than one constructor in a class. You have already seen this in both Java's `Date` class and our `Day` class. (You saw two of the three constructors available in the `Date` class and both of the constructors available in our `Day` class.)

Constructors work the same way in Java as they do in C++. But keep in mind that all Java objects are constructed on the heap and that a constructor must be combined with new. It is a common C++ programmer error to forget the new operator:

```
Employee number007("James Bond", 100000, hireDate);
    // C++, not Java
```

That works in C++, but does not work in Java.

The Methods of the Employee Class

The first three methods in our Employee class should not pose many problems. They are much like the methods you saw in the previous chapter. Notice, however, that all of these methods can access the private instance fields by name. This is a key point: instance fields are always accessible by the methods of their own class.

For example,

```
public void raiseSalary(double byPercent)
{   salary *= 1 + byPercent / 100;
}
```

sets a new value for the salary instance field in the object that executes this method. (This particular method does not return a value.) For example, the call

```
number007.raiseSalary(5);
```

raises number007's salary by increasing the number007.salary variable by 5%.

Of the remaining methods in this class, the most interesting is the one that returns the year hired. Recall that it looks like this:

```
public int hireYear()
{   return hireDay.getYear();
}
```

Notice that this method returns an integer value, and it does this by applying a method to the hireDay instance variable. This makes perfect sense because hireDay is an instance of our Day class, which indeed has a getYear method.

Finally, lets look more closely at the rather simple getName method.

```
public String getName()
{   return name
}
```

This is an obvious example of an accessor method. Because it works directly with a field in the class, it is sometimes called a *field accessor method*. It simply returns the current state of the name field.

For the class implementor, it is obviously more trouble to write both a private field and a public accessor method than to simply write a public data field. But programmers using the class are not inconvenienced—if `number007` is the name of the instance of the `Employee` class, they simply write `number007.getName()`, rather than `number007.name`.

The point is that the `name` field has become "read-only" to the outside world. Only operations of the class can modify it. In particular, should the value ever be wrong, only the class operations need to be debugged.

By the way, the function is called `getName()` because it can't be called `name()`—that is already taken by the instance variable itself. (And, in any case, the convention in Java is that accessor methods begin with a lowercase "get".)

Now, because secret agents come and go, one might want to modify the class at some later point to allow for a field mutator that resets the name of the current "007." But this would be done by the maintainers of the class as the need arises.

The point to keep in mind is that, in most classes, private data fields are of a technical nature and of no interest to anyone but the implementor of the operations. When the user of a class has a legitimate interest in both reading and setting a field, the class implementors need to supply *three* items:

- a private data field
- a public field accessor method
- a public field mutator method

This is a lot more tedious than supplying a single public data field, but there are considerable benefits:

1. The internal implementation can be changed without affecting any code other than the operations of the class.

Of course, the accessor and mutator methods may need to do a lot of work—especially when the data representation of the instance fields is changed. But that leads us to our second benefit.

2. Mutator methods can perform error-checking, whereas code that simply assigns to a field cannot.

Our `Day` class is a good example of a class that should *not* have mutators for each field. Suppose we had methods called `setDay`, `setMonth`, and `setYear` that do the obvious things. Suppose `d` was an instance of our `Day` class. Now consider the code:

```
d.setDay(31);
d.setMonth(3);
d.setYear(1996);
```

If the date encapsulated in `d` was currently at February 1, then the `setDay` operation described above would set it to an invalid date of February 31. What do you think `setDay` should do in this case? At first glance, this appears to be only a nuisance, but if you think this through carefully, you will find that there is no good answer.

Should an invalid `setDay` abort the program? Well, how *would* you then safely set the date from February 1 to March 31? Of course, you could set the month first:

```
d.setMonth(3);
d.setDay(31);
```

That will work. Now, how do you change it back to February 1? This time, you can't set the month first. This function would be a real hassle to use.

So perhaps `setDay` should just quietly adjust the date? If you set the date to February 31, then maybe the date should be adjusted to March 3 or 4, depending on whether the year is a leap year or not. The Java `Date` class does exactly that. We think this is a lousy idea. Consider again our effort to set the date from February 1 to March 31.

```
d.setDay(31); // now it is March 3 or 4
d.setMonth(3); // still March 3 or 4
```

Or perhaps `setDay` should temporarily make an invalid date and count on the fact that the programmer won't forget to adjust the month. Then we lose a major benefit of encapsulation, the guarantee that the object state is never corrupted.

We hope we have convinced you that a mutator that sets only the day field is not worth the trouble. It is obviously better to supply a single `setDate(int, int, int)` function that does the error-checking needed. (This also fits one's mental model better—after all, one sets a date and not a day, month, and year.)

Private Methods

When implementing a class, we make all data fields private, but what about the methods? While `public` data are dangerous, `private` methods occur quite frequently. These methods can be called only from other operations of the class. The reason is simple: to implement operations, you may wish to break up the code into many separate functions. Many of these functions are not particularly useful to the public. (For example, they may be too close to the current implementation or require a special protocol or calling order.) Such methods are best implemented as `private` operations.

• To implement a private method in Java, simply change the `public` keyword to `private`.

As an example, consider how our `Day` class might require a method to test whether or not a year is a leap year. By making the method private, we are under no obligation to keep it available if we change to another implementation. The method may well be *harder* to implement, or *unnecessary* if the data representation changes: this is irrelevant. The point is that as long as the operation is private, the designers of the class can be assured that it is never used outside the other class operations and can simply drop it. Had the method been public, we would be forced to reimplement it if we changed the representation, because other code might have relied on it. In sum, choose private methods:

- for those functions that are of no concern to the class user and

- for those functions that could not easily be supported if the class implementation were to change.

Static Methods

The last method modifier we want to talk about in this chapter is the `static` modifier. You saw the `static` modifier used to create class constants in Chapter 3. Classes can have both static variables and static methods. Static fields do not change from one instance of a class to another, so you should think of them as belonging to a class. Similarly, static methods belong to a class and do not operate on any instance of a class. This means that you can use them without creating an instance of a class. For example, all of the methods in the `Console` class are static methods. This is why a syntax like

```
x = Console.readDouble();
```

makes perfect sense.

The general syntax for using a static method from a class is:

```
ClassName.staticMethod(parameters);
```

Because static methods do not work with an instance of the class they can only access static fields. In particular, if a method needs to access a non-static instance field of an object, it cannot be a static method.

Static variables and methods in Java are the same as static data members and member functions in C++. As in C++, the term "static" makes no sense. The original purpose of `static` in C/C++ was to denote local variables that don't go away when the local scope is exited. In that context, the term "static" indicates that the variable stays around and is still there when the block is entered again. Then `static` got a second meaning in C/C++, to denote functions and global variables with file scope that could not be accessed from other files. Finally, C++ reused the keyword for a third, unrelated interpretation, to denote variables and functions that belong to a class but not to any particular object of the class. That is the same meaning that the keyword has in Java.

As another example, consider the header for the `main` method:

```
public static void main(String [] args)
```

Since `main` is `static`, you don't need to create an instance of the class in order to call it—and the Java interpreter doesn't either. For example, if your `main` function is contained in the class `Mortgage` and you start the Java interpreter with

```
javac Mortgage
```

then the interpreter simply starts the `main` function without creating an object of the `Mortgage` class. Because of this, `main` can only access static instance fields in the class. It is actually not uncommon for `main` to create an object of its own class!

```
class Application
{    . . .
    public static void main(String [] args)
    {    Application a = new Application();
        . . .
    }
}
```

This allows you to refer to instance variables of the class via the `a` object variable.

As a more serious example of a class that combines both static and public methods, the following class provides a random-number generator that is a significant improvement over the one supplied with Java. (Java uses a simple "linear congruential generator" that can be non-random in certain situations by displaying undesirable regularities. This is especially true when it is used to plot random points in space or for certain kinds of simulations.) The idea for the improvement is simple (we found it in Donald E. Knuth's *Semi-Numerical Algorithms*, which is Volume 2 of his *Art of Computer Programming* [Addison-Wesley, 1981]); instead of using the random number supplied by a call to

```
java.lang.Math.random();
```

we created a class that:

1. adds the convenience of generating random integers in a specific range and

2. is more "random" than the one supplied with Java (but takes about twice as long).

The class works in the following way:

1. It fills up a small array with random numbers, using the built-in random-number generator. The size of the array and the array itself are made class constants (*i.e.*, declared with `private static final`). This way, all instances of the `randomInteger` class can share this information. (This is obviously more efficient than regenerating this information in each instance.)

2. It has a public method, called draw, for drawing a random integer in the specified range. (You will need to create an instance of our RandomIntGenerator class in order to use this method.)

3. The draw method, in turn, uses a static method called nextRandom that actually implements the algorithm described in Knuth's *Semi-Numerical Algorithms*, p. 32. The way this works is the method calls the built-in random number generator twice: the first time tells us which random array element to take, and the second time, we use the resulting random number to replace the "used-up" element in the array. (It is conceptually clearer to have these operations done in a static method, since all instances of our RandomIntGenerator class will share these operations.)

4. The class constructor defines the range of integers.

Here's the code:

```java
package corejava;

public class RandomIntGenerator
{   public RandomIntGenerator(int l, int h)
    {   low = l;
        high = h;
    }

    public int draw()
    {   int r = low
            + (int)((high - low + 1) * nextRandom());
        if (r > high) r = high;
        return r;
    }

    public static void main(String[] args)
    {   RandomIntGenerator r1
            = new RandomIntGenerator(1, 10);
        RandomIntGenerator r2
            = new RandomIntGenerator(0, 1);
        int i;
        for (i = 1; i <= 100; i++)
            System.out.println(r1.draw() + " " + r2.draw());
    }

    private static double nextRandom()
    {   int pos =
            (int)(java.lang.Math.random() * BUFFER_SIZE);
        if (pos == BUFFER_SIZE) pos = BUFFER_SIZE - 1;
        double r = buffer[pos];
        buffer[pos] = java.lang.Math.random();
        return r;
    }
}
```

```
    private static final int BUFFER_SIZE = 101;
    private static double[] buffer
        = new double[BUFFER_SIZE];
    static //initialization of static data
    {   int i;
        for (i = 0; i < BUFFER_SIZE; i++)
            buffer[i] = java.lang.Math.random();
    }

    private int low;
    private int high;
}
```

Following is an example using our random integer generator. Note that the test program is simply included in the `RandomIntGenerator` class.

```
  class RandomIntGenerator
  {   . . .
      public static void main(String[] args)
      {   RandomIntGenerator r1 = new RandomIntGenerator(1, 10);
          RandomIntGenerator r2 = new RandomIntGenerator(0, 1);
          int i;
          for (i = 1; i <= 100; i++)
              System.out.println(r1.draw() + " " + r2.draw());
      }
  }
```

More on Object Construction and Destruction

Overloading

Recall that both Java's `Date` class and our `Day` class had more than one constructor. We could use:

```
  Date today = new Date()
```

or

```
  Date preMillenium =  new Date(1999,12,31)
```

This capability is called *overloading*. Overloading occurs if several methods have the same name (in this case the `Date` constructor method), but different arguments. The Java interpreter must sort out which method to call. (This is usually called *overloading resolution*.) It picks the correct method by matching the argument types in the headers of the various methods with the types of the values used in the specific method call. (Even if there are no arguments, you must use the empty parentheses.) A compile-time error occurs if the compiler cannot match the arguments or if more than one match is possible.

Java allows you to overload any method—not just constructor methods.

Overloading is something we will return to in the next chapter. Method over-loading (sometimes called *ad-hoc polymorphism*) must be distinguished from true polymorphism, which Java also does support. This, too, is discussed in the next chapter.

Instance Field Initialization

Since you can overload the constructor methods in a class, you can obviously build in many ways to set the instance fields of your classes. It is always a good idea to make sure that regardless of the constructor call, every instance field is set to something meaningful. Actually, Java does set all instance fields to a default value (numbers to zero, objects to null) if you don't set them explicitly. But it is considered poor programming practice to rely on this.

In this regard, instance variables differ from local variables in a method. Local vari-ables must be initialized explicitly.

For example, if our Day class did not have any constructors, then the day, month, and year fields would be initialized with zero whenever you made a new Day object. (That wouldn't be a good idea. In the Julian/Gregorian calen-dar, there is no year 0—the year 1 B.C. is immediately followed by 1 A.D. For that reason, we supply explicit constructors.)

If all constructors of a class need to set a particular instance variable to the same value, then there is a convenient syntax for doing the initialization. You simply assign to the field in the class definition. For example, when you initialize a Customer object, you would want to set the nextOrder instance variable to 1 all the time. This can be done as in the following code:

```
class Customer
{   public Customer(String n)
    {   name = n;
        accountNumber = Account.getNewNumber();
    }
    public Customer(String n, int a)
    {   name = n;
        accountNumber = a;
    }
    . . .
    private String name;
    private int accountNumber;
    private int nextOrder = 1;
}
```

Now the nextOrder field is set to 1 in all Customer objects.

We recommend that you use this convenient syntax whenever a field is set to the same constant value by all constructors.

A *default constructor* is a constructor with no parameters. If your class has no constructors whatsoever, Java provides a default constructor for you. It sets *all* the instance variables to their default values. So all numeric data contained in the instance fields would be zeroed out and all object variables would point to `null`.

This only applies when your class has no constructors. If you design your class with a constructor, then Java insists that you provide a default constructor if you want the users of your class to have the ability to create an instance via a call to:

```
new ClassName()
```

For example, the `Customer` class defines no constructors that use no parameters, so it is illegal for the users of the class to call:

```
c = new Customer(); // ERROR--no default constructor
```

In C++, you cannot directly initialize data members of a class. All data must be set in a constructor.

Java has no analog for the C++ initializer list syntax, such as:

```
Customer::Customer(String n)
:    name(n),
     accountNumber(Account.getNewNumber())
{}
```

C++ uses this special syntax to call the constructor for member objects. In Java, there is no need for it because objects have no member objects, only pointers to other objects.

The **this** Object

Occasionally, you want to access the current object in its entirety and not a particular instance variable. Java has a convenient shortcut for this—the `this` keyword. In a method, the keyword `this` refers to the object on which the method operates.

For example, many Java classes have a method called `toString()` that prints out the object. (For example, Java's `Date` class has this method.) You can print out the current date stored in a date variable by saying `this.toString()`.

More generally, provided your class implements a `toString()` method, you can print it out simply by calling:

```
System.out.println("Customer.computeOverdue: " + this)
```

This is a useful strategy for debugging. We will later see other uses for the `this` object.

There is a second meaning for the `this` keyword. If *the first line of a constructor* has the form `this(.  .)`, then the constructor calls another constructor of the same class. Here is a typical example:

```
class Customer
{   public Customer(String n)
    {   this(n, Account.getNewNumber());
    }
    public Customer(String n, int a)
    {   name = n;
        accountNumber = a;
    }
    . . .
}
```

When you call `new Customer("James Bond")`, then the `Customer(String)` constructor calls the `Customer(String, int)` constructor.

This is a useful device to factor out (combine) common code between constructors.

In sum, as you have seen, constructors are somewhat complex in Java. Before a constructor is called, all instance fields are initialized to the value you specified in the class or to their default values (zero for numbers, `null` for objects). The first line of your constructor may call another constructor.

The `this` object in Java is identical to the `this` pointer in C++. However, in C++ it is not possible for one constructor to call another. If you want to factor out common initialization code in C++, you must write a separate member function.

Object Destruction and the `finalize()` Method

Many languages, such as C++ and Delphi, have explicit destructor methods for the cleanup code that may be needed. The most common activity in a destructor is reclaiming the memory set aside for objects. Since Java does automatic garbage collection, manual memory reclamation is not needed, and Java does not support destructors.

Of course, some objects utilize a resource other than memory, such as a file or a handle to another object that uses system resources. In this case, it is important that the resource be reclaimed and recycled when it is no longer needed.

Java does allow you to add a `finalize()` method to any class. The `finalize()` method will be called before the garbage collector sweeps away the object. In practice, *do not rely on the finalize method* for recycling any resources that are in short supply—you simply cannot know when this method will be called.

If a resource needs to be closed as soon as you have finished using it, you need to manage it manually. Add a `dispose` method that *you* call to clean up what needs cleaning. Just as importantly, if a class you use has a `dispose` method, you will want to call it to reclaim what the designers of the class thought was important to reclaim. In particular, if your class has an instance field that has a `dispose` method, provide a `dispose` method that invokes the field's `dispose`.

A `CardDeck` *Class*

To put together the information in this chapter, we want to show you the code needed for the simplest card game of all. The program chooses two cards at random, one for you and one for the computer. The highest card wins.

The underlying object structure in this example is this: a class called `Card` is used to build up a class called `CardDeck`. A card stores its value (a number between 1 and 13 to denote ace, 2, . . . 10, jack, queen, or king) and its suit (a number between 1 and 4 to denote clubs, diamonds, hearts, or spades). Don't worry about the `final` for the class and for some of the methods in this example. We will explain the significance of this use of the `final` keyword as applied to classes and methods in the next chapter.

```
final class Card //don't worry about the final for now
{
    public static final int ACE = 1;
    public static final int JACK = 11;
    public static final int QUEEN = 12;
    public static final int KING  = 13;
    public static final int CLUBS = 1;
    public static final int DIAMONDS = 2;
    public static final int HEARTS = 3;
    public static final int SPADES = 4;

    . . .

    private int value;
    private int suit;
}
```

Here's the constructor for the Card object. As you might expect, it takes two integers, one for the value and one for the suit.

```
public Card(int v, int s)
{   value = v;
    suit = s;
}
```

The card deck stores an array of cards.

```
class CardDeck
{   . . .
    private Card[] deck;
    int cards;
}
```

The cards field counts how many cards are still in the deck. At the beginning, there are 52 cards, and the count will go down as we draw cards from the deck.

Here's the constructor for the CardDeck class:

```java
public CardDeck()
{   deck = new Card[52];
    fill();
    shuffle();
}
```

Notice that this constructor initializes the array of Card objects. After the array of cards is allocated, it will automatically be filled with cards and shuffled.

The fill method fills the card deck with 52 cards.

```java
final public void fill()
{   int i;
    int j;
    cards = 0;
    for (i = 1; i <= 13; i++)
        for (j = 1; j <= 4; j++)
        {   deck[cards] = new Card(i, j);
            cards++;
        }
}
```

The idea of the shuffle procedure is to choose randomly which of the cards becomes the last one. We then swap the last card with the chosen card and repeat the process with the remainder of the pile.

Here's the full code for the CardDeck class. Note the code for the game in the main function.

```java
import corejava.*;

public class CardDeck
{   public CardDeck()
    {   deck = new Card[52];
        fill();
        shuffle();
    }

    public void fill()
    {   int i;
        int j;

        for (i = 1; i <= 13; i++)
            for (j = 1; j <= 4; j++)
                deck[4 * (i - 1) + j - 1] = new Card(i, j);
        cards = 52;
    }
```

```java
public void shuffle()
{   int next;
    for (next = 0; next < cards - 1; next++)
    {   int r = new
            RandomIntGenerator(next, cards - 1).draw();
        Card temp = deck[next];
        deck[next] = deck[r];
        deck[r] = temp;
    }
}

public final Card draw()
{   if (cards == 0) return null;
    cards--;
    return deck[cards];
}

public static void main(String[] args)
{   CardDeck d = new CardDeck();
    int i;
    int wins = 0;
    int rounds = 10;

    for (i = 1; i <= rounds; i++)
    {   Card yours = d.draw();
        System.out.print("Your draw: " + yours + " ");
        Card mine = d.draw();
        System.out.print("My draw: " + mine + " ");
        if (yours.rank() > mine.rank())
        {   System.out.println("You win");
            wins++;
        }
        else
            System.out.println("I win");
    }
    System.out.println
("Your wins: " + wins + " My wins: " + (rounds - wins));

}

    private Card[] deck;
    private int cards;
}
```

Here's the complete code for the Card class. Note how we encapsulate the integers that represent the card's suit and value and only return information about them. Also note that once a card object is constructed, its contents can never change.

```java
public final class Card
{  public static final int ACE = 1;
   public static final int JACK = 11;
   public static final int QUEEN = 12;
   public static final int KING  = 13;
   public static final int CLUBS = 1;
   public static final int DIAMONDS = 2;
   public static final int HEARTS = 3;
   public static final int SPADES = 4;

   public Card(int v, int s)
   {  value = v;
      suit = s;
   }

   public int getValue()
   {  return value;
   }

   public int getSuit()
   {  return suit;
   }

   public int rank()
   {  if (value == 1)
         return 4 * 13 + suit;
      else
         return 4 * (value - 1) + suit;
   }

   public String toString()
   {  String v;
      String s;
      if (value == ACE) v = "Ace";
      else if (value == JACK) v = "Jack";
      else if (value == QUEEN) v = "Queen";
      else if (value == KING) v = "King";
      else v = String.valueOf(value);
      if (suit == DIAMONDS) s = "Diamonds";
      else if (suit == HEARTS) s = "Hearts";
      else if (suit == SPADES) s = "Spades";
      else /* suit == CLUBS */ s = "Clubs";
      return v + " of " + s;
   }

   private int value;
   private int suit;
}
```

Packages

Java allows you to group classes in a collection called a *package*. Packages are convenient for organizing your work and for separating your work from code libraries provided by others.

For example, we give you a number of useful classes in a package called `corejava`. The standard Java library is distributed over a number of packages, including `java.lang`, `java.util`, `java.net`, and so on. The standard Java packages are examples of a hierarchical package. Just as you have nested subdirectories on your hard disk, you can organize packages using levels of nesting. All standard Java packages are inside the `java` package hierarchy.

One reason for nesting packages is to guarantee the uniqueness of package names. Suppose someone else has the bright idea of calling their package `corejava`. By nesting it inside a package hierarchy, such as `cornell-horstmann.corejava`, we could have kept our package distinct from any other `corejava` package. You can have as many levels of nesting as you like. In fact, to absolutely guarantee a unique package name, Sun recommends that you use your company's Internet domain name (which presumably is unique) written in reverse order as a package prefix. One of the authors of this book has the registered Internet domain name `horstmann.com`, so we might have called the `corejava` package

```
COM.horstmann.corejava
```

When you write a package, you must put the name of the package on top of your source file, *before* the code that defines the classes in the package. For example, the files in our `corejava` package start like this:

```
package corejava;
```

If you look into the `Date.java` file of the Java library, you will see the line:

```
package java.util;
```

This means that the `Date.java` file is part of the `java.util` package. The `package` statement must be the first statement in the file after any comments.

If your source file has no package declaration, Java adds the classes in it to its default package.

Using Packages

You can use the public classes in a package in two ways. The first is simply to give the full name of the package. For example:

```
int i = corejava.Console.readInteger();
java.util.Date today = new java.util.Date();
```

That is obviously tedious. The simpler, and more common, approach is to use the import keyword. You can then refer to the classes in the package without giving their full names. You can import a specific class or the whole package. You place the import statement before the source code of the class that will use it. For example:

```
import corejava.*; // imports all the clases in the
                   // corejava package
import java.util.*;
int i = Console.readInteger();
Date today = new java.util.Date();
```

You can also import a specific class inside a package. In this case, you adjust the import statement as in the following:

```
import corejava.Console; // imports only the Console class
```

Normally, importing all classes in a package is simpler. It has no negative effect on compile time or code size, so there is generally no reason not to do it. However, if two packages each have classes with the same name, then you can't import them both.

Finally, you can only use the * to import a single package. You cannot use import java.* to import all packages with the java prefix.

How the Compiler Locates Packages

All files of a package must be located in a subdirectory that matches the full package name. For example, all files in our corejava package must be in the subdirectory corejava. All files in the java.util package are in a subdirectory java\util (java/util on Unix).

These subdirectories need not branch off directly from the root directory; they can branch off from any directory named in the CLASSPATH variable. Suppose your CLASSPATH is as follows:

```
CLASSPATH=c:\java\lib;c:\corejava-book;.
```

Suppose your code contains the lines:

```
import java.util.*;
import corejava.*;
```

If you use the class Console, the compiler looks for the following files:

```
c:\java\lib\Console.class
```

```
c:\java\lib\corejava\Console.class
```

```
c:\java\lib\java\util\Console.class
```

```
c:\corejava-book\Console.class
```

```
c:\corejava-book\java\util\Console.class
```

```
c:\corejava-book\corejava\Console.class
.\Console.class
.\java\util\Console.class
.\corejava\Console.class
```

When it finds a matching file, it checks that the package name matches the path and that the file contains a public class named `Console` inside the package.

Actually, if you look inside `c:\java\lib`, you won't find the subdirectory `java\util`. Instead, there is a single ZIP file, `classes.zip`. If you look inside that ZIP file with a ZIP viewer like WinZip, you will see the paths and the class files. If you like, you can also zip up your own packages in a file named `classes.zip` that is located on the class path.

In addition, the compiler always searches the `java.lang` package. You never need to specify it, nor do you need to import it.

When you make a package, it is your responsibility to place the object files in the correct subdirectory. For example, if you compile a file that starts with the line

```
package acme.util;
```

then you must put the resulting class file into the subdirectory `acme\util`. The compiler won't do it for you.

C++ programmers usually confuse `import` with `#include`. The two have nothing in common. In C++, you must use `#include` to include the declarations of external features, because the C++ compiler does not look inside any files except the one that it is compiling and explicitly included header files. The Java compiler will happily look inside other files provided you tell it where to look.

In Java, you can entirely avoid the `import` mechanism by explicitly naming all packages, such as `java.util.Date`. In C++, you cannot avoid the `#include` directives.

The only benefit of the `import` statement is convenience. You can refer to a class by a name shorter than the full package name. For example, after an `import java.util.*` (or `import java.util.Date`) statement, you can refer to the `java.util.Date` class simply as `Date`.

The analogous construction in C++ is the *namespace* feature. Think of the `package` and `import` keywords in Java as the analogs of `namespace` and `using` in C++.

Package Scope

We have already encountered the access modifiers `public` and `private`. Features tagged as `public` can be used by any class. Private features can only be used by the class that defines them. If you don't specify either `public` or `private`, then the feature (that is, the class, method or variable) can be accessed by all methods in the same *package*.

For example, if the class `Card` is not defined as a public class, then only other classes in the same package (such as `CardDeck`) can access it. For classes, that is a very reasonable default. However, methods should generally be either explicitly public or private, and instance and static variables should be private.

> Every source file can contain, at most, one public class, which must have the same name as the file.

Class Design Hints

Without trying to be comprehensive or tedious, we want to end this chapter with some hints that may make your classes more acceptable in well-mannered OOP circles.

1. *Always keep data private.*

This is first and foremost: doing anything else violates encapsulation. You may need to write an accessor or mutator method occasionally, but you are still better off keeping the instance fields private. Bitter experience has shown that how the data are represented may change, but how they are used will change much less frequently. When data are kept private, changes in their representation do not affect the user of the class, and bugs are easier to detect.

2. *Always initialize data.*

Java won't initialize local variables for you, but it will initialize instance variables of objects. Don't rely on the defaults, but initialize the variables explicitly, either by supplying a default or by setting defaults in all constructors.

3. *Don't use too many basic types in a class.*

The idea is to replace multiple *related* uses of basic types with other classes. This keeps your classes easier to understand and to change. For example, replace the following instance fields in a `Customer` class

```
private String street;
private String city;
private String state;
private int zip;
```

with a new class called `Address`. This way, one can easily cope with changes to addresses.

4. *Not all fields need individual field accessors and mutators.*

You may need to get and set a person's salary. You certainly won't need to change his or her hiring date once the object is constructed. And, quite often, objects have instance variables that you don't want others to get or set, for example, the array of cards in the card deck.

5.   *Use a standard form for class definitions.*

We always list the contents of classes in the following order:

> public features
>
> package scope features
>
> private features

Within each section, we list:

> constants
>
> constructors
>
> methods
>
> static methods
>
> instance variables
>
> static variables

After all, the users of your class are more interested in the public interface than in the details of the private implementation. And they are more interested in methods than in data.

6.   *Break up classes with too many responsibilities.*

This hint is, of course, vague: "too many" is obviously in the eye of the beholder. However, if there is an obvious way to make one complicated class into two classes that are conceptually simpler, seize the opportunity. (On the other hand, don't go overboard; 10 classes, each with only one method, is usually overkill.)

Here is an example of a bad design. In our card game, we could do without the Card class by having the deck store two arrays: one for the suits and one for the values. That would make it hard to draw and return a card, so we would need to fake it with functions that can look up the properties of the top card on the deck.

```
class CardDeck // bad design
{  public void CardDeck() { . . . }
   public void shuffle() { . . . }
   public int getTopValue() { . . . }
   public int getTopSuit() { . . . }
   public int topRank() { . . . }
   public void draw() { . . . }

   private int[] value;
   private int[] suit;
   private int cards;
}
```

As you can see, this is implementable, but it is clumsy. It makes sense to introduce the `Card` class because the cards are meaningful objects in this context.

7.   *Make the names of your classes and methods reflect their responsibilities.*

Just as variables should have meaningful names that reflect what they do, so should classes. (The standard library certainly contains some dubious example, such as the `Date` class that describes time and the `getDay` method that returns the weekday, not the day.)

A good convention is that a class name should be a noun (`Order`) or a noun preceded by an adjective (`RushOrder`) or a gerund (an "ing" word—`BillingAddress`). As for methods, follow the standard convention that accessor methods begin with a lowercase `get` (`getDay`), and mutator methods use a lowercase `set` (`setSalary`).

CHAPTER

5

Going Further with OOP: Inheritance

The last chapter introduced OOP. This chapter explains most of the remaining concepts you need to know, particularly with regard to deriving new classes from existing classes. You can reuse or change the methods of existing classes, as well as add new instance fields and new methods. This concept is usually called *inheritance* and was briefly touched upon in the last chapter. It is, however, vital to Java programming. (For example, as you will see in the next chapter, you cannot even put up a window in Java without using inheritance!)

As with the previous chapter, if you are coming from a procedure-oriented language like C or COBOL, you will want to read this chapter carefully. The same holds true for *all* users of VB (even VB4 users—the crippled object model in VB4 does not allow for inheritance).

For experienced C++ programmers, or those coming from another object-oriented language like Smalltalk, this chapter will seem largely familiar, but there are *many* differences between how inheritance is implemented in Java and how it is done in C++ or in other object-oriented languages. You will probably want to read the later sections of this chapter carefully.

First Steps with Inheritance

Let's return to the Employee class that we discussed in the previous chapter. Suppose (alas) you work for a company at which managers are treated substantially differently than other employees. Their raises are computed differently; they have access to a secretary; and so on. This is the kind of situation that in OOP cries out for inheritance. Why? Well, you need to define a new class, Manager, and add functionality, but you can retain some of what you have already programmed in the Employee class, and *all* the instance fields of the original class can be preserved. More abstractly, there is an obvious "is–a" relationship between `Manager` and `Employee`. Every manager *is an* employee: this is the hallmark of inheritance.

Here is some code for extending the `Employee` class to be a `Manager` class.

```
class Manager extends Employee
{    public Manager(String n, double s, Day d)
     {    super(n, s, d);
          secretaryName = "";
     }

     public void raiseSalary(double byPercent)
     {    // add 1/2% bonus for every year of service
          Day today = new Day();
          double bonus = 0.5 * (today.getYear() - hireYear());
          super.raiseSalary(byPercent + bonus);
     }

     public String getSecretaryName()
     { return secretaryName;
     }

     public void setSecretaryName(String name)
     { secretaryName = name;
     }

     private String secretaryName;
}
```

Let's go over the new features of this class, line by line. First, notice that the header for this class is a little different:

```
class Manager extends Employee
```

The keyword `extends` indicates that you are making a new class that derives from an existing class. The existing class is called the *superclass, base class,* or *parent class*. The new class is called the *subclass, derived class,* or *child class*. The terms superclass and subclass are those most commonly used by Java programmers, although we prefer the parent/child analogy, which also ties in nicely with the "inheritance" theme.

The `Employee` class is a superclass, but not because it is superior to its subclass or contains more functionality. *In fact, the opposite is true:* subclasses have *more* functionality than their superclasses. For example, as you will see when we go over the rest of the `Manager` class code, it encapsulates more data and has more functionality than its superclass `Employee`. As another example, you will see in the next chapter a superclass `Window`, which we extend to many useful subclasses, such as `FileDialog`.

The prefixes *super* and *sub* come from the language of sets used in theoretical computer science and mathematics. The set of all employees *contains* the set of all managers, and this is described by saying it is a *superset* of the set of managers. Similarly, the set of all file dialog windows is *contained* by the set of all windows, so it is a *subset* of the set of all windows.

Next, notice the constructor for the `Manager` class:

```
public Manager(String n, double s, Day d)
{   super(n, s, d);
    secretaryName = ""
}:
```

The keyword `super` always refers to the superclass (in this case, `Employee`). So the line

```
super(n, s, d);
```

is shorthand for "call the constructor of the `Employee` class with n, s, and d as parameters." The reason for this line is that every constructor of a subclass is also responsible for constructing the data fields of the superclass. Unless the subclass constructor is happy with the default constructor of the superclass, it must explicitly use `super` with the appropriate parameters.

The call to `super` must be the first line in the constructor for the subclass.

Next, as this example shows, subclasses can have more instance fields than the parent class. Following good programming practices, we set the `secretaryName` instance field to the empty string in order to initialize it. (By default, it would have been initialized to `null`.)

If you compare the `Manager` class with the `Employee` class, you will see that many of the methods are not repeated. This is because, unless otherwise specified, a subclass uses the methods of the superclass. In particular, when inheriting from a superclass, you need to indicate only the *differences* between the subclass and superclass. The ability to reuse methods in the superclass is automatic. Therefore, we do not need to give a new definition of, for example, a `getName` method, since the one in the superclass does what we need. However, do note that we are giving a new definition of the `raiseSalary` method:

```
public void raiseSalary(double byPercent)
{   // add 1/2% bonus for every year of service
    Day today = new Day();
    double bonus = 0.5 * (today.getYear() - hireYear());
    super.raiseSalary(byPercent + bonus);
}
```

We are also adding accessor and mutator methods to set the current name of the secretary.

The need to redefine methods is one of the main reasons to use inheritance; this is a good example. Life being the way it is, raises for managers are calculated differently than those for non-managers. In this case, suppose you give a companywide raise of three percent. For the managers, the `raiseSalary` method does the following:

1. It calculates a bonus percentage increase based on time employed.

2. Then, because of the use of `super` in the line

```
super.raiseSalary(byPercent + bonus);
```

the method looks to the `raiseSalary` method of the superclass and passes it a parameter that adds the original parameter and a bonus of half a percent for each year of service since the hire year.

The result is that when you give all employees a raise of three percent, the managers will *automatically* be given a larger raise. Here's an example of this at work: we make a new manager and set the manager's secretary's name:

```
Manager boss = new Manager("Carl Cracker", 75000,
    new Day(1987,12,15));
boss.setSecretaryName("Harry Hacker");
```

We make an array of three employees:

```
Employee[] staff = new Employee[3];
```

We populate the array with a mix of employees and managers:

```
staff[0] = boss;
staff[1] = new Employee("Harry Hacker", 35000,
    new Day(1989,10,1));
staff[2] = new Employee("Tony Tester", 38000,
    new Day(1990,3,15));
```

We raise everyone's salary by three percent:

```
for (i = 0; i < 3; i++) staff[i].raiseSalary(3);
```

Now `staff[1]` and `staff[2]` each get a raise of three percent because they are `Employee` objects. However, `staff[0]` is a `Manager` object and gets a higher raise. Finally, let's print out all employee records and the name of the secretary.

```
for (i = 0; i < 3; i++) staff[i].print();
System.out.println(boss.getName() + "'s current secretary is "
    + boss.getSecretaryName());
```

Because we didn't define a special `print` method for managers, all three objects are printed with the `Employee` print method. (We could have changed the `print` method in the `Manager` class in order to print out the current name of a manager's secretary.)

Here's the full sample code that shows you the `Manager` class at work.

```java
import java.util.*;
import corejava.*;

public class ManagerTest
{  public static void main(String[] args)
   {  Employee[] staff = new Employee[3];

      staff[0] = new Employee("Harry Hacker", 35000,
         new Day(1989,10,1));
      staff[1] = new Manager("Carl Cracker", 75000,
         new Day(1987,12,15));
      staff[2] = new Employee("Tony Tester", 38000,
         new Day(1990,3,15));
      int i;
      for (i = 0; i < 3; i++) staff[i].raiseSalary(5);
      for (i = 0; i < 3; i++) staff[i].print();
   }
}

class Employee
{  public Employee(String n, double s, Day d)
   {  name = n;
      salary = s;
      hireDay = d;
   }
   public void print()
   {  System.out.println(name + " " + salary + " "
         + hireYear());
   }
   public void raiseSalary(double byPercent)
   {  salary *= 1 + byPercent / 100;
   }
   public int hireYear()
   {  return hireDay.getYear();
   }

   private String name;
   private double salary;
   private Day hireDay;
}

class Manager extends Employee
{  public Manager(String n, double s, Day d)
   {  super(n, s, d);
   }
```

```
public void raiseSalary(double byPercent)
{   // add 1/2% bonus for every year of service
    Day today = new Day();
    double bonus = 0.5 * (today.getYear() - hireYear());
    super.raiseSalary(byPercent + bonus);
}
}
```

Inheritance is similar in Java and C++. Java uses the `extends` keyword instead of the "`:`" token. Java uses the keyword `super` to refer to the base class. In C++, you would use the name of the base class with the `::` operator instead. For example, the `raiseSalary` function of the `Manager` class would call `Employee::raiseSalary` instead of `super.raiseSalary`. In a C++ constructor, you do not call `super`, but you use the initializer list syntax to construct the base class. The `Manager` constructor looks like this in C++:

```
Manager::Manager(String n, double s, Day d) // C++
: Employee(n, s, d)
{
}
```

Inheritance need not stop at deriving one layer of classes. We could have an `Executive` class that derives from `Manager`, for example. The collection of all classes extending from a common parent is called an *inheritance hierarchy*. The path from a particular class to its ancestors in the inheritance hierarchy is an *inheritance chain*.

There is usually more than one chain of descent from a distant ancestor class. You could derive a `Programmer` class from `Employee` class or a `Secretary` class from `Employee`, and they would have nothing to do with the `Manager` class (or with each other). This process can continue as long as is necessary.

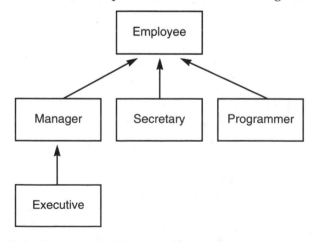

Figure 5-1: Employee Inheritance Hierarchy

Working with Subclasses

One way to know whether or not inheritance is right for your program is to keep in mind that any object of the subclass must be useable in place of the superclass object. If this is not true, do not use inheritance. (This is a more concrete way of thinking of the "is–a" relationship that is the hallmark of inheritance.) In particular, subclass objects are useable in any code that uses the superclass.

For example, you can assign a subclass object to a superclass variable. We did that in the sample code of the preceding section.

```
Employee[] staff = new Employee[3];
Manager boss = new Manager("Carl Cracker", 75000,
    new Day(1987,12,15));
staff[0] = boss;
```

In this case, the variables `staff[0]` and `boss` refer to the same area of memory. However, `staff[0]` "forgets" that it refers to a `Manager` and just considers itself an `Employee` object.

Similarly, a subclass object can be passed as an argument to any method that expects a superclass parameter.

The converse is false in general: a superclass object cannot usually be assigned to a subclass object. For example, it is not legal to make the assignment:

```
boss = staff[i]; // Error
```

The reason is clear: the subclass object may have more fields than the superclass object (as it does in this case), and the subclass methods have to be able to access those fields. If the fields are not accessible, run-time errors will result. Always keep in mind that subclass objects have at least as many data items as objects from the superclass because fields can only be added, not taken away, in inheritance.

Java does not support multiple inheritance. (For ways to recover much of the functionality of multiple inheritance, see the section on Interfaces in this chapter.)

Objects Know How to Do Their Work: Polymorphism

It is important to understand what happens when a method call is applied to objects of various types in an inheritance hierarchy. Remember that in OOP, you are sending messages to objects, asking them to perform actions. When you send a message that asks a subclass to apply a method using certain parameters, here is what happens:

- The subclass checks whether or not it has a method with that name and with *exactly* the same parameters. If so, it uses it.

If not,

- Java moves to the parent class and looks there for a method with that name and those parameters. If so, it calls that method.

Since Java can continue moving up the inheritance chain, parent classes are checked until the chain of inheritance stops or until Java finds a matching method. (If Java cannot find a matching method in the whole inheritance chain, you get a compile-time error.) Notice that methods with the same name can exist on many levels of the chain. This leads to one of the fundamental rules of inheritance:

- A method defined in a subclass with the same name and parameter list as a method in one of its ancestor classes hides the method of the ancestor class from the subclass.

For example, the `raiseSalary` method of the `Manager` class is called instead of the `raiseSalary` method of the `Employee` class when you send a `raiseSalary` message to a `Manager` object.

> The name and parameter list for a method is usually called the method's *signature*. For example, `raiseSalary(double)` and `raiseSalary(boolean)` are two methods with different signatures. In Java, having methods in a class or in a superclass and a subclass with the same signature but differing return types will give you a compile-time error. For instance, you cannot have a method `void raiseSalary(double)` in the `Employee` class and a function `int raiseSalary(double)` in the `Manager` class.

An object's ability to decide what method to apply to itself, depending on where it is in the inheritance hierarchy, is usually called *polymorphism*. The idea behind polymorphism is that while the message may be the same, objects may respond differently. Polymorphism can apply to any method that is inherited from a superclass.

The key to making polymorphism work is called *late binding*. This means that the compiler does not generate the code to call a method at compile time. Instead, every time you define a method with an object, the compiler generates code to calculate which method to call, using type information from the object. This process is usually called late binding, *dynamic binding*, or *dynamic dispatch*. The regular function call mechanism is called *static binding*, since the operation to be executed is completely determined at compile time. Static binding depends on the method alone; dynamic binding depends on the type of the object variable *and* the position of the actual object in the inheritance hierarchy.

Many Java users follow C++ terminology and refer to *virtual functions* for functions that are dynamically bound.

In Java, you do not need to declare a method as virtual. This is the default behavior. If you do *not* want a function to be virtual, you tag it as `final`. (We discuss this in the next section.)

To sum up, inheritance and polymorphism let the application spell out the general way it wants things to proceed. The individual classes in the inheritance hierarchy are responsible for carrying out the details—using polymorphism to determine which methods to call.

Polymorphism in an inheritance hierarchy is sometimes called *true polymorphism*, to distinguish it from the more limited kind of name overloading that is not resolved dynamically, but is resolved statically at compile time.

Preventing Inheritance: Final Classes

Occasionally, you want to prevent someone from deriving a class from one of your classes. Classes that cannot be parent classes are called *final* classes, and you use the `final` modifier in the definition of the class to indicate this. For example, the `Card` class from the last chapter was final, so its header began:

```
final class Card
```

You can also make a specific method in a class `final`. If you do this, then no subclass can override that method. (All methods in a `final` class are automatically `final`.) A class or method is made `final` for one of two reasons:

1. **Efficiency**

    Dynamic binding has more overhead than static binding—thus, virtual methods run slower. The dynamic dispatching mechanism is slightly less efficient than a straight procedure call. More importantly, the compiler cannot replace a trivial method with inline code because it is possible that a derived class would override that trivial code. The compiler can put final methods in line. For example, if `e.getName()` is final, the compiler can replace it with `e.name`. (So you get all the benefits of direct access to instance fields *without violating encapsulation*.)

    Microprocessors hate procedure calls because they interfere with their strategy of getting and decoding the next instructions while processing the current one. Replacing calls to trivial procedures with inline code is a big win. This is more important for a true compiler than for an interpreter like the current version of Java, but Java compilers are in the works!

2. Safety

The flexibility of the dynamic dispatch mechanism means that you have no control over what happens when you call a method. When you send a message, such as e.getName(), it is possible that e is an object of a derived class that redefined the getName method to return an entirely different string. By making the method final, you avoid this possible ambiguity.

We used final methods and final classes in the Card class of the preceding chapter. We knew that nobody would derive a new class from the Card class, so we made it final for efficiency reasons. The String class in the Java library is final for probably the same reasons.

In C++, a member function is not virtual by default, and you can tag it as inline in order to have function calls replaced with the function source code. However, there is no mechanism that would prevent a derived class from overriding a member function. In C++, it is possible to write classes from which no other class can derive, but it requires an obscure trick, and there are few reasons to do so.

Casting

Just as you occasionally need to convert an integer to a double, you also need to convert an object from one class to another. As was the case with converting basic types, this is called *casting*. To actually make a cast, use a syntax similar to the one you used for casting between variables of the basic types. Surround the target type with parentheses and place it before the object you want to cast. For example:

```
Manager boss = (Manager)staff[0];
```

There is only one reason why you would want to make a cast—to use an object in its full capacity after its actual type has been downplayed. For example, in the Manager class, the staff array had to be an array of Employee objects since *some* of its entries were regular employees. We would need to cast the managerial elements of the array back to Manager in order to access any of its new fields. (Note that in the sample code for the first section, we made a special effort to avoid the cast. We initialized the boss variable with a Manager object before storing it in the array. We needed the correct type in order to find the secretary of the manager.)

As you know, in Java, every object variable has a type. The type describes the kind of object the variable refers to and what it can do. For example, staff[i] refers to an Employee object (so it can also refer to a Manager object).

You rely on these descriptions in your code, and the compiler checks that you do not promise too much when you describe a variable. If you assign a subclass object to a superclass variable, you are promising less, and the compiler will simply let you do it. If you assign a superclass object to a subclass variable, you are promising more, and you must confirm that you mean what you say to the compiler with the (Subclass) cast notation.

What happens if you try to cast down an inheritance chain and you are "lying" about what an object contains?

```
Manager boss = (Manager)staff[1]; // Error
```

When the program runs, Java notices the broken promise, generates an exception (see the sidebar in this chapter and Chapter 10), and the program will usually die. It is good programming practice to find out whether or not your object is an instance of another object before doing a cast. This is accomplished with the instanceof operator. For example:

```
if (staff[1] instanceof Manager)
{   boss = (Manager)staff[1];
     . . .
}
```

Finally, the compiler will not let you make a cast if there is no chance for the cast to succeed. For example, the cast

```
Window w = (Window)staff[1];
```

will not succeed because Window is not a subclass of Employee.

To sum up, you can only cast within an inheritance hierarchy. You should use instanceof to check a hierarchy before casting from a parent to a child class.

Actually, performing a cast is not usually a good idea. In our example, you do not need to cast an Employee object to Manager for most purposes. The print and raiseSalary methods will work correctly on both types, because the dynamic binding automatically locates the correct method. The only reason to perform the cast is to use a method that is unique to managers, such as getSecretaryName. If it is important to get the name of a secretary for an object of type Employee, you should redesign that class and add a getSecretaryName method, which simply returns an empty string. That makes more sense than trying to remember which array locations stored which type, or to perform tedious type inquiries. Remember, it takes only one bad cast to terminate your program.

Java uses the inheritance syntax from the "bad old days" of C, but it works like the safe `dynamic_cast` operation of C++. For example,

```
Manager boss = (Manager)staff[1]; // Java
```

is the same as

```
Manager* boss = dynamic_cast<Manager>(staff[1]); // C++
```

with one important difference. If the cast fails, it does not yield a `null` object, but throws an exception. In this sense, it is like a C++ cast of *references.* This is a pain in the neck. In C++, you can take care of the type test and type conversion in one operation.

```
Manager* boss = dynamic_cast<Manager>(staff[1]); // C++
if (boss != NULL) . . .
```

In Java, you use a combination of the `instanceof` operator and a cast.

```
if (staff[1] instanceof Manager)
{  Manager boss = (Manager)staff[1];
   . . .
}
```

Abstract Classes

As you move up the inheritance hierarchy, classes become more general and probably more abstract. At some point, the ancestor class becomes *so* general that you think of it more as a framework for other classes than as a class with specific instances you want to use. Consider, for example, an electronic messaging system that integrates your e-mail, faxes, and voice mail. It must be able to handle text messages, fax messages, and voice messages.

Following the principles of OOP, the program will need classes called `TextMessage`, `VoiceMessage`, and `FaxMessage`. Of course, a mailbox needs to store a mixture of these messages, so it will have the common parent class `Message` as well.

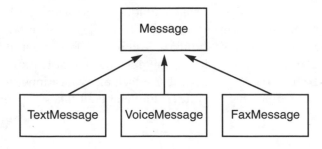

Figure 5-2: Abstract Classes

Why bother with so high a level of abstraction? The answer is that it makes the design of your classes cleaner. (Well, it does once you are familiar with OOP.) Ultimately, one of the keys to OOP is to understand how to factor out common operations to a higher level in the inheritance hierarchy. In our case, all messages have a common method, namely `play()`. It is easy to figure out how to play a voice message—you send it to the loudspeaker. You play a text message by showing it in a text window and a fax message by showing it in a graphics window. But how do you implement `play()` in the parent class `Message`?

The answer is that you can't. In Java, you use the `abstract` keyword to indicate that a method cannot yet be specified in a class. For added clarity, a class with one or more abstract methods must itself be declared abstract.

```
public abstract class Message
{   . . .
    public abstract void play();
}
```

Abstract classes can have (some) concrete data and methods. For example, the `Message` class can store the sender of the mail message and have a concrete method that returns the sender's name.

```
abstract class Message
{   public Message(String from) { sender = from; }

    public abstract void play();
    public String getSender() { return sender; }

    private String sender;
}
```

The key point is that, in addition to the ordinary methods you have seen, an abstract class has at least one *abstract method*. An abstract method promises that all nonabstract descendants of this abstract class will implement that abstract method. Abstract methods act as placeholder methods that are implemented in the subclasses.

It is common to think that abstract classes should have only abstract methods. This is not true: it always makes sense to move as much functionality as possible into a superclass, whether or not it is abstract. In particular, move common instance fields and *nonabstract* operations to the abstract superclass. Only those operations that cannot be implemented in the superclass should be given to the subclasses.

In C++, an abstract method is called a *pure virtual function* and is tagged with a trailing = 0 , such as in

```
class Message // C++
{  public:
      virtual void play() = 0;
   . . .
}
```

As in Java, a C++ class is abstract if it has at least one pure virtual function. But there is no special syntax to denote abstract classes.

To see a realization of this abstract class and the `play` method, try this code for the `TextMessage` class:

```
class TextMessage extends Message
{  public TextMessage(String from, String t)
   { super(from); text = t; }

   public void play() { System.out.println(text); }

   private String text;
}
```

Notice that we only need to give a concrete definition of the abstract `play` method in the `TextMessage` class.

Here's the code for the sample messaging program. Don't worry too much about the code for playing the wave file in this example; it uses a few language features, such as streams and exceptions, that we will discuss in later chapters. It also uses an undocumented feature of Java that lets you play audio clips from within an application as opposed to an applet. This is a teaching example, so we kept the user interface simple and ugly to allow you to focus on the OOP aspects instead of being distracted by GUI code. When you run the program, you can leave a text message by typing it in or leave a voice message by typing in the name of an audio file. We supply you with two sample audio files on the CD, or you can use your own. They must be in .au format.

```
import java.io.*;
import sun.audio.*;
import corejava.*;

public class MailboxTest
{  public static void main(String[] args)
   {  Mailbox mbox = new Mailbox();
      while (true)
      {  System.out.println(mbox.status());
         String cmd = Console.readString
               ("play, text, voice, quit> ");
```

```java
            if (cmd.equals("play"))
            {   Message m = mbox.remove();
                if (m != null)
                {   System.out.println("From: " + m.getSender());
                    m.play();
                }
            }
            else if (cmd.equals("text"))
            {   String from = Console.readString("Your name: ");
                boolean more = true;
                String msg = "";
                System.out.println
                    ("Enter message, 'exit' when done");

                while (more)
                {   String line = Console.readString();
                    if (line.equals("exit"))
                        more = false;
                    else msg = msg + line + "\n";
                }
                mbox.insert(new TextMessage(from, msg));
            }
            else if (cmd.equals("voice"))
            {   String from = Console.readString("Your name: ");
                String msg
                    = Console.readString("Audio file name: ");
                mbox.insert(new VoiceMessage(from, msg));
            }
            else if (cmd.equals("quit"))
                System.exit(0);
        }
    }
}

abstract class Message
{   public Message(String from) { sender = from; }

    public abstract void play();
    public String getSender() { return sender; }

    private String sender;
}

class TextMessage extends Message
{   public TextMessage(String from, String t)
    { super(from); text = t; }

    public void play() { System.out.println(text); }
```

```java
      private String text;
}

class VoiceMessage extends Message
{   public VoiceMessage(String from, String f)
    { super(from); filename = f; }

    public void play()
    {   AudioPlayer ap = AudioPlayer.player;
        try
        {   AudioStream as
                = new AudioStream(new FileInputStream(filename));
            ap.start(as);
        }
        catch(IOException e) {}
    }

    private String filename;
}

class Mailbox
{   public Message remove()
    {   if (nmsg == 0) return null;
        Message r = messages[out];
        nmsg--;
        out = (out + 1) % MAXMSG;
        return r;
    }

    public void insert(Message m)
    {   if (nmsg == MAXMSG) return;
        messages[in] = m;
        nmsg++;
        in = (in + 1) % MAXMSG;
    }

    public String status()
    {   if (nmsg == 0) return "Mailbox empty";
        else if (nmsg == 1) return "1 message";
        else if (nmsg < MAXMSG) return nmsg + " messages";
        else return "Mailbox full";
    }

    private final int MAXMSG = 10;
    private int in = 0;
    private int out = 0;
    private int nmsg = 0;
    private Message[] messages = new Message[MAXMSG];
}
```

Catching Exceptions

We will cover exception handling fully in Chapter 10, but once in a while you will encounter code that involves exceptions. Here is a quick introduction on what the exceptions are and how to handle them.

When an error occurs at run time, a Java program can "throw an exception." For example, code that attempts to open a file can throw an exception if the file unexpectedly cannot be opened. Throwing an exception is less violent and less fatal than terminating the program, because it provides the option of "catching" the exception and dealing with it.

> If an exception is not caught anywhere, the program will terminate, and a message will be printed to the console giving the type of the exception.

Without going into too much detail, here is the basic syntax. To run code that might throw an exception, you have to place it inside a "try" block. Then you have to provide an emergency action to deal with the exception, in the unlikely case that one actually occurs.

```
try
{   code that might
    throw exceptions
}   catch(ExceptionType e)
{   emergency action
}
```

We used that mechanism in the code that plays an audio clip.

```
try
{   AudioStream as
        = new AudioStream(new FileInputStream(filename));
    ap.start(as);
}
catch(IOException e) {}
```

The above says, in effect, "Do not end the program if you have an I/O (input/output) error—just ignore the error and do not play the clip."

The compiler is somewhat selective as to which exceptions *must* be handled. For example, when you access an array or perform a cast, you need not supply an exception handler, even though the array index or the cast might be invalid, causing the code to throw an exception. However, for other operations, such as input and output, you must specify what you want to happen when there is a problem.

Exceptions are a complex topic, and it is not generally a good idea to ignore them when they happen. But a full discussion will have to wait until Chapter 10.

> The Java and C++ exception mechanisms are similar. Chapter 10 explains the differences.

Interfaces

Suppose you wanted to write a general sorting routine that would work on many different kinds of Java objects. You now know how to organize this in an object-oriented fashion. You have the class `Sortable` with the method `compare` that determines whether or not one sortable object is less than, equal to, or greater than another.

Now you can implement a generic sorting algorithm. Here is an implementation of a shell sort, for sorting an array of `Sortable` objects.

```
abstract class Sortable
{   public abstract int compare(Sortable b);

    public static void shell_sort(Sortable[] a)
    {   int n = a.length;
        int incr = n / 2;
        while (incr >= 1)
        {   for (int i = incr; i < n; i++)
            {   Sortable temp = a[i];
                int j = i;
                while (j >= incr
                    && temp.compare(a[j - incr]) < 0)
                {   a[j] = a[j - incr];
                    j -= incr;
                }
                a[j] = temp;
            }
            incr /= 2;
        }
    }
}
```

This seems quite elegant. You would then use polymorphism to get the sorting routine in all the subclasses of the `Sortable` abstract class (by overriding the `compare` method in the subclass).

For example, to sort an array of employees (ordering them by—what else—their salary), we

1.   derive `Employee` from `Sortable`,

2.   implement the `compare` method for employees,

3.   call `shell_sort` on the employee array.

Here's an example of the extra code needed to do this in our `Employee` class:

```
class Employee extends Sortable
{  . . .
   public int compare(Sortable b)
   {  Employee eb = (Employee)b;
      if (salary < eb.salary) return -1;
      if (salary > eb.salary) return 1;
      return 0;
   }

   public static void main(String[] args)
   {  Employee[] staff = new Employee[3];
      . . .
      Sortable.shell_sort(staff);
      . . .
   }
}
```

There is, unfortunately, a major problem with implementing this strategy in Java. For example, we wrote a `Tile` class that models tiled windows on a screen desktop. Tiled windows are rectangles plus a "z-order." Windows with a larger z-order are displayed in front of those with a smaller z-order. To reuse code, we inherit `Tile` from `Rectangle`, a class that is already defined in the `java.awt` package.

```
class Tile extends Rectangle
{  public Tile(int x, int y, int w, int h, int zz)
   {  super(x, y, w, h);
      z = zz;
   }

   private int z;
}
```

Now we would like to sort an array of tiles by comparing z-orders. If we try to apply the procedure for making tiles sortable, we get stuck at step (1). We cannot derive `Tile` from `Sortable`—it already derives from `Rectangle`!

The point is that, in Java, a class can have only one superclass. Other programming languages, in particular C++, allow a class to have more than one superclass. This is called *multiple inheritance*.

Instead, Java introduces the notion of *interfaces* to recover much of the functionality that multiple inheritance gives you. The designers of Java chose this road because multiple inheritance makes compilers either very complex (as in C++) or very inefficient (as in Eiffel). (Interfaces also allow you to implement "callback functions" in Java—see the section on callbacks later in this chapter for more on this important topic.)

So what is an interface? Essentially, it is a promise that your class will imple-ment certain methods with certain signatures. You even use the keyword implements to indicate that your class will keep these promises. The way in which these methods are implemented is up to the class, of course. The impor-tant point, as far as the compiler is concerned, is that the methods have the right signature.

For example, suppose you wanted to create an interface called Sortable that could be used by any class that will sort. The code for the Sortable interface might look like this:

```
public interface Sortable
{   public int compare(Sortable b);
}
```

This code promises that any class that implements the Sortable interface will have a compare method that will take a Sortable object. A Sortable object, in turn, is any instance of a class that implements Sortable (therefore, any class that has a compare method). Of course, the way in which the compare method works (or even whether or not it works as one would expect) in a spe-cific class depends on the class that is implementing the Sortable interface. The key point is that any class can promise to implement Sortable—regard-less of whether or not its superclass promises the same. All descendants of such a class would implement Sortable, since they all would have access to a com-pare method with the right signature.

To tell Java that your class implements Sortable, you have the class header read something like this:

```
class Tile extends Rectangle implements Sortable
```

Then all you need to do is implement a compare method inside the class.

```
class Tile extends Rectangle implements Sortable
{   public int compare(Sortable b)
    {   Tile tb = (Tile)b;
        return z - tb.z;
    }
    . . .

    private int z;
}
```

Here is the complete code for the tile example. Note that we needed to put the static shell_sort method in a separate class, Sort. You cannot put static methods into interfaces. (There is no reason for this restriction—it is merely an oversight in the language design.)

```java
import java.awt.*;

public class TileTest
{   public static void main(String[] args)
    {   Tile[] a = new Tile[20];

        int i;
        for (i = 0; i < a.length; i++)
            a[i] = new Tile(i, i, 10, 20,
                (int)(100 * Math.random()));

        Sort.shell_sort(a);

        for (i = 0; i < a.length; i++)
            System.out.println(a[i]);
    }
}

interface Sortable
{   public int compare(Sortable b);
}

class Sort
{   static void shell_sort(Sortable[] a)
    {   int n = a.length;
        int incr = n / 2;
        while (incr >= 1)
        {   for (int i = incr; i < n; i++)
            {   Sortable temp = a[i];
                int j = i;
                while (j >= incr
                    && temp.compare(a[j - incr]) < 0)
                {   a[j] = a[j - incr];
                    j -= incr;
                }
                a[j] = temp;
            }
            incr /= 2;
        }
    }
}

class Tile extends Rectangle implements Sortable
{   public Tile(int x, int y, int w, int h, int zz)
    {   super(x, y, w, h);
        z = zz;
    }
```

```
    public int compare(Sortable b)
    {   Tile tb = (Tile)b;
        return z - tb.z;
    }

    public String toString()
    {   return super.toString() + "[z=" + z + "]";
    }

    private int z;
}
```

C++ has multiple inheritance and all the complications that come with it, such as virtual base classes, dominance rules, and transverse pointer casts. Few C++ programmers use multiple inheritance, and some say it should never be used. Other programmers recommend using multiple inheritance only for "mix-in" style inheritance, in which a class is derived from base classes with no data and only virtual functions. These are the same as Java interfaces!

Properties of Interfaces

Although interfaces are not instantiated with new, they have certain properties similar to ordinary classes. For example, once you set up an interface you can declare that an object variable will be of that interface type with the same notation used to declare a variable to be of a specific class type:

```
Sortable x = new Tile(. . .);
Tile y = new Tile(. . .);

if (x.compare(y) < 0) . . .
```

Also, nothing prevents you from extending one interface in order to create another. This allows for multiple chains of interfaces that go from a greater degree of generality to a greater degree of specialization. For example, suppose you had an interface called Moveable.

```
public interface Moveable
{   public void move(double x, double y);
}
```

Then you could imagine an interface called Powered that extends it:

```
public interface Powered extends Moveable
{   public String powerSource();
}
```

Unfortunately, the Java documentation often refers to *classes* when it means *classes or interfaces.* You have to use contextual clues to decide whether the reference is only to classes or to both classes and interfaces.

Although you cannot put instance fields in an interface, you can supply constants. For example:

```
public interface Powered extends Moveable
{   public string powerSource(PoweredVehicle);
    public final int speedLimit = 95;
}
```

Classes can implement multiple interfaces. This gives you the maximum amount of flexibility in defining a class's behavior. For example, Java has an important interface built into it called `Cloneable`; if your class implements `Cloneable`, the `clone` method in the `Object` class will make a bitwise copy of your class's objects. If your class doesn't implement `Cloneable`, then the `clone` method causes a run-time error when any code attempts to make a clone of your object. Suppose you want clonability and sortability. Then you implement both interfaces.

```
class Tile extends Rectangle implements Cloneable, Sortable
```

Interfaces and Callbacks

Suppose you want to implement a `Timer` class in Java. You want to be able to program your class to:

- start the timer,

- have the timer measure some time interval,

- then carry out some action when the correct time has elapsed.

For this to be practical, the `Timer` class needs a way of communicating with the calling class. This is usually called a *callback function*. Interfaces are the only way to implement callback functions in Java. To see why, let's peek inside the `Timer` class.

```
class Timer extends Thread
{   . . .
    public void run()
    {   while (true)
        {   sleep(interval);
            // now what?
        }
    }
}
```

(Don't worry about the fact that this class has to extend Java's built-in `Thread` class. Threads have many uses—one of the simplest is to sleep until some time has elapsed. You will read more about threads in Chapter 12.)

The object constructing a `Timer` object must somehow tell the timer what to do when the time is up. In C++, the code creating the timer gives it a pointer to a function, and the timer calls that function at the end of every interval. Java has no function pointers. It uses interfaces instead. So the `//now what` comment in the preceding code is replaced by a method call that was declared inside an interface.

Thus, in addition to the `Timer` class, we need the interface `Timed`. It has a single method called *tick*.

```
interface Timed
{   public void tick(Timer t);
}
```

Any class wanting to be called from a timer must implement that interface.

```
class AlarmClock implements Timed
{   AlarmClock()
    {   Timer t = new Timer(this);
        t.setInterval(1000); // 1000 milliseconds
    }

    public void tick(Timer t)
    {   if(t.time() >= wakeUpTime)
            wakeUp.play();
    }
}
```

Here's the code for the `Timer` class. Notice how the constructor of the `Timer` class receives the pointer to the object that needs to be notified. It is notified through the `tick()` method, which passes the `this` reserved variable that identifies it to the `tick` method in the `Timed` interface.

```
class Timer extends Thread
{   Timer(Timed t) { owner = t; }
           . . .
    public void run()
    {   while (true)
        {   sleep(interval);
            owner.tick(this);
        }
    }
    Timed owner;
}
```

This code explains only how an interface can be used to supply a notification mechanism and, hence, callback functions; for the rest of the timer implementation, please turn to Chapter 12.

Java has no function pointers. Whenever you would like to use a function pointer, you must use polymorphism, either by deriving from a base class or by implementing an interface. You can only derive from one base class, but you can implement any number of interfaces. It is quite common in Java to have trivial interfaces for callback protocols.

More on `Object`: The Cosmic Superclass

The `Object` class is the ultimate ancestor—every class in Java extends `Object`. You don't have to say:

```
class Employee extends Object
```

The parent class `Object` is taken for granted if no parent is explicitly mentioned. Because *every* class in Java extends `Object`, it is important to be familiar with the services provided by the `Object` class. We will go over the basic ones in this chapter and refer you to later chapters or to the on-line documentation for what is not covered here. (Several methods of `Object` come up only when dealing with threads—see Chapter 12 for more on threads.)

The `equals` method in `Object` tests whether or not one object is equal to another. The `equals` method in the `Object` parent class determines whether or not two objects point to the same area of memory. Other classes in the Java hierarchy are free to override `equals` for a more meaningful comparison. You will often find yourself overriding `equals` in your classes.

Here are versions of the API descriptions of the basic parts of the `Object` class:

`java.lang.Object`

• `Class getClass()`

returns a `Class` object that contains information about the object. As you will see in the next section, Java has a run-time representation for classes that is encapsulated in the `Class` class that you can often use to your advantage.

• `boolean equals(Object obj)`

compares two objects for equality; returns true if the objects point to the same area of memory, and false otherwise.

• `Object clone()`

creates a clone of the object. Java allocates memory for the new instance and copies the memory allocated for the current object.

- `String toString()`

returns a string that represents the value of this object. Almost all classes override this method in order to give you a printed representation of the object's current state. For example, you have seen `toString` used with the `Date` class to give a string representation of the date.

Object Wrappers

Occasionally, you need to convert a basic type like `int` to an object. All basic types have class counterparts. For example, there is a class `Integer` corresponding to the basic type `int`. These kinds of classes are usually called *object wrappers*. The wrapper classes have obvious names: `Integer`, `Long`, `Float`, `Double`, `Character`, and `Boolean`. (The first four inherit from the common parent wrapper `Number`.) The wrapper classes are `final`. (So you can't override the `toString` method in `Integer` in order to display strings in Roman numerals, sorry.)

The major reason for which wrappers were invented is *generic programming*. The container classes that we describe in Chapter 9 can store arbitrary objects. But they cannot store numbers unless they are turned into objects of a class.

Here is a simpler example that illustrates this concept. Suppose you want to find the index of an element in an array. This is a generic situation, and by writing the code for objects, you can reuse it for employees, dates, or whatever.

```
static int find(Object[] a, Object key)
{   int i;
    for (i = 0; i < a.length; i++)
        if (a[i].equals(key)) return i;
    return -1; // not found
}
```

For example,

```
Employee[] staff;
Employee harry;
. . .
int n = find(staff, harry);
```

But what if you want to find a number in an array of floating-point numbers? Here is where wrappers come in handy. By using `Double` objects instead of `double` variables, you can take advantage of the generic code.

You will often see the number wrappers for another reason. The designers of Java found the wrappers a convenient place to put certain basic functions, like converting strings of digits. The place is convenient, but the functionality, unfortunately, isn't.

To convert a string to an integer, you use the following:

```
int x = Integer.parseInt(s);
```

This has nothing to do with `Integer` objects—`parseInt` is a static method. But the `Integer` class was a good place to put it. Unfortunately, there is no corresponding `parseDouble` in the `Double` class. Instead, you must use the cumbersome

```
double x = new Double(s).doubleValue();
```

What this does is:

1.   use a constructor in the `Double` class that accepts a string of digits in the form of a double and gives you a `Double` object,

2.   use the `doubleValue` method in the `Double` class that returns an actual double.

(VB users are probably longing for a simple Val function.)

You will find this everywhere in Java code. Actually, in real life you have to contend with the possibility that the string has leading or trailing spaces, or that it may contain non-digits. So a correct version would be as follows:

```
try
{   x = new Double(s.trim()).doubleValue();
}
catch(NumberFormatException e)
{   x = 0;
}
```

We found this so cumbersome that we wrote our own string-to-number conversions in the `corejava` package. You simply use this:

```
x = Format.atof(s);
```

The API notes show some of the more important methods of the `Integer` class. The other number classes implement some (but not all) of the corresponding methods.

`java.lang.Integer`

• `int intValue()`

returns the value of this `Integer` object as an int (overrides the `intValue` method in the `Number` class).

• `static String toString(int i)`

returns a new `String` object representing the specified integer in base 10.

- `static String toString(int i, int radix)`

lets you return a representation of the number i in the base specified by the `radix` parameter.

- `static int parseInt(String s)`

returns the integer's value, assuming the specified `String` represents an integer in base 10.

- `static int parseInt(String s, int radix)`

returns the integer's value, assuming the specified `String` represents an integer in the base specified by the `radix` parameter.

- `static Integer valueOf(String s)`

returns a new `Integer` object initialized to the integer's value, assuming the specified `String` represents an integer in base 10.

- `static Integer valueOf(String s, int radix)`

returns a new `Integer` object initialized to the integer's value, assuming the specified `String` represents an integer in the base specified by the `radix` parameter.

In C++, there is no cosmic root class. It is not needed, because templates do a better job for generic programming. But Java has no templates, so one has to make do with a common ancestor class.

C++ programmers may be surprised that the cast from `Employee[]` to `Object[]` is legal. Even if `Object` was a base class of `Employee` in C++, the equivalent cast from `Employee**` to `Object**` would not be legal. (Of course, the cast from `Employee*` to `Object*` is legal in C++.)

There is a security reason behind this restriction. If the cast `"Derived** -> Base**"` were permitted, you could corrupt the contents of an array. Consider this code:

```
Employee** a; // C++
Object** p = a; // not legal, but suppose it was
p[0] = new AudioClip();
    // legal, AudioClip also inherits from Object
for (i = 0; i < n; i++) a[i].raiseSalary(3);
    // ouch, now the audio clip gets a raise!
```

If you try the equivalent Java code, you will notice that the `Object[]` array still remembers its original type (`Employee[]` in our example). It will throw an exception if you try to insert any nonemployee object into it. This ensures that a generic array cannot be corrupted.

Reading a Page in the HTML Documents

At this point, you have seen all the basic terms that Java uses to describe its methods, classes, and interfaces. Once you are comfortable with this information, you will often consult the API documentation. Figures 5-3 and 5-4 show the pages of API documentation for the `Double` class. As you can see, the API documentation pages are always organized in the same way:

1. the name of the class (or interface),

2. the inheritance chain for this class (starting from `java.lang.Object`),

3. the name of the class along with the access modifiers such as public or final, the classes it extends, and the interfaces it implements (for example, as you can see in Figure 5-5, `Double` extends `Number`, which extends `Object`).

4. a (more or less useful) discussion of the class (occasionally, this includes some sample code),

5. a list of all the methods in the class, with the constructors given first,

6. a more detailed discussion of the methods.

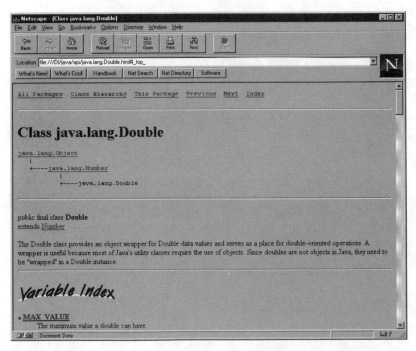

Figure 5-3

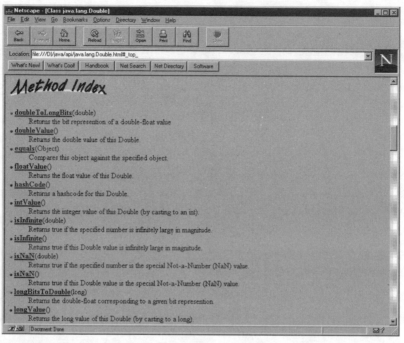

Figure 5-4

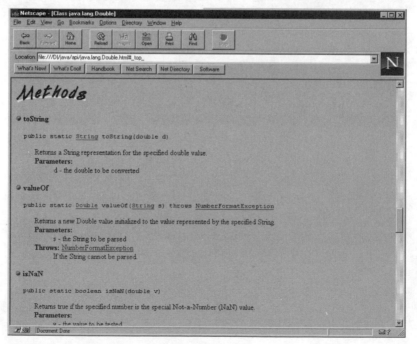

Figure 5-5

The Class `Class` (Run-Time Type Identification)

While your program is running, Java always maintains what is called run-time type identification (RTTI) on all objects, which keeps track of the class to which each object belongs. This is used by Java to select the correct methods at run time. You can also access the information. The class that holds this information is called `Class`. The `getClass()` method in the `Object` class returns an instance of this class type.

Probably the most commonly used method of `getClass` is `getName`. It gets the name of the class. You can use it in a simple `println`; for example, the code

```
System.out.println(e.getClass().getName() + " "
          + e.getName());
```

prints

```
Employee Harry Hacker
```

if e is an employee, and the code prints

```
Manager Harry Hacker
```

if e is a manager.

Aside from asking an object for the name of its corresponding class object, you can ask for a class object corresponding to a string by using the static `forName` method.

Another example of a useful method is one that lets you create an instance of a new class on the fly. This method is called, naturally enough, `newInstance()`. For example:

```
e.getClass().newInstance();
```

would create a new instance of the same class type as e, (either an employee or a manager). The `newInstance` method calls the default constructor (the one that takes no arguments) to initialize the newly created object.

The combination of `forName` and `newInstance` lets you create an object from a class name stored in a string.

```
String s = "Manager";
Manager m = (Manager) Class.forName(s).newInstance();
```

The `newInstance` method corresponds to a *virtual constructor* in C++. The `Class` class is similar to the `type_info` class in C++, and the `getClass` method is equivalent to the `typeid` operator. The Java `Class` is quite a bit more versatile than `type_info`, though. The C++ `type_info` can only reveal a string with its name, not create new objects of that type.

java.lang.Class

- String getName()

returns the name of this class.

- Class getSuperclass()

returns the superclass of this class as a Class object.

- Class[] getInterfaces()

returns an array of Class objects that give the interfaces implemented by this class; returns an array of length 0 if this class implements no interfaces. Somewhat confusingly, interface descriptions are also stored in Class objects.

- boolean isInterface()

returns true if this class is an interface and false if not.

- String toString()

returns the name of this class or this interface. The word *class* precedes the name if it is a class; the word *interface* precedes the name if it is an interface. (This method overrides the toString method in Object.)

- static Class forName(String className)

returns a new instance of this class.

Protected Access

As you know, instance fields in a class are usually tagged as private and methods are tagged as public. Any features declared private are not visible to other classes. This is also true for subclasses. A subclass cannot access the private data members of its superclass.

For example, the raise method of the Manager class cannot access the hireDay field directly when computing the bonuses. It has to use the public interface like all other methods.

```
class Manager extends Employee
{   . . .
    public void raiseSalary(double byPercent)
    {    // add 1/2% bonus for every year of service
        Day today = new Day();
        double bonus = 0.5 * (today.getYear() -
            hireYear()); // can't use hireDay.year
        super.raiseSalary(byPercent + bonus);
    }
}
```

There are, however, times when you want a subclass to have access to a method or to data. In that case, you declare the feature as protected. For example, if the base class Employee declares the hireDay object as protected instead of private, then the Manager methods can access it directly.

In practice, you should use the protected attribute with caution. Suppose your class is used by other programmers, and it contains protected data. Unbeknownst to you, other programmers may derive classes from your class and start accessing the protected instance fields. In this case, you can no longer change the implementation of your class without upsetting the other programmers. That is against the spirit of OOP, which encourages data encapsulation.

Protected methods make more sense. A class may declare a method as protected if it is tricky to use. This indicates that the subclasses (which, presumably, know their ancestors well) can be trusted to use the method correctly, but other classes cannot.

A good example is the clone method in the class Object. Let us remind you why you sometimes want to clone an object. When you make a copy of a variable, the original and the copy are references to the same object. (See Figure 5-6.) This means a change to either variable also affects the other.

```
Day bday = new Day(1959, 6, 16);
Day d = bday;
d.advance(100); // oops--also changed bday
```

If you would like to indicate that d should be a new object that begins as identical to bday but may later change to a different state, then you use the clone() method.

```
Day bday = new Day(1959, 6, 16);
Day d = (Day)bday.clone();
    // must cast--clone returns an object
d.advance(100); // ok--bday unchanged
```

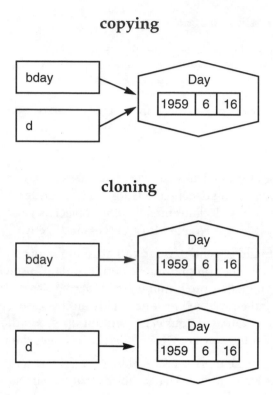

Figure 5-6

But it isn't quite so simple. The clone method is a protected method of Object, which means that your code cannot simply call it. Only the Day class can clone Day objects. There is a reason for this. Think about the way in which the Object class can implement clone. It knows nothing about the object at all, so it can only make a bit-by-bit copy. If all data fields in the object are numbers or other basic types, a bitwise copy is just fine. It is simply another object with the same base types and fields. But if the object contains pointers (that is, other objects), then the bitwise copy contains exact copies of the pointer fields, so the original and the cloned objects still share some information.

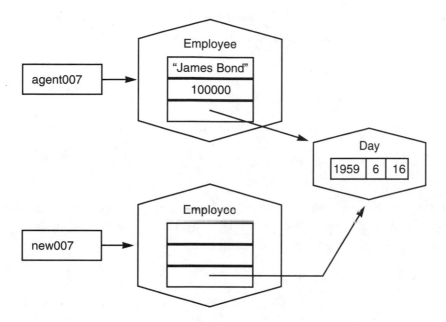

Figure 5-7

It is up to the derived class to make a judgment whether or not

1. the default `clone` method is good enough,

2. the default `clone` method can be patched up by calling `clone` on the object instance variables,

3. the situation is hopeless and `clone` should not be attempted.

The third option is actually the default. To choose either the first or the second option, a class must

1. implement the `Cloneable` interface and

2. redefine the `clone` method with the public access privilege.

The appearance of the `Cloneable` interface is another nuisance. Objects are so paranoid about cloning that they generate a run-time exception if an object requests cloning but does not implement that interface. (There are no methods at all in the `Cloneable` interface. It serves simply as a tag.)

Here is the drudgery that the Day class has to do to redefine clone.

```
public class Day implements Cloneable
{   . . .
  public Object clone()
  {   try
      {   return super.clone();
      } catch (CloneNotSupportedException e)
      {   // this shouldn't happen, since we are Cloneable
          return null;
      }
  }
}
```

And that is the easy case. If we want to clone employees, we have to call the Object clone method to make a bitwise copy, then clone the Day object.

```
public class Employee implements Cloneable
{   . . .
  public Object clone()
  {   try
      {   Employee e = (Employee)super.clone();
          e.hireDay = hireDay.clone();
          return e;
      }   catch (CloneNotSupportedException e)
      {   // this shouldn't happen, since we are Cloneable
          return null;
      }
  }
}
```

As you can see, cloning is a subtle business, and it makes sense that it is defined as protected in the Object class.

As it happens, protected features in Java are visible to all subclasses as well as all other classes in the same package. This is slightly different from the C++ meaning of protected. To placate the C++ crowd, yet another access modifier, private protected, has been provided. It denotes visibility by subclasses, but not by other classes in the same package. This subtle difference is probably not worth worrying about in practice.

Here is a summary of the five access modifiers in Java that control visibility.

1. visible to the class only (private)

2. visible to the world (public)

3. visible to the class and all subclasses (private protected)

4. visible to the package and all subclasses (protected)

5. visible to the package (the default—no modifier needed)

Design Hints for Inheritance

1. Common operations and fields belong in the superclass.

This is why we put the `sender` field into the `Message` class, rather than replicating it in `TextMessage` and `VoiceMessage`.

2. Use inheritance to model the "is–a" relationship.

Inheritance is a handy code saver, and sometimes people overuse it. For example, suppose we need a `Contractor` class. Contractors have names and hire dates, but they do not have salaries. Instead, they are paid by the hour, and they do not stay around long enough to get a raise. There is the temptation to derive `Contractor` from `Employee` and add an `hourlyWage` field.

```
class Contractor extends Employee
{   public Contractor(String name, double wage, Day hireDay)
    {   super(name, 0, hireDay);
        hourlyWage = wage;
    }
    private double hourlyWage;
}
```

This is *not* a good idea, however, and it will cause you no end of grief when you implement methods for printing paychecks or tax forms. You will end up writing more code than you would have by not inheriting in the first place.

The contractor/employee relationship fails the "is–a" test. A contractor is not a special case of an employee.

3. Don't use inheritance unless *all* inherited methods make sense.

Suppose we want to write a `Holiday` class . Surely every holiday is a day, so we can use inheritance.

```
class Holiday extends Day {  . . .  }
```

Unfortunately, this is somewhat subtle. When we say that `Holiday` extends `Day`, we have to consider that we are talking about the *class* `Day`, as specified by its public methods. One of the public methods of `Day` is advance. And advance can turn holidays into non-holidays, so it is not an appropriate operation for holidays.

```
Holiday xmas;
xmas.advance(10);
```

In that sense, a holiday is a day *but* not a `Day` .

4. Use polymorphism, not type information.

Whenever you find code of the form

```
if (x is of type 1)
   action1(x);
else if (x is of type 2)
   action2(x);
```

think polymorphism.

Do `action1` and `action2` represent a common concept? If so, make the concept a method of a common parent class or interface of both types. Then you can simply call

```
x.action();
```

and have the dynamic dispatch mechanism launch the correct action.

Code with polymorphic methods or interface implementations is much easier to maintain and extend than code with type tests.

CHAPTER

6

Graphics
Programming
with AWT

Until now, you have only learned how to write programs that take input from the keyboard, fuss with it, and then display the results on the console screen. This type of program is old-fashioned and clearly not what users want. Modern programs don't work this way and neither do Web pages. This chapter helps you begin the process of writing Java programs that use a graphical user interface (GUI) for output. In particular, you will learn how to write programs that use windows with multiple fonts, display images, and so on. (The next chapter shows you how to add interface elements such as menus and buttons.) When you finish these two chapters, you will know what is needed to write *stand-alone* graphical applications. Chapter 8 shows how to program applets embedded in Web pages that use these features.

Even if you are not concerned with graphics programming in the sense of displaying curves and such, you should read the first five sections of this chapter.

Java gives you a class library for basic GUI programming. It is called the Alternative Window Toolkit or AWT. Even though it is called the "alternative" toolkit, you don't have another realistic alternative at this time—you must use AWT for graphical Java programming. Unfortunately, AWT is somewhat primitive, not very well documented, and not particularly powerful. On the other hand, it is platform independent. (This means that Sun Microsystems has programmed AWT to be portable to various operating systems, such as Windows 95 and Solaris. People have ported it to such platforms as Linux.)

The most obvious way in which AWT shows itself as primitive is that applications built with AWT simply do not look as nice as native Windows or Macintosh applications. But, from the programmer's point of view there are far more serious problems: quite a few tasks that ought to be simple turn out to be quite complex in AWT. For this reason, many Java programmers believe that what AWT really stands for is "awkward window toolkit."

If you have programmed Microsoft Windows applications using VB, Delphi, or Visual C++, you are probably familiar with graphical layout tools. These tools let you design the visual appearance of your application and then generate much of the code for you. Currently, there are no such tools available for Java programming. (Many tools such as Borland's Latte have been announced; however, these will not be available for a while.) What this means to the programmer now is that you must build the user interface manually, and this often requires writing *a lot of code*.

The First Graphics Program

In this section, you will see what is probably the simplest graphical interface: a window! This is shown in Figure 6-1. As you will see, building this interface is not completely trivial. The window requires some sophisticated code to work correctly.

Figure 6-1

In AWT, a top-level window (that is, a window that is not contained inside another window) is called a *frame*. Frames are Java objects, so it should not be surprising that a program that creates a frame (window) must follow the following steps:

1. Create the frame by a call to `new`.

2. Resize the frame.

3. Call the `show` method in the `Frame` class in order to display the window (frame).

Here is the program, but *please don't run this program yet:* there is one very important rule when developing programs that use AWT:

Save all of your work-in-progress before running the program.

The problem is that it is sometimes hard to kill off a program that uses AWT, as you will soon see.

```
import java.awt.*; //see Chapter 4 for more on import

class NotHelloWorld1
{   public static void main(String[] args)
    {   Frame f = new Frame();
        f.resize(300, 200);
        f.show();
    }
}
```

Figure 6-1 shows the result of the program: just an empty window with a border and a title. Let's go over the code, line by line. First, we have imported the AWT package. Next is the standard header for a new class. The key line

```
Frame f = new Frame();
```

declares and makes a new `Frame` object. At this point, Java will build the data structure that contains all the necessary information for the underlying windowing system to display a frame window. This does not yet display the frame. You need to invoke the `show` method in order to display the frame. However, before you can show a frame, you need to size it. Here we make the window 300 pixels wide by 200 pixels high. If you don't explicitly size a frame, all frames will be sized at 0 by 0 pixels, and so will not be visible.

All measurements in AWT are made in pixels, and the first coordinate (*x*-coordinate) gives the width and the second (*y*-coordinate), the height.

Unfortunately, you don't know the resolution of the user's screen. A program that looks nice on a laptop screen will look like a postage stamp on a high-resolution screen. For now, we will just use values that we hope work acceptably on most displays. Feel free to change the window dimensions if you have a higher-resolution or larger screen. A better approach is to measure the size of a font and derive the screen dimensions from those measurements. See the section on Text and Fonts for information on font metrics.

OK, suppose you do run this program. How do you (try to) close the window? If you look carefully at the window shown in Figure 6-1, you will find it has a close box in its upper, right-hand corner. Unfortunately, clicking on this close box doesn't close the window. Clicking on the upper, left-hand corner reveals a menu (see Figure 6-2), but selecting Close from the menu doesn't work either.

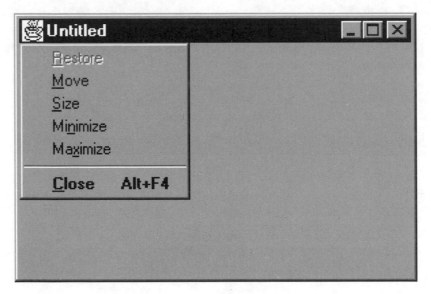

Figure 6-2

Guess what, nothing obvious will get this application to close. You will soon see how to write programs that can be closed properly, but right now you need a way to kill a wayward windowed Java application.

- Under Windows 95 or NT, *carefully* press CTRL+ALT+DEL. You get a dialog box similar to the one shown in Figure 6-3, which lists all running programs. Select the Java program and click on the **End Task** button. If a dialog box comes up that alerts you that the program isn't responding, confirm that you want to end it. You have to be careful when pressing CTRL+ALT+DEL. If you press the key combination twice, your computer reboots immediately, and you lose all work in all open applications.

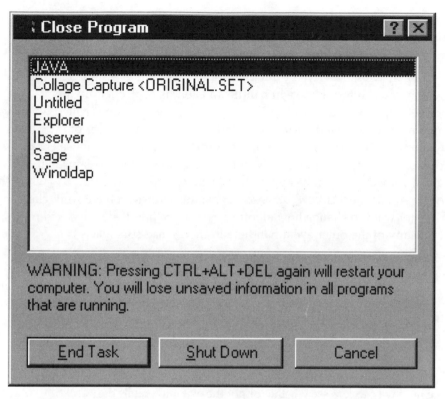

Figure 6-3

- Under Solaris, you can select **Destroy** from the program menu or terminate the program with extreme prejudice with the kill -9 command.

Obviously, you can't very well tell a user of your program that the natural way to end your program is via something like a CTRL+ALT+DEL "three-finger salute." Unfortunately, in Java the default behavior for a frame is to ignore all requests for its destruction—thus necessitating drastic actions to terminate the program.

What we need is something that is like a standard frame in most respects, except that it destroys itself when the user asks it to. As you saw in the previous chapter, Java has a powerful language construct to deal with just this situation: inheritance. We need to derive a new window class from the standard Frame class that somehow can respond to a request to destroy itself.

The key is that a frame can already respond to user events via what are called *event handlers*. (People coming from a Windows programming background will, of course, be familiar with event-driven programming. If you are coming from another background, think of it this way: in an event-driven program, objects sit around waiting for messages [events]. If they receive one, they see if they have some preprogrammed response to that message.)

In Java, each event is derived from the Event class and is assigned an *event id* for which you can test. How you handle an event is controlled by the handleEvent method in the Event class. Thus, this method is called whenever a frame receives an event it can understand. There are a number of interesting events to which frames can respond, for example: keystrokes, mouse clicks, and, of course, the destroy request. We will look at all the event types in Chapter 7. For now, we want to exit the application (i.e., use System.exit(0)) when the event ID equals the WINDOW_DESTROY constant defined in the Event class. (We do not want to change how all other events are handled so we will not override any of the other event handlers in the Frame superclass.)

The handleEvent function returns a Boolean value. You return true if you handle the event, false if you don't. Here's the code snippet that shows you how the event handler works for our class:

```
public boolean handleEvent(Event e)
{   if (e.id == Event.WINDOW_DESTROY)
        System.exit(0);
    return super.handleEvent(e);
}
```

Notice how we check to see whether or not the event id equals the WINDOW_DESTROY constant. In this case, the function calls the System.exit(0) method, which closes any Java application. Notice that this method won't return out of the call to System.exit, so it doesn't matter that we are not having the handleEvent method returning true—even though we are, in fact, handling the destroy event. Notice as well that all other events are still handled by the Frame super-class. You will see in Chapter 7 what happens to an event when a particular window refuses to handle it. You should normally return true when you handle an event in the handleEvent method. However, if the WINDOW_DESTROY event occurs, we call exit and the method does not return.

Having briefly gone through what it means to write event-handling code you can now understand the following code, which gives you a closeable window.

```
import java.awt.*;

class NotHelloWorld2 extends Frame
{   public boolean handleEvent(Event e)
    {   if (e.id == Event.WINDOW_DESTROY)
            System.exit(0);
        return super.handleEvent(e);
    }
```

```
    public static void main(String[] args)
    {   Frame f = new NotHelloWorld2();
        f.resize(300, 200);
        f.show();
    }
}
```

This derivation process via inheritance from classes like `Frame` is the key to working with the AWT library. Every time you need a user interface component that is similar to one of the basic AWT components, you use inheritance to supply the additional functionality.

Displaying Text in a Window

Now that you can close a window without having to reboot your computer, let us try to build the first non-trivial windowed application. Rather than displaying "Not a Hello, World program" in text mode in a console window as in Chapter 3, we will display the message in a window, as in Figure 6-4.

Figure 6-4

Anytime you want to put text or graphics into a window, you need to override the `paint` method from the `Frame` class, so, of course, you need to write a new class for this that overrides not only the `WINDOW_DESTROY` event handler but also the `paint` method. The `paint` method has one parameter of type `Graphics`. The `Graphics` parameter is similar to a device context in Windows or a graphics context in X11 programming.

VB Programmers rarely need a device context, but they are there just the same. For now, think of a `Graphics` object as being like a Picture box (which actually encapsulates a graphics context). On a `Graphics` object, like a Picture box, you have certain methods for drawing, changing colors and pen styles, and the like.

A `Graphics` object remembers a collection of settings for drawing images and text, such as the currently selected font or the current color. All drawing in Java must go through a `Graphics` object. Displaying text (usually called *rendering text*) is considered a special kind of drawing. For example, a `Graphics` object has a `drawString` method that has the following syntax:

```
drawString(String s, int xCoord, int yCoord)
```

In our case, we want to draw the string "Not a Hello, World" in our original window, roughly one quarter of the way across and halfway down. Although we don't yet know how to exactly measure the size of the string, we'll start the string at (75, 100). (You will see how to draw lines and other shapes in the section on Text and Fonts.) Here's the code:

```
import java.awt.*;

class NotHelloWorld3 extends Frame
{   public boolean handleEvent(Event e)
    {   if (e.id == Event.WINDOW_DESTROY)
            System.exit(0);
        return super.handleEvent(e);
    }
    public void paint(Graphics g)
    {   g.drawString("Not a Hello, World program", 75, 100);
    }
    public static void main(String[] args)
    {   Frame f = new NotHelloWorld3();
        f.resize(300, 200);
        f.show();
    }
}
```

More on Event-Driven Programming: Update and Paint Functions

Just like Microsoft Windows or X Windows programming, and unlike most DOS programs, a graphical Java program is event driven. The programmer describes what needs to occur when a particular event happens. However, as with all event-driven programs, the sequence of events is beyond the control of the programmer since users may perform operations in any order.

For example, parts of an application may need to be redrawn in response to a user action or external circumstances. Perhaps the user increases the size of the window or minimizes and then restores the application. If another window has popped up and then disappeared, the covered application windows are corrupted and will need to be redrawn. (The graphics system does not usually save the pixels underneath.) And, of course, when a window is first displayed, its initial elements must be drawn.

There is no way to make graphics persistent in Java; you will always need to write the code in a paint method to redraw.

Each time a window needs to be redrawn, for any reason, the event handler calls its `update` function. The default implementation for `update` (in the base class called `Component`) is to erase the background and to call `paint`. In most cases, we can leave `update` alone and just redefine `paint`. For example, in the preceding section, we defined `paint` to draw a message on the screen.

The `update`, like the `paint`, procedures take a single parameter of type `Graphics`. As with the `paint` procedure, you use the `Graphics` object to render graphics on the window and to inquire and modify the graphics state.

Text and Fonts

To display text, you must first select a font. A font is specified by its name, such as "Helvetica," the style (plain, **bold**, *italic*, or ***bold italic***), and the point size. Unfortunately, there is no way to find out what fonts have been installed on the system of the user of your program, so it seems wise to stick to the following fonts:

Helvetica

TimesRoman

Courier

Dialog

Symbol

These font names are always mapped by Java to fonts that actually exist on the client machine. For example, on a Windows system, Helvetica is mapped to Arial. You are free to ask for other fonts by name, but don't be surprised if your user doesn't have Troglodyte Bold installed and your text doesn't show up right.

As you might expect, `Font` is an object in Java, so we need to create it via a call to `new` before we can use it. In this case, `Font` requires parameters that define its properties in the constructor. The syntax is

```
Font(String name, Font property, int size)
```

where one uses something like `Font.BOLD` to get bold.

Here's the code in a `paint` method that would let you display "Not a Hello, World program" in Helvetica 14-point bold at the same location as before.

```
public void paint(Graphics g)
{   Font f = new Font("Helvetica", Font.BOLD, 14);
    g.setFont(f);
    g.drawString("Not a Hello, World program", 75, 100);
}
```

Actually, since we now have the freedom to choose fonts, let's display the text with a mixture of roman and italic letters, "Not a *Hello, World* program." We need two fonts, the base font, `f`, and its italicized version.

```
Font f = new Font("Helvetica", Font.BOLD, 14);
Font fi = new Font("Helvetica", Font.BOLD + Font.ITALIC, 14);
```

Now we have a problem. We need to know how long the string `Not a` is in Helvetica Bold 14 point so that we can tack the `Hello, World` string behind it. To measure a string, you need to use the `FontMetrics` class to derive properties of the font to be used with the `Graphics` object. This class reveals global size properties of the font and measures the sizes of strings rendered in the font. For example, the `stringWidth` method of `FontMetrics` takes a string and returns its current width in pixels.

You cannot mix fonts in Java without carefully positioning the strings yourself. There is no notion of a last point referenced.

In Java, you need to become familiar with terminology taken from typesetting in order to handle fonts properly. Many of the properties used in typesetting correspond to methods of the `FontMetrics` class.

For example, the *ascent* is the distance from the baseline to the top of an *ascender*, which is the upper part of a letter like "b" or "k", or an uppercase character. The *descent* is the distance from the baseline to a *descender*, which is the lower portion of a letter like "p" or "g". These correspond to the `getAscent` and `getDescent` methods of the `FontMetrics` class.

You also need the `getLeading` and `getHeight` methods of the `FontMetrics` class, which correspond to what typesetters call *leading* and *height*. Leading is the space between the descent of one line and the ascent of the next line. The height of a font is the distance between successive baselines, which is the same as descent + leading + ascent.

Some characters, typically those with diacritics such as "Ã", extend above the normal ascent. (There is, in fact, a slight chance that such characters may overlap with descenders from the preceding line.) The *maximum ascent* is the largest height of such a character. Similarly, the *maximum descent* is the largest depth of a descender. You would use the ascent and descent measurements for line spacing and the maximum ascent and descent if you need to determine the maximum screen area occupied by a font.

These vertical measurements are properties of the font. In contrast, horizontal measurements are properties of the individual characters. In a proportionally spaced font such as Times or Helvetica, different characters have different sizes. For example, a "w" is much wider than an "l". In fact, the size of a word may not even equal the sum of the sizes of its characters because some fonts move certain character pairs closer together, a process called *kerning*. For example, the pair "Av" is often kerned. The `stringWidth` method of the `FontMetrics` object of a font computes the width of any string and thus takes into account any kerning that may have occurred.

The following code displays the mixed font text "Not a *Hello, World* program."

```
public void paint(Graphics g)
{   Font f = new Font("Helvetica", Font.BOLD, 14);
    Font fi = new Font("Helvetica", Font.BOLD + Font.ITALIC, 14);
    FontMetrics fm = g.getFontMetrics(f);
    FontMetrics fim = g.getFontMetrics(fi);
    String s1 = "Not a ";
    String s2 = "Hello, World";
    String s3 = " Program";
    int cx = 75;
    int cy = 100;
    g.setFont(f);
    g.drawString(s1, cx, cy);
    cx += fm.stringWidth(s1);
    g.setFont(fi);
    g.drawString(s2, cx, cy);
    cy += fim.stringWidth(s2);
    g.setFont(f);
    g.drawString(s3, cx, cy);
}
```

Actually, this code is a little unrealistic. The allocation of fonts and font metrics is time consuming, and it is usually best to allocate these items only once. We'll do that in the code below, simply by making the fonts and metrics into variables of the frame class and setting them once in a `setFonts` method. We call the `setFonts` method from `paint`. We would have preferred to set the fonts in the constructor, but the graphics context is not yet set up when the frame is constructed.

While we are at it, we want to make one final improvement: centering the string in the window. The `size` method of `Component`, a parent class of `Frame`, returns the size of the frame. Unless the user resizes the window, it will be the same 300 by 200 that we set in `main`. However, that is the size of the whole window, including borders and title bars. The `insets` method returns a structure giving the measurements of the borders around the four sides (i.e., the useable, or client, area.) We can use this information to properly center the string.

Note that this program repositions text so that the string stays centered when the user resizes the window.

Think of `size` as corresponding to Height and Width and `insets` as corresponding to ScaleHeight and ScaleWidth.

Here is the program listing. Figure 6-5 shows the screen display.

Figure 6-5

```java
import java.awt.*;

class NotHelloWorld4 extends Frame
{   public boolean handleEvent(Event evt)
    {   if (evt.id == Event.WINDOW_DESTROY) System.exit(0);
        return false;
    }

    private Font f;
    private Font fi;
```

```
    private FontMetrics fm;
    private FontMetrics fim;
    private boolean fontsSet = false;

    private void setFonts(Graphics g)
    {   if (fontsSet) return;
        f = new Font("Helvetica", Font.BOLD, 14);
        fi = new Font("Helvetica", Font.BOLD + Font.ITALIC, 14);
        fm = g.getFontMetrics(f);
        fim = g.getFontMetrics(fi);
        fontsSet = true;
    }

    public void paint(Graphics g)
    {   setFonts(g);
        String s1 = "Not a ";
        String s2 = "Hello, World";
        String s3 = " Program";
        int w1 = fm.stringWidth(s1);
        int w2 = fim.stringWidth(s2);
        int w3 = fm.stringWidth(s3);

        Dimension d = size();
        Insets in = insets();
        int client_width = d.width - in.right - in.left;
        int client_height = d.height - in.bottom - in.top;
        int cx = (client_width - w1 - w2 - w3) / 2;
        int cy = client_height / 2;
        g.drawRect(0, 0, client_width - 1, client_height - 1);

        g.setFont(f);
        g.drawString(s1, cx, cy);
        cx += w1;
        g.setFont(fi);
        g.drawString(s2, cx, cy);
        cx += w2;
        g.setFont(f);
        g.drawString(s3, cx, cy);

    }

    public static void main(String args[])
    {   Frame f = new NotHelloWorld4();
        f.resize(300, 200);
        f.show();
    }
}
```

`java.awt.Font`

• `Font(String name, int style, int size)`

creates a new font object.

Parameters:

name	the font name (e.g., "Times Roman")
style	the style (`Font.PLAIN`, `Font.BOLD`, `Font.ITALIC` or `Font.BOLD + Font.ITALIC`)
size	the point size (e.g., 12)

`java.awt.FontMetrics`

• `int getAscent()`

gets the font ascent—the distance from the baseline to the tops of uppercase characters.

• `int getDescent()`

gets the font descent—the distance from the baseline to the bottoms of descenders.

• `int getLeading()`

gets the font leading—the space between the bottom of one line of text and the top of the next line.

• `int getHeight()`

gets the total height of the font—the distance between the two baselines of text (descent + leading + ascent).

• `int getMaxAscent()`

gets the maximum height of all characters in this font.

• `int getMaxDescent()`

gets the maximum descent of all characters in this font.

• `int stringWidth(String str)`

computes the width of a string.

Parameters:

    `str`   the string to be measured

```
java.awt.Graphics
```
• `void setFont(Font font)`

selects a font for the graphics context. That font will be used for subsequent text-drawing operations.

Parameters:

    `font`   a font

• `FontMetrics getFontMetrics()`

gets the metrics of the current font.

• `void drawString(String str, int x, int y)`

draws a string in the current font and color.

Parameters:

    `str`   the string to be drawn

    `x`   the *x*-coordinate of the start of the string

    `y`   the *y*-coordinate of the baseline of the string

Colors

The `setColor` method call selects a color that is used for all subsequent drawing operations. To draw in multiple colors, you select a color, draw, then select another color.

The `setColor` method takes a parameter of type `Color`. You can either pick one of the 13 standard colors listed in Table 6-1, or specify a color by its red, green, and blue components.

```
g.setColor(Color.pink);
g.drawString("Hello", 75, 100);
g.setColor(new Color(0, 128, 128)); // a dull blue-green
g.drawString("World", 75, 125);
```

Table 6-1: Standard Colors

black	green	red
blue	lightGray	white
cyan	magenta	yellow
darkGray	orange	
gray	pink	

To set the *background color*, you use the `setBackground` method of the
Component class, an ancestor of `Frame`. In fact, you should set the background
before displaying the frame for the first time.

```
f.resize(300, 200);
f.setBackground(Color.white);
f.show();
```

`java.awt.Color`

• `Color(int r, int g, int b)`

creates a color object.

Parameters:

      r   the red value (0–255)

      g   the green value (0–255)

      b   the blue value (0–255)

`java.awt.Graphics`

• `void setColor(Color c)`

changes the current color. All subsequent graphics operations will use the new
color.

Parameters:

      c   the new color

`java.awt.Component`

• `void setBackground(Color c)`

sets the background color.

Parameters:

c   the new background color

Drawing Graphical Shapes

The drawLine, drawArc, and drawPolygon methods in java.awt.Graphics are used to draw straight and curved lines.

```
java.awt.Graphics
```
• void drawLine(int x1, int y1, int x2, int y2)

draws a line between the points with coordinates (x1,y1) and (x2,y2).

Parameters:

x1   the first point's *x*-coordinate

y1   the first point's *y*-coordinate

x2   the second point's *x*-coordinate

y2   the second point's *y*-coordinate

• void drawArc(int x, int y, int width, int height,
       int startAngle, int arcAngle)

draws an arc bounded by the rectangle with the upper left corner (x, y) and the given width and height. The arc starts at startAngle and spans the arcAngle. (That is, the end angle is startAngle + arcAngle.) Angles are measured in degrees and follow the usual mathematical conventions: 0 degrees is at the three-o'clock position, and positive angles indicate counterclockwise rotation. The "PacMan" figure in the example below illustrates the usage of the parameters.

Parameters:

x   the *x*-coordinate

y   the *y*-coordinate

width   the width of the rectangle

height   the height of the rectangle

startAngle   the beginning angle

arcAngle   the angle of the arc (relative to *startAngle*)

In Java, a *polygon* is a sequence of line segments. (That is different from the usual definition in which a polygon is required to be closed.) The easiest way to draw a polygon in Java is to:

- create a polygon object,

- add points to the object,

- use the `drawPolygon(Polygon p)` method described here to draw the polygon.

(There is another `drawPolygon` method that takes two arrays, one for each of the *x*- and *y*-coordinates of the endpoints of the line segments, but it is less convenient.)

`java.awt.Graphics`

- `void drawPolygon(Polygon p)`

draws a path joining the points in the `Polygon` object.

Parameters:

    p   a polygon

- `void drawPolygon(int[] xPoints, int[] yPoints, int nPoints)`

draws a path joining a sequence of points.

Parameters:

    xPoints   an array of *x*-coordinates of the corner points

    yPoints   an array of *y*-coordinates of the corner points

    nPoints   the number of corner points

Polygons with very closely spaced points are useful to render curved shapes.

(We give an example of this in the next program, in which we draw a spiral made up of many vertices.)

Now let's draw these figures. We will draw a PacMan shape (by using an arc and two line segments), a pentagon (with one side missing because the `drawPolygon` function does not close polygons), and a spiral (actually a polygon with many closely spaced points).

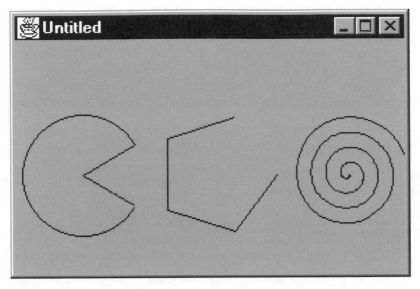

Figure 6-6

```java
import java.awt.*;

class DrawPoly extends Frame
{   public boolean handleEvent(Event evt)
    {   if (evt.id == Event.WINDOW_DESTROY) System.exit(0);
        return false;
    }

    public void paint(Graphics g)
    {   int r = 45; // radius of circle bounding PacMan(R)
        int cx = 50; // center of that circle
        int cy = 100;
        int angle = 30;; // opening angle of mouth

        int dx = (int)(r * Math.cos(angle * Math.PI / 180));
        int dy = (int)(r * Math.sin(angle * Math.PI / 180));

        g.drawLine(cx, cy, cx + dx, cy + dy); // lower jaw
        g.drawLine(cx, cy, cx + dx, cy - dy); // upper jaw
        g.drawArc(cx - r, cy - r, 2 * r, 2 * r, angle, 360 - 2 * angle);
        Polygon p = new Polygon();
        cx = 150;
        int i;
        for (i = 0; i < 5; i++)
            p.addPoint((int)(cx + r * Math.cos(i * 2 * Math.PI / 5)),
                (int)(cy + r * Math.sin(i * 2 * Math.PI / 5)));
```

```
    g.drawPolygon(p);

    Polygon s = new Polygon();
    cx = 250;
    for (i = 0; i < 360; i++)
    {   double t = i / 360.0;
        s.addPoint((int)(cx + r * t * Math.cos(8 * t * Math.PI)),
            (int)(cy + r * t * Math.sin(8 * t * Math.PI)));
    }
    g.drawPolygon(s);
}

public static void main(String args[])
{   Frame f = new DrawPoly();
    f.resize(300, 200);
    f.show();
}
}
```

The `drawRect...` and `drawOval` functions render the outlines of rectangles and ellipses (called ovals in AWT).

`java.awt.Graphics`

• void drawRect(int x, int y, int width, int height)

draws the outline of the rectangle. Note that the third and fourth parameters are *not* the opposite corner points.

Parameters:

      x   the *x*-coordinate of the top left corner

      y   the *y*-coordinate of the top left corner

      width   the width of the rectangle

      height   the height of the rectangle

• void drawRoundRect(int x, int y, int width, int height,
    int arcWidth, int arcHeight)

draws the outline of the rectangle, using curved arcs for the corners.

Parameters:

x	the *x*-coordinate of the top left corner
y	the *y*-coordinate of the top left corner
width	the width of the rectangle
height	the height of the rectangle
arcWidth	the horizontal diameter of the arcs at the corners
arcHeight	the vertical diameter of the arcs at the corners

- void draw3dRect(int x, int y, int width, int height, boolean raised)

draws the outline of the rectangle. Note that the third and fourth parameters are *not* the opposite corner points.

Parameters:

x	the *x*-coordinate of the top left corner
y	the *y*-coordinate of the top left corner
width	the width of the rectangle
height	the height of the rectangle
raised	true to have the rectangle appear above the window

- void drawOval(int x, int y, int width, int height)

draws the outline of an ellipse. The parameters specify the bounding rectangle.

Parameters:

x	the *x*-coordinate of the top left corner of the bounding rectangle
y	the *y*-coordinate of the top left corner of the bounding rectangle
width	the width of the bounding rectangle
height	the height of the bounding rectangle

The following program shows the various rectangle styles and the oval.

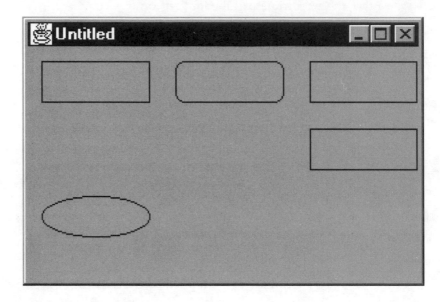

Figure 6-7

```java
import java.awt.*;

class DrawRect extends Frame
{   public boolean handleEvent(Event evt)
    {   if (evt.id == Event.WINDOW_DESTROY) System.exit(0);
        return false;
    }

    public void paint(Graphics g)
    {   g.setColor(Color.blue);
        g.drawRect(10, 10, 80, 30);
        g.drawRoundRect(110, 10, 80, 30, 15, 15);
        g.draw3DRect(210, 10, 80, 30, true);
        g.draw3DRect(210, 60, 80, 30, false);
        g.drawOval(10, 110, 80, 30);
    }

    public static void main(String args[])
    {   Frame f = new DrawRect();
        f.resize(300, 200);
        f.show();
    }
}
```

Filling Shapes

The interiors of closed shapes (rectangles, ellipses, polygons, and pie chart segments) can be filled with a color. The method calls are similar to the draw calls of the preceding section, except that draw is replaced by fill.

- void fillRect(int x, int y, int width, int height)
- void fillRoundRect(int x, int y, int width, int height,
    int arcWidth, int arcHeight)
- void fill3dRect(int x, int y, int width, int height, boolean
    raised)
- void fillOval(int x, int y, int width, int height)
- void fillArc(int x, int y, int width, int height,
    int startAngle, int arcAngle)
- void fillPolygon(Polygon p)
- void fillPolygon(int[] xPoints, int[] yPoints, int nPoints)

To *fill* rectangles and ovals simply means to color the inside of the shape with the current color. There is one minor point: When you *fill* a rectangle, you get one pixel less on the right and on the bottom of the rectangle than when you *draw* it. When you look closely at the output of the test program, you can see that the top and left line segments of the drawn rectangles are covered by the subsequent fills, but the right and bottom line segments are not. This is different from Windows API, where the end points of lines and rectangles are neither drawn nor filled.

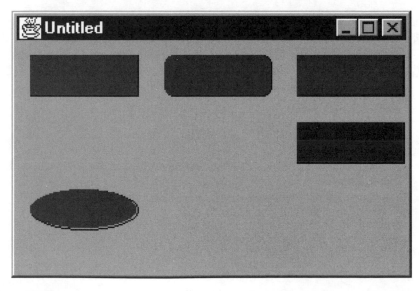

Figure 6-8

```
import java.awt.*;

class FillRect extends Frame
{   public boolean handleEvent(Event evt)
    {   if (evt.id == Event.WINDOW_DESTROY) System.exit(0);
        return false;
    }

    public void paint(Graphics g)
    {   g.drawRect(10, 10, 80, 30);
        g.drawRoundRect(110, 10, 80, 30, 15, 15);
        g.draw3DRect(210, 10, 80, 30, true);
        g.draw3DRect(210, 60, 80, 30, false);
        g.drawOval(10, 110, 80, 30);
        g.setColor(Color.red);
        g.fillRect(10, 10, 80, 30);
        g.fillRoundRect(110, 10, 80, 30, 15, 15);
        g.fill3DRect(210, 10, 80, 30, true);
        g.fill3DRect(210, 60, 80, 30, false);
        g.fillOval(10, 110, 80, 30);
    }
    public static void main(String args[])
    {   Frame f = new FillRect();
        f.resize(300, 200);
        f.show();
    }
}
```

Note that filling arcs and polygons is quite different from drawing them. Arcs are filled as pie segments, by joining the center of the enclosing rectangle with the two end points of the arc and filling the interior. To see this, look at the filled PacMan in the screen picture in Figure 6-9.

Polygons, on the other hand, are closed before they are filled. If they have gaps in the interior, they are filled according to the "alternating" rule. The effect shows up nicely in the filled spiral in the sample code.

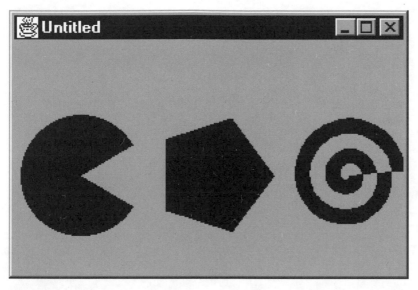

Figure 6-9

```
import java.awt.*;

class FillPoly extends Frame
{   public boolean handleEvent(Event evt)
    {   if (evt.id == Event.WINDOW_DESTROY) System.exit(0);
        return false;
    }

    public void paint(Graphics g)
    {   int r = 45; // radius of circle bounding PacMan(R)
        int cx = 50; // center of that circle
        int cy = 100;
        int angle = 30;; // opening angle of mouth

        int dx = (int)(r * Math.cos(angle * Math.PI / 180));
        int dy = (int)(r * Math.sin(angle * Math.PI / 180));

        g.fillArc(cx - r, cy - r, 2 * r, 2 * r, angle, 360 - 2 * angle);

        Polygon p = new Polygon();
        cx = 150;
        int i;
        for (i = 0; i < 5; i++)
            p.addPoint((int)(cx + r * Math.cos(i * 2 * Math.PI / 5)),
                (int)(cy + r * Math.sin(i * 2 * Math.PI / 5)));
```

```
        g.fillPolygon(p);

        Polygon s = new Polygon();
        cx = 250;
        for (i = 0; i < 360; i++)
        {   double t = i / 360.0;
            s.addPoint((int)(cx + r * t * Math.cos(8 * t * Math.PI)),
                (int)(cy + r * t * Math.sin(8 * t * Math.PI)));
        }
        g.fillPolygon(s);
    }

    public static void main(String args[])
    {   Frame f = new FillPoly();
        f.resize(300, 200);
        f.show();
    }
}
```

Paint Mode

When you paint shapes on top of one another, the shape last drawn simply writes on top of everything under it. In addition to this *overwrite* paint mode, AWT also supports a second method of combining new shapes with the old window contents; this is usually called *XOR* paint mode.

The XOR paint mode is used for highlighting a portion of the screen. Suppose you draw a filled rectangle over a part of the screen. If you draw on top of pixels that are already in the current color, then they are changed to the color specified in the setXORMode call. If you draw on top of pixels in the color of the setXORMode parameter, they are changed to the current color. Any other colors under the highlighted area are changed in some way. The key point is that XOR is a *toggle*. If you draw the same shape twice in XOR mode, the second drawing erases the first, and the screen looks just as it did at the outset.

Usually, you use the background color as the argument to setXORMode.

```
import java.awt.*;

class XOR extends Frame
{   public boolean handleEvent(Event evt)
    {   if (evt.id == Event.WINDOW_DESTROY) System.exit(0);
        return false;
    }
```

```
    public void paint(Graphics g)
    {   g.setColor(Color.red);
        g.fillRect(10, 10, 80, 30);
        g.setColor(Color.green);
        g.fillRect(50, 20, 80, 30);
        g.setColor(Color.blue);
        g.fillRect(130, 40, 80, 30);
        g.setXORMode(Color.green);
        g.fillRect(90, 30, 80, 30);

    }

    public static void main(String[] args)
    {   Frame f = new XOR();
        f.resize(300, 200);
        f.setBackground(Color.black);
        f.show();
    }
}
```

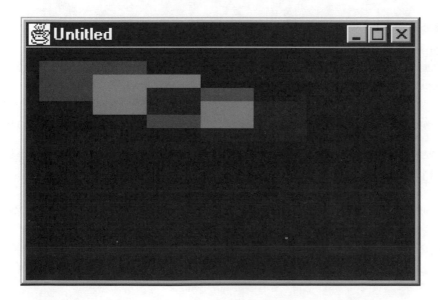

Figure 6-10

```
java.awt.Graphics
```
• void setPaintMode()

sets the graphics context to use "paint mode," in which new pixels replace old ones.

• void setXORMode(Color xor_color)

sets the graphics context to use "XOR mode." The color of a pixel is determined as old_color ^ new_color ^ xor_color. If you draw the same shape twice, then it is erased and the screen is restored to its original appearance.

Parameters:

xor_color   the color to which the current color should change during drawing

Images

We can build up simple images by drawing lines and shapes. Complex images, such as photographs, must be generated externally, for example with a scanner or special image-manipulation software, then stored in a file. Once they are in a file they can be read into a Java application. To read a graphics file into an application, you need to use a so-called Toolkit object. A Toolkit object can read most standard graphics formats, for example, GIF and JPEG files. To get a Toolkit object, use the static getDefaultToolkit method of the Toolkit class. Here is the code you need:

```
String name = "blue-ball.gif";
Image image = Toolkit.getDefaultToolkit.getImage(name);
```

Now the variable image contains the GIF file image and you can display it.

```
public void paint(Graphics g)
{   g.drawImage(image, 0, 0, this);
}
```

The drawImage command renders the image in the window. Our next sample program takes this a little bit further and *tiles* the window with the graphics image (see Figure 6-11).

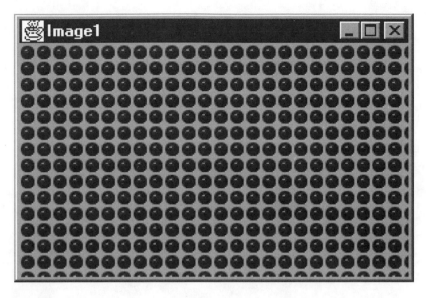

Figure 6-11

Here is the program:

```java
import java.awt.*;
import java.awt.image.*;
import java.net.*;

class Image1 extends Frame
{   public boolean handleEvent(Event evt)
    {   if (evt.id == Event.WINDOW_DESTROY) System.exit(0);
        return false;
    }

    public Image1()
    {   setTitle("Image1");

        image = Toolkit.getDefaultToolkit()
            .getImage("blue-ball.gif");
    }

    public void paint(Graphics g)
    {   Dimension d = size();
        Insets in = insets();
        int client_width = d.width - in.right - in.left;
        int client_height = d.height - in.bottom - in.top;
```

```
        int image_width = image.getWidth(this);
        int image_height = image.getHeight(this);

        g.drawImage(image, 0, 0, this);
        for (int i = 0; i <= client_width / image_width; i++)
            for (int j = 0; j <= client_height / image_height; j++)
                if (i + j > 0) g.copyArea(0, 0, image_width,
                image_height, i * image_width, j * image_height);
    }

    Image image;

    public static void main(String args[])
    {   Frame f = new Image1();
        f.resize(300, 200);
        f.show();
    }
}
```

The tiling occurs in the paint program. We compute the sizes of the client area of the window and of the image using insets. Then we draw one copy of the image in the top left corner and use the `copyArea` call to copy it into the entire window.

By the way, if you look at the `Image1` constructor, you will note a call to

```
    setTitle("Image1");
```

This call sets the title bar of the window.

```
java.awt.Toolkit
```
• `Toolkit getDefaultToolkit()`

returns the default toolkit.

• `Image getImage(String filename)`

returns an image that will read its pixel data from a file.

Parameters:

> `filename`   the file containing the image (e.g., a GIF or JPEG file)

`java.awt.Graphics`

- `boolean drawImage(Image img, int x, int y, int width,`
  `int height, ImageObserver observer)`

draws an image. Note: This call may return before the image is drawn.

Parameters:

`img`	the image to be drawn
`x`	the *x*-coordinate of the upper left corner
`y`	the *y*-coordinate of the upper left corner
`width`	the desired width of image
`height`	the desired height of image
`observer`	the object to be notified of the rendering process (may be null)

- `boolean drawImage(Image img, int x, int y, ImageObserver`
  `observer)`

draws a scaled image. Note: This call may return before the image is drawn.

Parameters:

`img`	the image to be drawn
`x`	the *x*-coordinate of the upper left corner
`y`	the *y*-coordinate of the upper left corner
`observer`	the object to be notified of the rendering process (may be null)

`java.awt.Frame`

- `setTitle(String title)`

sets the title string.

Parameters:

`title`	the string to use in the title bar

Buffering

If you run the `Image1` program on a moderately slow computer, you can watch how it slowly fills the window. When something the user does requires that the window be repainted (i.e., causes a call to the `paint` method), the window again *slowly* fills with the images.

Thus, this naive image handling does not work well if you are concerned about performance or if the image arrives slowly over a network connection. In the remainder of this chapter, we explain how the professionals deal with images. If the discussion gets too technical, just skip this section and come back when you actually have to deal with images.

First, you may have noticed that the immediately preceding program sometimes flickers when it redraws the screen. That is because `update`, and not the `paint` method, is called when AWT notifies the window of the need to redraw. The default action of `update` is to erase the screen and then to repaint it. In our case, erasing the screen is not necessary because we completely cover it with the image. This problem is simple to solve. We just override `update` by calling `paint` directly.

```
void update(Graphics g)
{    paint(g);
}
```

To speed up the screen refresh, we first build the entire screen image in its own image buffer. We can then paint the screen by drawing just that one buffer into it. That makes the drawing much smoother and faster. The cost is the time and memory needed to fill the buffer. As an added benefit, we only need to recompute the buffer when the user makes the screen area larger.

Windows users should think of what is occurring after the buffer is filled as corresponding to using the BitBlt API call.

If you are using VB4, think of this as corresponding to a call to PaintPicture.

You create a buffer with the `createImage` command. To draw into that buffer, rather than directly into the window, we need to work with the graphics context that is attached *to the buffer*. (The graphics context parameter of the `update` and `paint` functions is attached to the screen window.) This is done with the `getGraphics` method call of the image class, which returns a `Graphics` object (i.e., a graphics context).

Here is the code for this:

```
Image buffered_image = createImage(client_width,
client_height);
Graphics bg = buffered_image.getGraphics();
// all drawing commands that use bg fill the buffered_image
bg.drawImage(image, 0, 0, this);
for (int i = 0; i <= client_width / image_width; i++)
   for (int j = 0; j <= client_width / image_width; j++)
      if (i + j > 0) // skip the first tile
         bg.copyArea(0, 0, image_width, image_height,
            i * image_width, j * image_height);
bg.dispose();
```

Notice the last line

```
bg.dispose();
```

Don't forget to dispose of a graphics context when you are done with it. Graphics contexts occupy more than just memory. They attach to finite resources in the operating systems, so you can't just rely on the garbage collection mechanism to release and then recycle them.

Finally, when the image has been built, we want to display it in the window.

```
void paint(Graphics g)
{   // if the window size has increased, recompute
buffered_image
    . . .
    g.drawImage(buffered_image, 0, 0, null);
}
```

```
java.awt.Component
```

• `void update(Graphics g)`

updates the component without erasing the current image.

Parameters:

     g   the graphics context to use for the drawing

• `Image createImage(int width, int height)`

creates an off-screen image buffer to be used for double buffering.

Parameters:

    width   the width of the image

    height   the height of the image

`java.awt.Graphics`

• `void copyArea(int x, int y, int width, int height, int dx, int dy)`

copies an area of the screen.

Parameters:

x	the *x*-coordinate of the upper left corner of the source area
y	the *y*-coordinate of the upper left corner of the source area
width	the width of the source area
height	the height of the source area
dx	the horizontal distance from the source area to the target area
dy	the vertical distance from the source area to the target area

• `void dispose()`

disposes of this graphics context and releases operating system resources. You should always dispose of the graphics contexts that you allocate, but not the ones handed to you by `paint` or `update`.

`java.awt.Image`

• `Graphics getGraphics()`

gets a graphics context to draw into this image buffer.

Image Updating

The buffering technique you saw works well if you draw lines or text into the buffer. However, *it does not work for images*. If you try out the code that we have described so far, the paint procedure will probably paint a blank rectangle! The reason for that is subtle, but important.

AWT was written with the assumption that an image may arrive slowly over a network connection. The *first* call to the `drawImage` function recognizes that the GIF file has not yet been loaded. Instead of loading the file and returning to the caller when the image is actually loaded, Java spawns a new thread of execution to load the image, *and then returns to the caller without actually having completed that task*.

This is—to say the least—surprising to anyone who expects that a function won't return until it has done its job. But here the multi-threaded aspect of Java works against your assumptions. What will happen is that Java will run the code in your program in parallel with the code to load the image. Eventually, the image will be loaded and available. Of course, in the meantime, our code has tiled the entire buffer with copies of a blank array.

The solution of course is to find out when the GIF image is completely loaded and *then* tile the buffer. When we were trying to figure out how this is accomplished (and this is a technique you should be prepared to use yourself), we needed to look at the Java on-line documentation and then study the ancestors of the Frame class. Frame extends Window, which extends Container, which extends Component, which extends Object *and implements* ImageObserver.

Inheritance hierarchy

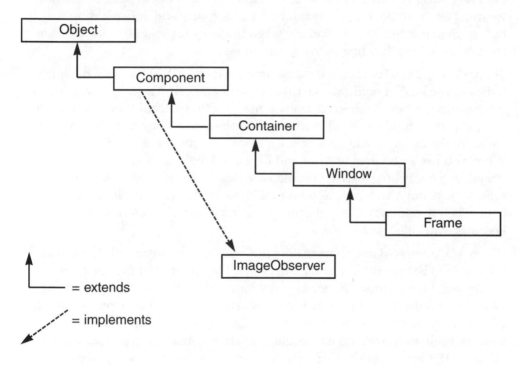

ImageObserver is an interface with a single method, imageUpdate. This is a *callback* function. That is, the thread that loads the image periodically calls the imageUpdate function of the object that was passed as the last argument of the drawImage call

```
bg.drawImage(image, 0, 0, this);
```

That parameter must be of type ImageObserver. Now you know why we passed this as the last parameter. The this object is our application object derived from `Frame`. Since `Frame` (indirectly) extends `ImageObserver`, `this` is a legal argument. (By the way, you pass `null` if you don't want to be notified of the image acquisition process.)

The default implementation of `imageUpdate` simply calls `update`. Now you know why the first program worked, and why it flickered more than it should have. During the first call to `paint`, the first call to `drawImage` returned immediately, and the first attempt at tiling didn't actually work. But as soon as the image was acquired, the `paint` procedure was called again and the screen was rendered correctly.

However, this mechanism fails if we use buffering. The sole reason for using buffering was not to render the screen again with every call to `paint`. Instead, we must let the initial image acquisition take its course and only build up the buffer when it is finished. To find out when the image is complete, we override the `imageUpdate` function in `ImageObserver`.

The `imageUpdate` function has six parameters (see API). The second parameter indicates the kind of notification used in a particular call. The image acquisition mechanism notifies the observer many times during the acquisition process. The `imageUpdate` function is called when the image size is known, each time that a chunk of the image is ready, and, finally, when the entire image is complete. When you use an Internet browser and look at a Web page that contains an image, you know how these notifications are translated into actions. An Internet browser lays out a Web page as soon as it knows the sizes of the images in the page. Then it gradually fills in the images, as more detailed information becomes available.

We are not interested in incremental rendering. Our code just needs to wait for the image to be complete, copy the image into the buffer, start the tiling, and finally, paint the window. Timing is everything—if any one of these events happens out of order, then the image is not correctly rendered. In Chapter 12, you will learn an elegant way of controlling the timing by synchronizing different threads. Right now, we'll do it by brute force. In the first call to `paint`, we render the GIF file in a buffer of size 1 by 1, simply to force the loading of the GIF file. When the `imageUpdate` function finds that the image is complete, it calls `repaint`, which notices that the buffer needs to be filled, fills the buffer, and then displays it in the window.

```
import java.awt.*;
import java.awt.image.*;
import java.net.*;
import java.io.*;
```

```
class Image2 extends Frame
{  public boolean handleEvent(Event evt)
   {  if (evt.id == Event.WINDOW_DESTROY) System.exit(0);
      return false;
   }

   public Image2()
   {  setTitle("Image2");
      image = Toolkit.getDefaultToolkit().getImage
         ("blue-ball.gif");
   }

   public void update(Graphics g)
   {  paint(g);
   }

   public void paint(Graphics g)
   {  if (image_width <= 0 || image_height <= 0)
      {  buffered_image = createImage(1,1);
         Graphics bg = buffered_image.getGraphics();
         bg.drawImage(image, 0, 0, this);
         bg.dispose();
         return;
      }

      Dimension d = size();
      Insets in = insets();

      int client_width = d.width - in.right - in.left;
      int client_height = d.height - in.bottom - in.top;

      if (client_width > buffer_width || client_height >
         buffer_height)
      // size has increased
      {  buffer_width = client_width;
         buffer_height = client_height;

         buffered_image = createImage
            (buffer_width, buffer_height);
         Graphics bg = buffered_image.getGraphics();
         bg.drawImage(image, 0, 0, null);
         for (int i = 0; i <= buffer_width / image_width; i++)
            for (int j = 0; j <= buffer_height / image_height; j++)
               if (i + j > 0) bg.copyArea
                  (0, 0, image_width, image_height, i
                     * image_width, j * image_height);
         bg.dispose();
      }
```

```
        g.drawImage(buffered_image, 0, 0, this);
    }

    public boolean imageUpdate(Image img, int infoflags,
        int x, int y, int width, int height)
    {   if ((infoflags & ImageObserver.ALLBITS) != 0)
        {   // image is complete
            image_width = image.getWidth(null);
            image_height = image.getHeight(null);
            repaint();
            return false;
        }
        return true; // want more info
    }

    int buffer_width = 0;
    int buffer_height = 0;
    int image_width = 0;
    int image_height = 0;
    Image image;
    Image buffered_image;

    public static void main(String args[])
    {   Frame f = new Image2();
        f.resize(300, 200);
        f.show();
    }
}
```

```
java.awt.ImageObserver
```

- `boolean imageUpdate(Image img, int infoflags, int x, int y,
   int width, int height)`

this function is called to notify the observer of progress in the rendering process.

Parameters:

`img`	the image that is being acquired
`infoflags`	a combination of the following flags:

- `ABORT`   the image acquisition was aborted

- `ALLBITS`   all bits of the image are now available

- `ERROR`   an error was encountered in the acquisition process

- FRAMEBITS   a complete frame of a multi-frame image is now available for drawing
- HEIGHT   the height of the image is now known (and passed in the height argument of this call)
- PROPERTIES   the properties of the image are now available
- SOMEBITS   some (but not all) bits of the image are available. The x, y, width, and height arguments of this call give the bounding box of the new pixels
- WIDTH   the width of the image is now known (and passed in the width argument of this call)

x, y, width, height   further information about the image, dependent on infoflags

---

java.awt.Component

- void repaint()

causes a repaint of the component by calling update "as soon as possible."

- public void repaint(int x, int y, int width, int height)

causes a repaint of a part of the component by calling update "as soon as possible."

Parameters:

x   the *x*-coordinate of the top left corner of the area to be repainted

y   the *y*-coordinate of the top left corner of the area to be repainted

width   the width of the area to be repainted

height   the height of the area to be repainted

CHAPTER

7

- Panels

- Canvases

- Text Input

- Text Areas

- Making Choices

- Flow Layouts Revisited

- Border Layout

- Card Layout

- Grid Layout

- Grid Bag Layout

- Using No Layout Manager

- Custom Layout Managers

- Dialog Boxes

- Data Exchange

- Menus

- Keyboard Events

- Mouse Events

- Scroll Bars

Designing User Interfaces with AWT

This chapter shows you how to design a graphical user interface (GUI) in Java applications. The idea is that you construct the user interface with various building blocks such as buttons, input areas for text (text fields), and scroll bars. You can then program the interface to respond to various events. (After all, what good is a button if you can't tell when it is clicked, or a text field box if you can't detect keystrokes in it.)

In Java, the various GUI building blocks are usually called *components*.

Components, in turn, are placed inside a Java object called a *container*. For example, a dialog box in Java would be made up of the surrounding container and, inside of it, the components needed to make the dialog box useable, such as a text field and at least one button.

(This way of working should be familiar to Windows or X-Windows programmers. These building blocks are called *controls* in Windows programming and *widgets* in X-Windows programming. The best analogy to a container is probably the Windows notion of a *parent window*. In X-Windows there actually is a notion of a *container widget*, which is [probably] where the Java designers got the idea for a container.)

A VB *form* is a good analogy for the Java notion of a container.

The same user interface components are used to build both stand-alone programs and applets. (For GUI-based browser *applets* please see Chapter 8.)

To build a user interface you obviously need to decide how your interface should look. In particular, what components are needed and how should they appear? This is often easiest with old-fashioned paper and pencil since Java has no form designer like those in VB or Delphi. When you are satisfied with the design, you need to convert the design to Java code. Unfortunately, because of the lack of a form designer to generate code templates, you need to write code for *everything*. In particular, code (often lots of it) is needed to:

1. make the components in the user interface look the way you want them to,

2. position (lay out) the user interface components where you want them to be inside a window,

3. Handle user input, in particular, program the components to recognize the events to which you want them to respond.

We start this chapter with an example that demonstrates how things work in a simple situation. The rest of this chapter shows you how to use all the user interface components and layout mechanisms that AWT has to offer.

A Simple Example

Our first example is a window populated with *lots* of buttons—see Figure 7-1. When you click on one of the buttons, the background color of the window changes. Although this is not a terribly useful program, it will show you the basic methods for building an AWT-based user interface. For example, we need to position and size the buttons as well as make them respond to a mouse click. (Even this simple application requires 30 lines of code. This gives you an idea of how complex a sophisticated GUI application, with many different components responding to multiple events, will be!)

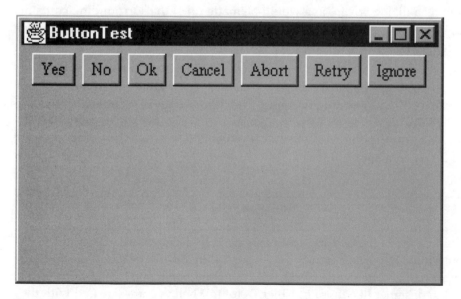

Figure 7-1

Let us go through the elements of this program one by one. First, as you learned in the last chapter, *every* graphics application uses a class derived from `Frame` to describe the top-level window. For a GUI-based program, you add the code to create the user interface elements in the class constructor of the derived class.

We begin by using the `setTitle` method that you saw in the last chapter to give a title to the window. Thus, the constructor begins:

```
public class ButtonTest extends Frame
{   public ButtonTest()
    {   setTitle("Button Test");
        . . .
    }
    . . .
}
```

Actually adding the buttons to the frame occurs through a call to a method named (quite mnemonically) `add`. For our example, the appropriate piece of the constructor is shown below. (The blank line is for a statement that lays out the buttons—we will cover this statement shortly.)

```
public class ButtonTest extends Frame
{   public ButtonTest()
    {   setTitle("Button Test:");
        // important line for the layout is missing next
        add(new Button("Yes"));
        add(new Button("No"));
        . . .
    }
    . . .
}
```

The idea is that the `add` method takes as a parameter the specific component to be added to the frame. Since a component is a Java object, it is usually convenient to create it when you add it to the frame—hence the call to new in the above example. Of course, we always use new with a constructor for the object concerned. Notice that, in this case, the `Button` constructor for the `Button` class actually lets us specify the string that we want to appear on the button.

If you want to set the color of the button, you must:

1. first give a name to the button instance,

2. invoke the `setBackground` method on it,

3. then add the button.

Here's an example of a fragment that would do this:

```
Button yellowButton = new Button("Yellow");
yellowButton.setBackground(color.yellow);
add(yellowButton);
```

Layout

Notice that, in the code above, we did not specify the positions of the buttons. This is true of AWT in general. You do not specify absolute positions for interface elements. This is very different from Windows programming, for example, for which you would specify the exact position of each button in a dialog box. (You may not have paid attention to this if you use a "resource editor" that lets you drag and drop buttons onto the dialog box or if you use VB or Delphi. But, if you look carefully into the resource description—the .RC file or the property sheet of the button—you will find the x and y positions of every button listed.)

There is a reason why AWT works this way: it is designed to be platform independent. In particular, you have no idea what fonts are installed on your user's computer, or how thick the buttons are in the user interface in his or her system. For example, Motif buttons have a different shape than Windows buttons.

(To some degree, Windows programmers have the same problem—they usually just don't bother compensating. For example, the user of a Windows program may have a high-resolution graphics adapter with large fonts or a simple VGA with small fonts. Similarly, buttons look different in the various versions of Windows. To partially compensate for this, button coordinates in Windows are not measured in pixels, but in "dialog units." These dialog units are derived from the size of the system font. This is a bit of a hack that actually works pretty well most of the time. Of course, users who install Troglodyte Bold as their system font probably get some overlapping buttons on their dialog boxes—the feeling in Redmond is, of course, if you choose to do this, you don't deserve better results.)

AWT has a much more general and elegant mechanism. When you add buttons in the container, you specify a general rule for the layout. The buttons are then laid out automatically, regardless of the size of the Window. In our program, the one line that was missing in the fragments above was for the statement that constructed a new *flow layout* for the class. Usually it is important that the layout be done *before* we add the interface elements. (Although in the case of flow layouts, strictly speaking, it isn't necessary.) The actual constructor thus begins like this:

```
public class ButtonTest extends Frame
{   public ButtonTest()
    {   setTitle("Button Test:");
        setLayout(new FlowLayout());
        add(new Button("Yellow"));
        add(new Button("Blue"));
        . . .
    }
    . . .
}
```

A flow layout object simply adds buttons until the current row is full, then starts a new row of buttons. Moreover, the flow layout object keeps each set of buttons centered in an individual row. You can see the flow layout in action when you resize the test application (see Figure 7-2). If you make the window narrower, the buttons are rearranged. That is a neat feature of Java and a great savings in programming time. Regardless of how the user resizes the window, you can be sure the buttons always stay neatly centered.

One point to keep in mind when using any layout manager (even one as simple as the flow layout manager) is that the add method being called belongs to the underlying panel, not to the layout manager. However, what is going on internally is that the layout manager is sent the information derived from the use of the add method.

Figure 7-2

Making the Buttons Responsive

Finally, you must learn how to make the program respond when a user clicks on one of the buttons. As you saw in the previous chapter, AWT programs can be event driven. The operating system sends event notifications to the running Java program when various events occur. Then, as an AWT programmer, you need to know:

- what events to expect and

- how to trap them (that is, which methods get called when the event occurs).

Then, all you need to do is:

- override those methods in your class and

- insert the desired actions into the methods that are called by the event handler.

When a button is clicked, the `action` method is the one that is triggered (called). It has two arguments: a description of the event (which we will analyze in greater detail later) and a generic argument that varies with different event types. For button events, the second argument is simply the string on the face of the button. In this program (as well as in most—if not all—applets), the strings of all the buttons are distinct, so we can use them to determine what happened. (If there were two buttons, both labeled "OK," we would need to work much harder to differentiate between the two—but, of course, having two OK buttons in the same window is rather poor GUI design.) Here's the framework code for the `action` method:

```java
public boolean action(Event evt, Object arg)
{   if (arg.equals("Yellow")) setBackground(Color.yellow);
    else if (arg.equals("Blue")) setBackground(Color.blue);
    else if . . .
    else return false; // action not handled
    repaint(); // force color change
    return true; // action handled
}
```

If you declare an object instance in Java with code like this

```java
Button yesButton = new Button("Yes");
```

your instinct would be to regard yesButton as the name of the button: unfortunately, this can lead you astray. A better analogy is to think of this as an alias for the button, much like the one you would get by using the Set command. There is no real notion of a name property of objects in Java.

The Complete Code for the Button Test Example

Since you now have seen at least one way to accomplish the three essential tasks of AWT user interface programs, you might want to see the whole code for the Button Test application. (The only significant addition is the `main` method to size the window and make sure the window will die if the user tries to close it!) You saw this kind of code in the last chapter. Here's the entire code:

```java
import java.awt.*;

public class ButtonTest extends Frame
{  public ButtonTest()
   {  setTitle("ButtonTest");
      setLayout(new FlowLayout());
      add(new Button("Yes"));
      add(new Button("No"));
      add(new Button("Ok"));
      add(new Button("Cancel"));
      add(new Button("Abort"));
      add(new Button("Retry"));
      add(new Button("Ignore"));
   }

   public boolean handleEvent(Event evt)
   {  if (evt.id == Event.WINDOW_DESTROY) System.exit(0);
      return super.handleEvent(evt);
   }

   public boolean action(Event evt, Object arg)
   {  if (arg.equals("Yes")) setBackground(Color.yellow);
      else if (arg.equals("No")) setBackground(Color.blue);
      else if (arg.equals("Ok")) setBackground(Color.orange);
      else if (arg.equals("Cancel"))
         setBackground(Color.cyan);
      else if (arg.equals("Abort"))
         setBackground(Color.pink);
      else if (arg.equals("Retry"))
         setBackground(Color.red);
      else if (arg.equals("Ignore"))
         setBackground(Color.white);
      else return false;
      repaint();
      return true;
   }

   public static void main(String[] args)
   {  Frame f = new ButtonTest();
      f.resize(320, 200);
      f.show();
   }
}
```

API Syntax Elements

`java.awt.Button`

* `Button(String s)`

constructs a button.

Parameters:

> s   the label that will appear on the face of the button

`java.awt.Container`

* `setLayout(LayoutManager m)`

sets the layout manager for this container.

* `add(Component c)`

adds a component to this container.

Panels

In our first example, we dumped all the buttons into a window and let the flow layout manager worry about arranging them. In practice, that would result in a very messy and unstructured dialog box in most situations. You obviously need a more precise method of locating components. In Java, you can think of dividing a top-level window into *panels*. Panels act as (smaller) containers for interface elements and can themselves be arranged inside the window. For example, you can have one panel for the buttons and another for the text fields. The result can be a precise positioning of components. What you do in Java is:

* build up a panel the way you want it to look,

* then add the panel to the window.

Think of a panel as corresponding to a picture box without a boundary—it is invisible to the user but still functions as a container.

For example, look at Figure 7-3. The three buttons at the bottom of the screen are all contained in a panel. The panel is put into the "south" end of the window.

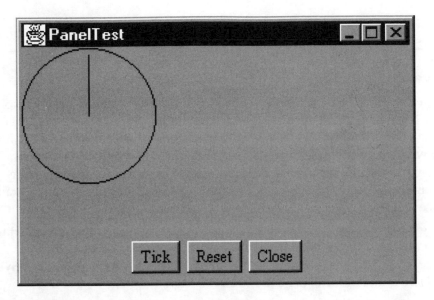

Figure 7-3

So suppose you want to add a panel with three buttons as in Figure 7-3. As you might expect, you first create a new instance of a `Panel` object, before you add the individual buttons to it. You then use the `setLayout` method of the `Panel` class to tell the panel that you will be using a `FlowLayout` manager in it. Finally you add the individual buttons, using the `add` method you have seen before. (And you add buttons under the control of the `FlowLayout` manager, so they have all the good properties you have seen before.)

Here's a code fragment that (after you import `java.awt.*` and add the other necessary code) adds a panel in the south end of a container.

```
public class PanelTest extends Frame
{   public PanelTest()
    {   setTitle("Panel test");
        Panel p = new Panel();
        p.setLayout(new FlowLayout());
        p.add(new Button("Tick"));
        p.add(new Button("Reset"));
        p.add(new Button("Close"));
        add("South", p);
    }
    //rest of the code goes here

}
```

> When Java displays a window, the panel boundaries are not visible to the user. Panels are just an organizing mechanism for the user interface designer.

Canvases

Once you start filling up a window with lots of interface elements and multiple panels, it is best not to draw directly onto the window surface any more. This is because your drawing may interfere with the buttons. Instead, you add a *canvas* to the window. A canvas is simply a rectangular area in which you can draw. (In contrast, a panel is a rectangular area into which you can place user interface components.) We use the canvas in the sample program for this section to draw the face of a clock.

Making a canvas is a bit more complex than using a panel, because you need to specify how to draw on the canvas. This means you must derive a new class from `Canvas` and then override (redefine) the `paint` procedure in your derived class. Here is an outline of the `ClockCanvas` class:

```
class ClockCanvas extends Canvas
{   public void paint(Graphics g)
    {   g.drawOval(0, 0, 100, 100);
        // draw hour and minute hand
        . . .
    }
    public void tick() { minutes++; repaint(); }
    public void reset() { minutes = 0; }
    private int minutes = 0;
}
```

Just as we derived classes from `Frame` in the previous chapter to draw on the entire frame, we now derive a new class from `Canvas` to draw on a specific area of the window. We also add methods to communicate with the canvas. (In our case, the `tick` and `reset` functions.)

Our sample program is getting a bit more complicated; it has two classes:

- The first class is derived from `Frame`. It describes how the main window is different from the default window. (In our case, the difference is simply that it has buttons and a canvas.)

- The second class is derived from `Canvas`. It describes how our canvas is different from the default. (It draws a clock face!)

Notice that we didn't need to extend the `Panel` class because the standard class already does everything necessary to manage the buttons we want to place on the window.

Here is the complete program:

```java
import java.awt.*;
public class PanelTest extends Frame
{   public PanelTest()
    {   setTitle("PanelTest");
        Panel p = new Panel();
        p.setLayout(new FlowLayout());
        p.add(new Button("Tick"));
        p.add(new Button("Reset"));
        p.add(new Button("Close"));
        add("South", p);
        clock = new ClockCanvas();
        add("Center", clock);
    }

    public boolean handleEvent(Event evt)
    {   if (evt.id == Event.WINDOW_DESTROY) System.exit(0);
        return super.handleEvent(evt);
    }

    public boolean action(Event evt, Object arg)
    {   if (arg.equals("Tick")) clock.tick();
        else if (arg.equals("Reset")) clock.reset();
        else if (arg.equals("Close")) System.exit(0);
        else return false;
        return true;
    }

    public static void main(String[] args)
    {   Frame f = new PanelTest();
        f.resize(300, 200);
        f.show();
    }

    private ClockCanvas clock;

}

class ClockCanvas extends Canvas
{   public void paint(Graphics g)
    {   g.drawOval(0, 0, 100, 100);
        double hourAngle = 2 * Math.PI * (minutes - 3 * 60)
            / (12 * 60);
        double minuteAngle = 2 * Math.PI * (minutes - 15)
            / 60;
        g.drawLine(50, 50,
            50 + (int)(30 * Math.cos(hourAngle)),
            50 + (int)(30 * Math.sin(hourAngle)));
```

```
    g.drawLine(50, 50,
        50 + (int)(45 * Math.cos(minuteAngle)),
        50 + (int)(45 * Math.sin(minuteAngle)));
    }

    public void reset()
    {   minutes = 0;
        repaint();
    }

    public void tick()
    {   minutes++;
        repaint();
    }

    private int minutes = 0;
}
```

API Definitions Used

`java.awt.Container`

• `Component add(String name, Component c)`

adds a component to this container.

Parameters:

name   a string that has a meaning for the layout manager. For example, "South" directs the `BorderLayout` manager (the default manager for frames) to add the component to the bottom of the container.

c   the component to be added

Text Input

Obviously, Java programs would have little use if they could only draw pretty pictures. You need to have a way to accept input from a user. In Java, the areas used to input text are called *text fields*.

The usual way to add a text field to a window is to actually add it to a panel—just as you would a button:

```
Panel p = new Panel();
TextField tf = new TextField("New text field", 20);
p.add(tf);
```

This code adds a text field and initializes the text field by placing the string `"New text field"` inside of it. The second parameter of this constructor sets the width. In this case the width is 20 "columns." Unfortunately, a column is a rather imprecise measurement. One column is the expected width of one character in the font you are using for the text. The idea is that if you expect the inputs to be n characters or less, you are supposed to specify n as the column width. In practice, this measurement doesn't work out too well, and you should add 1 or 2 to the maximum input length to be on the safe side.

> The column width that you set in the `TextField` constructor is not an upper limit on the number of characters the user can enter. The user can still type in longer strings, but the input scrolls when the text exceeds the length of the field, which is irritating.

In general, of course, you want to let the user add text (or edit the existing text) in a text field. Of course, quite often text fields start out blank. For this, just use the empty string as the first parameter for the `TextField` constructor:

```
TextField tf = new TextField("", 20);
```

You can change the contents of the text field at any time with the `setText` method. For example:

```
hourField.setText("12");
```

And you can find out what the user typed by calling the `getText` method. For example, if you want to trim any extraneous spaces from the data in a text field, use something like:

```
String hour = hourField.getText().trim();
```

To change the font in which the user text appears, use the `setFont` method in `java.awt.Component` (see the previous chapter for more on this method).

`java.awt.TextField`

• `TextField(String text, int cols)`

constructs a new `TextField`.

Parameters:

text	the text to be displayed
cols	the number of columns

`java.awt.TextComponent`

• `void setText(String t)`

changes the text of a text component.

Parameters:

t	the new text

`java.awt.TextComponent`

• `String getText()`

returns the text contained in this text component.

A Clock Example Program—First Steps

Let us put a few text boxes to work in the clock program that we mentioned a moment ago. Figure 7-4 shows the running application. Instead of a reset button, there are now two text fields for entering the hours and minutes. When you click on the "Set time" button, the clock changes.

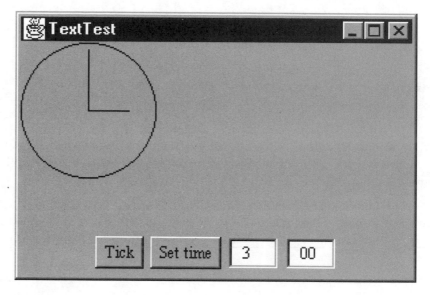

Figure 7-4

The program is essentially a straightforward extension of what you have seen before—except for two important points. The first is that you add text fields to a panel in a different fashion than the way in which you added buttons. Notice the contrast in the following code:

```
p.add(new Button("Set time"));
hourField = new TextField("12", 3);
p.add(hourField);
```

Why did we not just use p.add(new TextField("12", 3))? If we did this, we would have no handle for the text field component, so there would be no way to refer to it for future code. And we *do* need to remember the text fields in order to track them (in particular, to get text into them and to get the data out). (We don't need to have handles for buttons because they can be identified by their title strings.)

When the user clicks on the "Set time" button, we use the getText method to obtain the user input string. Unfortunately, that is what we get: a string. We need to convert the string to an integer. Java would like us to use the unbelievably complex incantation

```
int hours = Integer.parse1nt(hourField.getText().trim())
```

But this code won't work right when the user types a non-integer string, such as "two", into the text field, or even leaves the field blank. Try it out: the terminal window will display an ugly error message complaining about a `java.lang.NumberFormatException`.

We use our `atoi` helper function in the `corejava` package, but it does no error-checking at all, which isn't good for user interface design. We will tackle the issue of validating input in the next section.

```java
import java.awt.*;
import corejava.*;

public class TextTest extends Frame
{  public TextTest()
   {  setTitle("TextTest");
      Panel p = new Panel();
      p.setLayout(new FlowLayout());
      p.add(new Button("Tick"));
      p.add(new Button("Set time"));
      hourField = new TextField("12", 3);
      p.add(hourField);
      minuteField = new TextField("00", 3);
      p.add(minuteField);

      add("South", p);
      clock = new ClockCanvas();
      add("Center", clock);
   }

   public boolean handleEvent(Event evt)
   {  if (evt.id == Event.WINDOW_DESTROY) System.exit(0);
      return super.handleEvent(evt);
   }

   public boolean action(Event evt, Object arg)
   {  if (arg.equals("Tick")) clock.tick();
      else if (arg.equals("Set time"))
      {  int hours = Format.atoi(hourField.getText());
         int minutes = Format.atoi(minuteField.getText());
         clock.setTime(hours, minutes);
      }
      else return false;
      return true;
   }
```

```
        private TextField hourField;
        private TextField minuteField;
        private ClockCanvas clock;

        public static void main(String[] args)
        {   Frame f = new TextTest();
            f.resize(300, 200);
            f.show();
        }
    }

    class ClockCanvas extends Canvas
    {   public void paint(Graphics g)
        {   g.drawOval(0, 0, 100, 100);
            double hourAngle = 2 * Math.PI * (minutes - 3 * 60) / (12 * 60);
            double minuteAngle = 2 * Math.PI * (minutes - 15) / 60;
            g.drawLine(50, 50, 50 + (int)(30 * Math.cos(hourAngle)),
                50 + (int)(30 * Math.sin(hourAngle)));
            g.drawLine(50, 50, 50 + (int)(45 * Math.cos(minuteAngle)),
                50 + (int)(45 * Math.sin(minuteAngle)));
        }

        public void setTime(int h, int m)
        {   minutes = h * 60 + m;
            repaint();
        }

        public void tick()
        {   minutes++;
            repaint();
        }

        private int minutes = 0;
    }
```

Input Validation

The problems mentioned in the last section are commonplace—if you have a place to enter text, you will need to check that the input makes sense before you work with it. For most text fields you need to test whether or not:

- the input value is legal (that is, not blank and a number) and

- the number is within the correct range (*e.g.*, 0–59 for minutes).

In either case, if there are problems, then it is usually best to move the cursor back into the edit field with the faulty entry so that the user can correct the problem.

Because this is such a common task, we will develop a class for it. (We hope you find this class—or a version of your own that you build on it—useful in your own coding.)

The class `IntTextBox` that we will design next is a text box especially for integer input. It would, of course, be nice if we could simply block all keystrokes except `'0'` ... `'9'`, but unfortunately, that is not possible. The native user interface component (that is, the actual Windows or X-Windows text box) handles the keystrokes and puts the characters on the screen before telling AWT what has happened. At any rate, we do have to allow a minus sign and then must check that the user has typed no more than one minus sign in the first position.

A good time to check for valid inputs would be when the user moves the mouse out of the current field. The natural way to do this is in some sort of "lost focus" event. There is supposed to be a "lost focus" event generated whenever the text box loses the focus, but, at least for Windows 95, the current version of Java doesn't support one. Instead, our class requires the programmer to manually determine when to check the input. In our case, the best point at which to check is when the user clicks on the "Set time" button. The code is as follows:

```
if (hourField.isValid() && minuteField.isValid())
    clock.setTime(hourField.getValue(), minuteField.getValue());
```

The `isValid()` method has the side effect of moving the cursor back to the field if the content is not valid. For example, if the user entered 27 for the hour, then the first call to `hourField.isValid()` fails, and the clock won't be set. Furthermore, the code moves the cursor back into the `hourField` field.

See the following listing for the code of the `IntTextField` class. Don't worry about the exception and the `try` block—we will get to that in Chapter 10. Note how we use the `requestFocus` method call to shift the focus back into the text component if its content is not valid.

```
import java.awt.*;
import corejava.*;

public class ValidationTest extends Frame
{   public ValidationTest()
    {   setTitle("ValidationTest");
        Panel p = new Panel();
        p.setLayout(new FlowLayout());
        p.add(new Button("Tick"));
        p.add(new Button("Set time"));
        hourField = new IntTextField(12, 0, 23, 3);
        p.add(hourField);
```

```java
      minuteField = new IntTextField(0, 0, 59, 3);
      p.add(minuteField);

      add("South", p);
      clock = new ClockCanvas();
      add("Center", clock);
   }

   public boolean handleEvent(Event evt)
   {  if (evt.id == Event.WINDOW_DESTROY) System.exit(0);
      return super.handleEvent(evt);
   }

   public boolean action(Event evt, Object arg)
   {  if (arg.equals("Tick")) clock.tick();
      else if (arg.equals("Set time"))
      {  if (hourField.isValid() && minuteField.isValid())
            clock.setTime(hourField.getValue(),
               minuteField.getValue());
      }
      else return super.action(evt, arg);
      return true;
   }

   public static void main(String[] args)
   {  Frame f = new ValidationTest();
      f.resize(300, 200);
      f.show();
   }

   private IntTextField hourField;
   private IntTextField minuteField;
   private ClockCanvas clock;

}


class ClockCanvas extends Canvas
{  public void paint(Graphics g)
   {  g.drawOval(0, 0, 100, 100);
      double hourAngle = 2 * Math.PI * (minutes - 3 * 60) / (12 * 60);
      double minuteAngle = 2 * Math.PI * (minutes - 15) / 60;
      g.drawLine(50, 50, 50 + (int)(30 * Math.cos(hourAngle)),
         50 + (int)(30 * Math.sin(hourAngle)));
      g.drawLine(50, 50, 50 + (int)(45 * Math.cos(minuteAngle)),
         50 + (int)(45 * Math.sin(minuteAngle)));
   }
```

```java
    public void setTime(int h, int m)
    {   minutes = h * 60 + m;
        repaint();
    }

    public void tick()
    {   minutes++;
        repaint();
    }

    private int minutes = 0;
}
```

```java
package corejava;

import java.awt.*;

public class IntTextField extends TextField
{   public IntTextField(int def, int min, int max,
        int size)
    {   super("" + def, size);
        low = min;
        high = max;
    }

    public boolean isValid()
    {   int value;
        try
        {   value = Integer.valueOf(getText().trim()).intValue();
            if (value < low || value > high)
                throw new NumberFormatException();
        }
        catch (NumberFormatException e)
        {   requestFocus();
            return false;
        }
        return true;
    }

    public int getValue()
    {   return Format.atoi(getText());
    }

    private int low;
    private int high;
}
```

`java.awt.Component`

• `void requestFocus()`

requests that this component gets the input focus.

Text Areas

Sometimes you need to collect user input that is more than one line long. Use the `TextArea` component for this. When you place a text area in your program, a user can enter any number of lines of text; each line ends with `'\n'`. Figure 7-5 shows a text area.

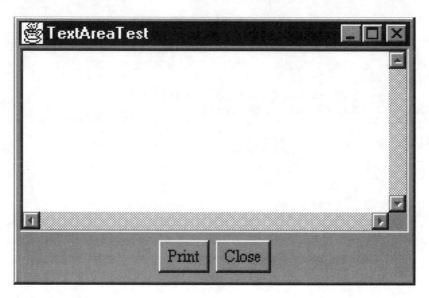

Figure 7-5

In the `TextArea` constructor, you specify the number of rows and columns for the component. For example:

```
Comments = new TextArea(8, 40); // 8 lines of 40 columns each
```

(where the columns parameter works as before—add a few more columns for safety's sake). And, as before, the user is not restricted to the number of rows and columns; the text simply scrolls when the user inputs too much.

Here is the complete code for the text area demo.

```java
import java.awt.*;

public class TextAreaTest extends Frame
{   public TextAreaTest()
    {   setTitle("TextAreaTest");
        Panel p = new Panel();
        p.setLayout(new FlowLayout());
        p.add(new Button("Print"));
        p.add(new Button("Close"));

        add("South", p);
        ta = new TextArea(8, 40);
        add("Center", ta);
    }

    public boolean handleEvent(Event evt)
    {   if (evt.id == Event.WINDOW_DESTROY) System.exit(0);
        return super.handleEvent(evt);
    }

    public boolean action(Event evt, Object arg)
    {   if (arg.equals("Print"))
            System.out.println(ta.getText());
        else if (arg.equals("Close"))
            System.exit(0);
        else return super.action(evt, arg);
        return true;
    }

    public static void main(String[] args)
    {   Frame f = new TextAreaTest();
        f.resize(300, 200);
        f.show();
    }

    private TextArea ta;
}
```

java.awt.TextArea

• TextArea(int rows, int cols)

constructs a new text area.

Parameters:

    rows   the number of rows

    cols   the number of columns

Selecting Text

The text field and text area classes have methods to select (highlight) the text contained in the component. They can also check which text is currently selected.

First, there is the `selectAll()` method, which highlights all the text in the field. You would use this method when presenting the user with an input that they either will want to use exactly as provided, or that they won't want to use at all. In the latter case, they can just type their own input and the first keystroke replaces the selection.

The `select` method selects a part of the text. The arguments of `select` are the same as for `substring`: the first index is the start of the substring, the last is one more than the end. For example, `t.select(10, 15)` selects the tenth to fourteenth character in the text control. End-of-line markers count as one character.

The `getSelectionStart` and `getSelectionEnd` methods return the current selection, and `getSelectedText` returns the highlighted text.

How users highlight text is system dependent. In Windows, you can use the mouse or the standard SHIFT + arrow keys.

`java.awt.TextComponent`

• `void selectAll()`

selects all text in the component.

• `void select(int selStart, int selEnd)`

selects a range of text in the component.

Parameters:

selStart	the first position to select
selEnd	one past the last position to select

• `int getSelectionStart()`

returns the first position of the selected text.

• `int getSelectionEnd()`

returns one past the last position of the selected text.

- `String getSelectedText()`

returns the selected text.

Text Editing

You can write code that modifies the contents of a text area (but not a text field). You can append text at the end, insert text in the middle, and replace text. To delete text, simply replace the text to be deleted with an empty string.

The following program shows how to implement a simple "find-and-replace" feature. Each time you click on the Replace button, the first match of the text in the first field is replaced by the text in the second field.

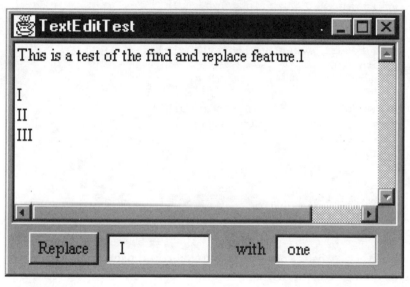

Figure 7-6

```java
import java.awt.*;

public class TextEditTest extends Frame
{   public TextEditTest()
    {   setTitle("TextEditTest");
        Panel p = new Panel();
        p.setLayout(new FlowLayout());
        p.add(new Button("Replace"));
        from = new TextField(10);
        p.add(from);
        p.add(new Label("with"));
        to = new TextField(10);
        p.add(to);
```

```
         add("South", p);
         ta = new TextArea(8, 40);
         add("Center", ta);
      }

      public boolean handleEvent(Event evt)
      {  if (evt.id == Event.WINDOW_DESTROY) System.exit(0);
         return super.handleEvent(evt);
      }

      public boolean action(Event evt, Object arg)
      {  if (arg.equals("Replace"))
         {  String f = from.getText();
            int n = ta.getText().indexOf(f);
            if (n >= 0 && f.length() > 0)
               ta.replaceText(to.getText(), n, n + f.length());
         }
         else return super.action(evt, arg);
         return true;
      }

      public static void main(String[] args)
      {  Frame f = new TextEditTest();
         f.resize(300, 200);
         f.show();
      }

      private TextArea ta;
      private TextField from, to;
   }
```

This is not a very realistic application, but you could use this feature to correct spelling or typing errors in URLs.

java.awt.TextArea

• void insertText(String str, int pos)

inserts a string into the text area.

Parameters:

str	the text to insert
pos	the position at which to insert (0 = first position. Newlines count as one character)

- `void appendText(String str)`

appends the given text to the end of the text already in the text area.

Parameters:

    `str`   the text to insert

- `void replaceText(String str, int start, int end)`

replaces a range of text with another string.

Parameters:

    `str`   the new text

    `start`   the start position of the text to be replaced

    `end`   one past the end position of the text to be replaced

Labeling Fields

Unlike buttons, text fields have no label. If you want to label a field, you need to construct a `Label` object and place it before the field. If you look at the previous program, you will see how one of the text fields is preceded by a label with the text `"with"`. Labels are simple plain-text strings. They have no decorations (for example, no boundaries). They also do not react to user input. However, labels can be positioned inside a container like any other component, using the techniques you have seen before. This lets you place them where you need them.

For example, in the code for the search-and-replace example,

```
p.add(new Label("with"));
```

used the flow layout object to position the label.

`java.awt.Label`

- `Label(String s)`

Parameters:

    `s`   the label text

- `public Label(String s, int align)`

Parameters:

    `s`   the label text

    `align`   one of `LEFT`, `CENTER`, or `RIGHT`

Making Choices

You now know how to collect text input from users, but there are many occasions where you would rather give a user a finite set of choices, rather than have them enter the data in a text field. Using something like a set of check boxes tells the user what choices he or she has. (It also saves you from the trouble of error-checking.) In this section, you will learn how to program check boxes and what Java calls choice lists (which are a special type of list box).

Check Boxes

If you just want to collect a "yes" or "no" input, use a check box component. The user checks the box by clicking inside it and turns off the check mark by clicking inside the box again. Figure 7-7 shows a simple program with two check boxes, one to turn on or off the "italic" attributes of a font and the other for boldface. Each time the user clicks one of the check boxes, we refresh the screen, using the new font attributes.

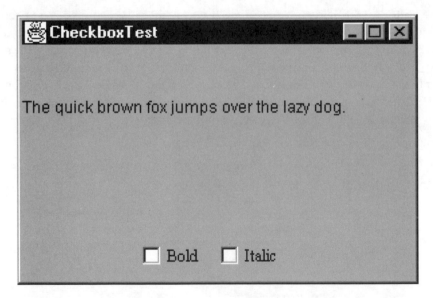

Figure 7-7

When creating a check box, you need to be able to identify the check box object, since you need this information to identify the sender of a check box event. Check boxes will need text next to them to identify them. You give the text that identifies the check box in the constructor. (The text will always appear to the right of the check box.)

```
class MyFrame extends Frame
{   public MyFrame()
    {   Panel p;
        bold = new Checkbox("Bold");
        p.add(bold);
        . . .
    }
    . . .
    private Checkbox bold;
}
```

When the user clicks on a check box, this triggers an action event. The `target` field of the event structure is the originating check box.

"Target" is really a misnomer. The check box is the source of the event.

The `getState` method then retrieves the current state of the check box. It is `false` if unchecked, `true` if checked.

Here is the event handler for the font application. When the state of either check box changes, the code retrieves the current states of both check boxes and then notifies the canvas of the new font attributes to use.

```
public boolean action(Event evt, Object arg)
{   if (evt.target.equals(bold) || evt.target.equals(italic))
    {   int m = 0;
        if (bold.getState()) m += Font.BOLD;
        if (italic.getState()) m += Font.ITALIC;
        fox.setFont(m);
    }
    . . .
}
```

Here is the complete program listing.

```
import java.awt.*;

public class CheckboxTest extends Frame
{   public CheckboxTest()
    {   setTitle("CheckboxTest");
        Panel p = new Panel();
        p.setLayout(new FlowLayout());
        p.add(bold = new Checkbox("Bold"));
        p.add(italic = new Checkbox("Italic"));
        add("South", p);
        fox = new FoxCanvas();
        add("Center", fox);
    }

    public boolean handleEvent(Event evt)
    {   if (evt.id == Event.WINDOW_DESTROY) System.exit(0);
```

```
            return super.handleEvent(evt);
        }

    public boolean action(Event evt, Object arg)
    {   if (evt.target.equals(bold)
            || evt.target.equals(italic))
        {   int m = (bold.getState() ? Font.BOLD : 0)
            + (italic.getState() ?
                Font.ITALIC : 0);
            fox.setFont(m);
        }
        else return super.action(evt, arg);
        return true;
    }
    public static void main(String[] args)
    {   Frame f = new CheckboxTest();
        f.resize(300, 200);
        f.show();
    }
    private FoxCanvas fox;
    private Checkbox bold;
    private Checkbox italic;
}

class FoxCanvas extends Canvas
{   public FoxCanvas()
    { setFont(Font.PLAIN);
    }

    public void setFont(int m)
    {   setFont(new Font("Helvetica", m, 12));
        repaint();
    }
    public void paint(Graphics g)
    {   g.drawString
      ("The quick brown fox jumps over the lazy dog.", 0, 50);
    }
}
```

```
java.awt.Checkbox
• Checkbox(String label)
```

Parameters:

      label   the label on the check box

- `boolean getState()`

returns the state of the check box.

- `void setState(boolean state)`

sets the check box to a new state.

Check Box Groups

In the previous example, the user could check either, both, or none of the two check boxes. In many cases, we want to require the user to check only one of several boxes. When another box is checked, the current one is automatically unchecked. Such a group of boxes is often called a *radio button group* because the buttons work like the station selector buttons on a radio. When you push in one button, the previously depressed button pops out. Figure 7-8 shows a typical example. We allow the user to select a font size among the choices "small", "medium", "large" and "extra large", but of course only one size can be selected at a time.

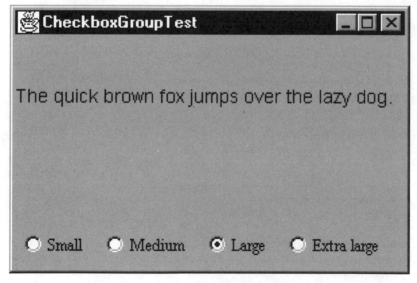

Figure 7-8

Implementing radio button groups is easy in AWT. You construct one object of type `CheckboxGroup` for every group of buttons. The object has no data; it simply serves as the common identifier of the group. You pass the group object into the constructors of the individual buttons.

```
CheckboxGroup g = new CheckboxGroup();
small = new Checkbox("Small", g, false);
medium = new Checkbox("Medium", g, true);
large = new Checkbox("Large", g, false);
extraLarge = new Checkbox("Extra large", g, false);
```

The third argument of the constructor is `true` for the box that should be checked initially, `false` for all others.

If you look again at Figures 7-7 and 7-8, you will note that the appearance of the selection indicators is different. Individual check boxes without a group are square and use a check mark. Grouped check boxes are round and use a dot.

Check Box Groups Event Notification

The event notification mechanism is simple for a check box group. When the user checks a box that is part of a group, Java generates an action event whose "target" is the checked box. You override `action` to test for these events. (Note that the unchecked box does not generate an action.)

```
public boolean action(Event evt, Object arg)
{   if (evt.target.equals(small))
        fox.setSize(8);
    else if (evt.target.equals(medium))
        fox.setSize(10);
    else if (evt.target.equals(large))
        fox.setSize(14);
    else if (evt.target.equals(extraLarge))
        fox.setSize(18);
    else return super.action(evt, arg);
    return true;
}
```

Here is the complete program.

```
import java.awt.*;

public class CheckboxGroupTest extends Frame
{   public CheckboxGroupTest()
    {   setTitle("CheckboxGroupTest");
        Panel p = new Panel();
        p.setLayout(new FlowLayout());
        CheckboxGroup g = new CheckboxGroup();
        p.add(small = new Checkbox("Small", g, false));
        p.add(medium = new Checkbox("Medium", g, true));
        p.add(large = new Checkbox("Large", g, false));
        p.add(extraLarge =
            new Checkbox("Extra large", g, false));
        add("South", p);
        fox = new FoxCanvas();
        add("Center", fox);
```

```
      }

   public boolean handleEvent(Event evt)
   {  if (evt.id == Event.WINDOW_DESTROY) System.exit(0);
      return super.handleEvent(evt);
   }

   public boolean action(Event evt, Object arg)
   {  if (evt.target.equals(small))
         fox.setSize(8);
      else if (evt.target.equals(medium))
         fox.setSize(10);
      else if (evt.target.equals(large))
         fox.setSize(14);
      else if (evt.target.equals(extraLarge))
         fox.setSize(18);
      else return super.action(evt, arg);
      return true;
   }
   public static void main(String[] args)
   {  Frame f = new CheckboxGroupTest();
      f.resize(300, 200);
      f.show();
   }

   private FoxCanvas fox;
   private Checkbox small;
   private Checkbox medium;
   private Checkbox large;
   private Checkbox extraLarge;
}

class FoxCanvas extends Canvas
{  public FoxCanvas()
   {  setSize(10);
   }

   public void setSize(int p)
   {  setFont(new Font("Helvetica", Font.PLAIN, p));
      repaint();
   }

   public void paint(Graphics g)
   {  g.drawString
    ("The quick brown fox jumps over the lazy dog.", 0, 50);
   }
}
```

```
java.awt.Checkbox
```
• Checkbox(String label, CheckboxGroup group, boolean state)

Parameters:

label	the label on the check box
group	the group to which this check box belongs
state	the initial state of the check box

Choice Boxes (Drop-Down Lists)

If you have more than a handful of alternatives, radio buttons are not a good choice, because they take up too much screen space. Instead, you should probably use a choice box which is a drop-down list box. When the user clicks on the field, this drops down a list of choices, and the user can then select one of them (see Figure 7-9).

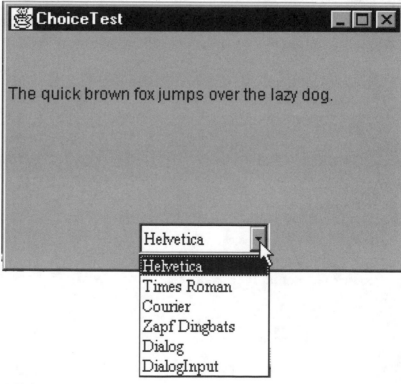

Figure 7-9

The `Choice` class implements these lists. In the example program, the user can choose a font style from a list of styles (Times Roman, Helvetica, Courier, etc.). You add the choice items with the `addItem` method. In our program, `addItem` is only called in the constructor, but you can call it any time.

```
style = new Choice();
style.addItem("Times Roman");
style.addItem("Helvetica");
. . .
```

Once added, items cannot be removed from a choice box.

When the user selects an item from a choice box, this generates an action event. The target of the action event is the component chosen, and the second argument of the call to `action` is the selected string.

```
public boolean action(Event evt, Object arg)
{    if (evt.target.equals(style))
     fox.setStyle((String)arg);
     . . .
}
```

AWT has no "combo box" control. (A combo box is a combination of a text box and a choice list, in which you can pick one of the choices or type in another input.)

`java.awt.Choice`

• void addItem(String item)

adds an item to this choice component.

Parameters:

    item   the item to add

The `List` Component

The `List` component is similar to the `Choice` component except that the user will always see the items. `List` components take up more screen space, but also make it obvious to the user what can be chosen from a list.

One other difference is that for a `List` component, but not a `Choice` component, you can allow the user to make multiple selections. If you permit multiple selection for a list box, the user can select any combination of the strings in the box, using whatever techniques are appropriate in the target operating system (SHIFT + Click or CTRL + Click for Windows, for example).

Figure 7-10 shows an admittedly silly example. The user can select the attributes for the fox, such as `"quick"`, `"brown"`, `"hungry"`, `"wild"`, and, because we ran out of attributes, `"static"`, `"private"`, and `"final"`. You can, thus, have the *static, final* fox jump over the lazy dog.

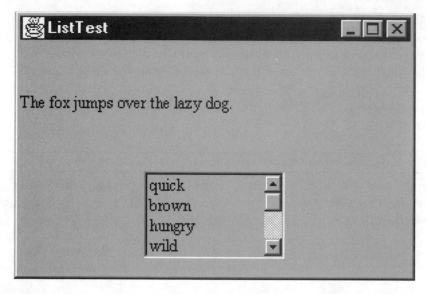

Figure 7-10

Here is a more realistic application: you are going to design an order-taking system; you will use a list box to give users a choice of items to order. Why a list box rather than a choice box? Well, your employer hopes that the customer will order most or all of the items, so you want to make it easy for him or her to select more than one.

The constructor of the list box has

- parameters that take the number of items you want to display at one time (if you add more items, they scroll) and

- a flag to indicate whether or not you want to allow multiple selection.

You initialize a list box just as you would a choice component (drop-down list): use the `addItem` method. If you want to activate an initial set of selections, use the select method.

```
words = new List(4, true); //4 items allow multiple selections
words.addItem("quick");
words.addItem("brown");
   . . .
words.addItem("final");
words.select(0);
words.select(1);
```

The method with which Java notifies a list box of relevant events is not quite as easy as that for the other components. Java triggers the `action` function *only* when the user double-clicks on an item in the list box. The problem is that this is not very intuitive for most users.

Instead, the most user-friendly solution is to track all changes in what the user is selecting. Every time the user selects an item, Java generates an event with the ID LIST_SELECT. Every time the user removes an item from the selection, an event with the ID LIST_DESELECT is generated. These events can be trapped in the handleEvent function.

As a general observation, we could have handled other events in handleEvent instead of action, but it is easier to override action, since it deals with fewer events. We will discuss this in detail in the section on event handling.

Once you are notified that an event has happened, you will want to find out what items are currently selected. This is phenomenally convenient in Java. The getSelectedItems method returns an *array of strings* containing all selected items. (If you have ever done this in C, you probably suffered through a lookup loop, a callback procedure, a memory allocation headache, or all of the above.)

Here is the event handler for our toy program.

```java
public boolean handleEvent(Event evt)
{   if (evt.target.equals(words) && (evt.id == Event.LIST_SELECT
         || evt.id == Event.LIST_DESELECT))
      fox.setAttributes(words.getSelectedItems());
}
```

Here is the program listing. Notice how the setAttributes function builds up the message string from the selected items.

```java
import java.awt.*;

public class ListTest extends Frame
{   public ListTest()
    {   setTitle("ListTest");

        words = new List(4, true);
        words.addItem("quick");
        words.addItem("brown");
        words.addItem("hungry");
        words.addItem("wild");
        words.addItem("silent");
        words.addItem("huge");
        words.addItem("private");
        words.addItem("abstract");
        words.addItem("static");
        words.addItem("final");

        Panel p = new Panel();
        p.add(words);
        add("South", p);
        fox = new FoxCanvas();
        add("Center", fox);
```

```
      }

   public boolean handleEvent(Event evt)
   {  if (evt.id == Event.LIST_SELECT
         || evt.id == Event.LIST_DESELECT)
      {  if (evt.target.equals(words))
            fox.setAttributes(words.getSelectedItems());
      }
      else if (evt.id == Event.WINDOW_DESTROY)
         System.exit(0);
      else return super.handleEvent(evt);
      return true;
   }

   FoxCanvas fox;
   List words;

   public static void main(String[] args)
   {  Frame f = new ListTest();
      f.resize(300, 200);
      f.show();
   }
}

class FoxCanvas extends Canvas
{  public FoxCanvas()
   {  setAttributes(new String[0]);
   }

   public void setAttributes(String[] w)
   {  text = "The ";
      for (int i = 0; i < w.length; i++)
         text += w[i] + " ";
      text += "fox jumps over the lazy dog.";
      repaint();
   }

   public void paint(Graphics g)
   {  g.drawString(text, 0, 50);
   }

   private String text;
}
```

```
java.awt.List
```
• `List(int rows, boolean multipleSelections)`

Parameters:

> rows   the number of items to show
>
> multipleSelections   true when multiple selections are allowed

• `String getItem(int index)`

gets an item from a list component.

Parameters:

> index   the position of the item to get

• `void select(int index)`

selects an item in a list component.

Parameters:

> index   the position of the item to select

• `String[] getSelectedItems()`

returns an array containing all selected items.

Sophisticated Layout Management

We have managed to lay out the user interface components of our toy applications by using a couple of panels and canvases, but for more complex tasks, that method is not going to be sufficient. In this section, we discuss all the layout managers that AWT provides to organize components.

> If none of the layout schemes fit your needs, break the surface of your window into separate panels, and lay out each panel separately. Then use another layout manager to organize the panels.

In AWT, *components* are laid out inside *containers*. A component is either a button, a text field or other user interface element, or another container. For example, as we have seen before, a window can contain a canvas (a basic component) and a panel (a component that is itself a container).

Because every container is itself a possible component, the class `Container` derives from `Component`. Figure 7-11 shows the inheritance hierarchy.

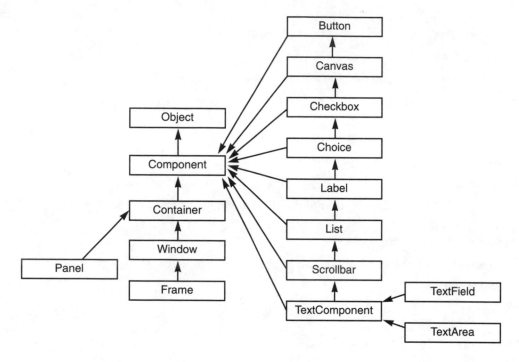

Figure 7-11

As usual, the complexities of real life muddy this issue somewhat. Indeed, panels are containers that can themselves be components, but frames are not. You would not want to stick several frames inside another container. Nevertheless, it is helpful to understand the roles of containers and components when browsing the AWT on-line documentation.

To organize the components in a container, you first specify a layout manager. For example,

```
panel.addLayout(new CardLayout());
```

will use the `CardLayout` class to lay out the panels. After you set the layout manager, you add components to the container. The details of doing this depend on the specific layout manager, but in all cases the information will be obtained from the `add` method of the underlying panel. With the flow layout manager that you have already seen, you can insert the components in random order.

```
panel.add(new Button("Ok"), 4);
```

With the border layout manager, you give a string to indicate component placement.

```
panel.add("South", new TextField());
```

With the grid bag layout, you need to add components sequentially.

```
panel.add(new Checkbox("italic"));
panel.add(new Checkbox("bold"));
```

Flow Layouts Revisited

The simplest layout manager is the one you have already seen: the flow layout. We have used the flow layout for laying out panels in quite a few test programs in this chapter. Components are lined up horizontally until there is no more room, and then a new line of components is started.

You can choose how you want to arrange the components in each line. The default is to center them in the container. The other choices are to align them to the left or to the right of the container. To select that alignment, you specify LEFT or RIGHT in the constructor of the FlowLayout object.

```
toolbar.setLayout(new FlowLayout(FlowLayout.LEFT));
```

When the container is resized, Java automatically reflows the components to fill the available space.

java.awt.FlowLayout

• FlowLayout(int align)

constructs a new FlowLayout with the specified alignment.

Parameters:

align	one of LEFT, CENTER, or RIGHT

Border Layout

The border layout divides the area to be laid out into five areas, called north, south, east, west, and center (see Figure 7-12).

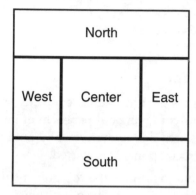

Figure 7-12

The borders are laid out first, and the remaining available space is occupied by the center. When the container is resized, the thickness of the borders is unchanged, but the center area changes its size.

You add components by specifying a string that says in what area the object should be placed. You can specify "North", "South", "East", "West", or "Center". Not all of the positions need to be occupied. Here's an example of using a border layout manager:

```
panel.add("East", new Scrollbar());
```

Border layout is the default for frames and other windows. You need not specify a layout manager for those containers if the border layout works for you.

It is not common to use all four border areas simultaneously. The following program shows a typical case, with scroll bars to the right and bottom, and a tool bar on the top. If you look closely, you will notice that the horizontal scroll bar extends below the vertical scroll bar. If you really want to achieve a more symmetrical and pleasant layout of the scroll bars, you need to use the grid bag layout.

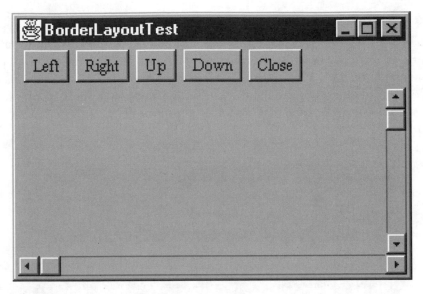

Figure 7-13

```java
import java.awt.*;

public class BorderLayoutTest extends Frame
{   public BorderLayoutTest()
    {   setTitle("BorderLayoutTest");
        Panel p = new Panel();
        p.setLayout(new FlowLayout(FlowLayout.LEFT));
        p.add(new Button("Left"));
        p.add(new Button("Right"));
        p.add(new Button("Up"));
        p.add(new Button("Down"));
        p.add(new Button("Close"));
        add("North", p);
        add("East", new Scrollbar(Scrollbar.VERTICAL));
        add("South", new Scrollbar(Scrollbar.HORIZONTAL));
    }

    public boolean handleEvent(Event evt)
    {   if (evt.id == Event.WINDOW_DESTROY) System.exit(0);
        return super.handleEvent(evt);
    }

    public static void main(String[] args)
    {   Frame f = new BorderLayoutTest();
        f.resize(300, 200);
        f.show();
    }
}
```

Card Layout

Windows 95 uses tabbed dialog boxes when there is a lot of related information to set that can still be organized conveniently into panels. The reason is simple: if you need to gather a lot of information from the user, it is not a good idea to cram dozens of fields into one dialog box. As an example of this, consider the "tabbed dialog" in Netscape that organizes a multitude of configuration options (Figure 7-14).

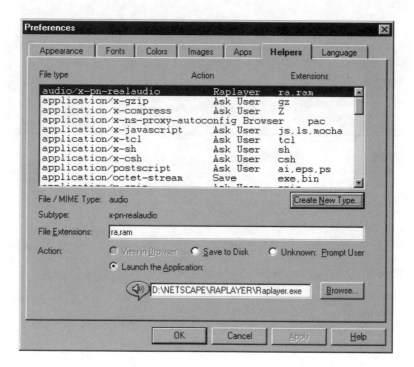

Figure 7-14

The settings are grouped onto individual "index cards," and you flip through them by clicking on one of the tabs.

Java does not have such an elegant looking dialog layout, but the `CardLayout` manager provides the bare rudiments of this functionality. (It gives you only a bit more functionality than using multiple panels would give—although it is more convenient to use.) Unlike the other layouts, which place the objects to be laid out *next to each other*, the card layout places them *behind each other*.

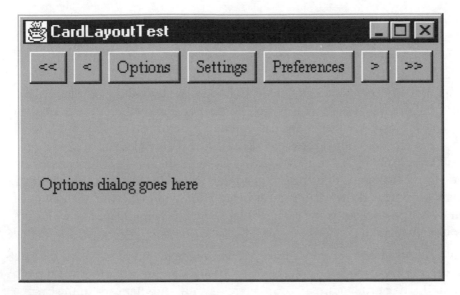

Figure 7-15

The window of this program consists of two areas. The top area is a panel containing a row of buttons that make the different cards show up in the top area. These are analogous to the "tabs" in the tabbed dialogs. For example, if you click on the "Options" button, the "Options" card will show up. Unlike tabbed dialog boxes, we also provided buttons to cycle through the cards and to go to the first and last card in the stack. That probably isn't terribly useful, and we only did it to show how it can be done. The second area holds cards managed by the `CardLayout` manager.

Here is the procedure to set up a card layout.

1. Make a panel of buttons, one for each card.

```
tabs = new Panel(new FlowLayout());
tabs.add(new Button("Options"));
tabs.add(new Button("Settings"));
. . .
```

2. Below it, place another panel. This one will be managed by the `CardLayout` object.

```
cards = new Panel();
layout = new CardLayout();
cards.setLayout(layout);
```

3. Then add the individual labels that identify the cards with the panel.

```
cards.add("Options", new SimpleDialog("Options"));
cards.add("Settings", new SimpleDialog("Settings"));
cards.add("Preferences", new SimpleDialog("Preferences"));
```

(Java internally keeps track of the fact that there are now three "cards" *i.e.*, labels that are filling up the cards. You do not add three different panels when using a card layout manager; instead you add individual cards via a call to add. In our case, the individual cards are identified by the strings "Options", "Settings", and "Dialog". Window's users might want to think of what is going on as analogous to using an MDI interface—with the panel being the parent window and the various cards being child windows. The analogy is, of course, not precise, since one cannot "tile" the cards being managed by a card layout manager.)

Finally, write an action procedure that makes the tab buttons switch the cards. You use the show method of the card layout manager in order to show a particular card. The next and previous methods show another card in the card sequence. The first and last methods show the first and last cards.

```
public boolean action(Event evt, Object arg)
{ if (evt.target instanceof Component &&
      ((Component)evt.target).getParent().equals(tabs))
   // it was one of the tab keys
   {  if (arg.equals("<"))
         layout.next(cards));
      else if (arg.equals(">"))
         layout.next(cards));
      else
         layout.show(cards, (String)arg);
   }
   . . .
}
```

(To keep this example simple, we didn't actually put any data-entry fields on any of the cards. There's just a label that says, "Options dialog goes here". In an actual program, of course, you would have a full-fledged container that is populated by the necessary components.)

Here is the code listing for the sample program.

```java
import java.awt.*;

public class CardLayoutTest extends Frame
{   public CardLayoutTest()
    {   setTitle("CardLayoutTest");

        tabs = new Panel();
        tabs.add(new Button("<<"));
        tabs.add(new Button("<"));
        tabs.add(new Button("Options"));
        tabs.add(new Button("Settings"));
        tabs.add(new Button("Preferences"));
        tabs.add(new Button(">"));
        tabs.add(new Button(">>"));
        add("North", tabs);

        cards = new Panel();
        layout = new CardLayout();
        cards.setLayout(layout);

        cards.add("Options", new SimpleDialog("Options"));
        cards.add("Settings", new SimpleDialog("Settings"));
        cards.add("Preferences",
            new SimpleDialog("Preferences"));

        add("Center", cards);
    }

    public boolean handleEvent(Event evt)
    {   if (evt.id == Event.WINDOW_DESTROY) System.exit(0);
        return super.handleEvent(evt);
    }

    public boolean action(Event evt, Object arg)
    {   if (evt.target instanceof Component &&
            ((Component)evt.target).getParent().equals(tabs))
        {   if (arg.equals("<<")) layout.first(cards);
            else if (arg.equals("<")) layout.previous(cards);
            else if (arg.equals(">")) layout.next(cards);
            else if (arg.equals(">>")) layout.last(cards);
            else layout.show(cards, (String)arg);
        }
        else return super.action(evt, arg);
        return true;
    }

    public static void main(String[] args)
```

```
  {   Frame f = new CardLayoutTest();
      f.resize(320, 200);
      f.show();
  }
  private Panel cards;
  private Panel tabs;
  private CardLayout layout;
}

class SimpleDialog extends Panel
{   SimpleDialog(String name)
    {   setLayout(new BorderLayout());
        add("Center", new Label(name + " dialog goes here"));
        Panel p = new Panel();
        p.add(new Button("Ok"));
        add("South", p);
    }
}
```

`java.awt.CardLayout`

• `void show(Container parent, String name)`

flips to a card of the card layout.

Parameters:

    parent   the container with the card layout

    name   the name of the card

• `void first(Container parent)`

flips to the first card.

Parameters:

    parent   the container with the card layout

• `void next(Container parent)`

flips to the next card.

Parameters:

    parent   the container with the card layout

• `void previous(Container parent)`

flips to the previous card.

Parameters:

    parent   the container with the card layout

- `void last(Container parent)`

flips to the last card.

Parameters:

    `parent`   the container with the card layout

Grid Layout

The grid layout arranges all components in rows and columns. The calculator program in Figure 7-16 uses a grid to arrange the calculator buttons. When you resize the window, the buttons grow and shrink.

Figure 7-16

In the constructor of the grid layout object, you specify how many rows and columns you need.

```
panel.setLayout(new GridLayout(5, 4));
```

You add the components, starting with the first entry in the first row, then the second entry in the first row, and so on.

```
panel.add(new Button("1"));
panel.add(new Button("2"));
```

Here is the source listing for the calculator program. This is a regular calculator, not the "reverse Polish" variety that is so oddly popular with Java fans.

```java
import java.awt.*;

public class Calculator extends Frame
{  public Calculator()
   {  setTitle("Calculator");

      display = new TextField("0");
      display.setEditable(false);
      add("North", display);

      Panel p = new Panel();
      p.setLayout(new GridLayout(4, 4));
      for (int i = 0; i <= 9; i++)
      p.add(new Button("" + (char)('0' + i)));
      p.add(new Button("+"));
      p.add(new Button("-"));
      p.add(new Button("*"));
      p.add(new Button("/"));
      p.add(new Button("%"));
      p.add(new Button("="));
      add("Center", p);
   }

   public boolean handleEvent(Event evt)
   {  if (evt.id == Event.WINDOW_DESTROY) System.exit(0);
      return super.handleEvent(evt);
   }

   public boolean action(Event evt, Object arg)
   {  if (arg instanceof String)
      {  String s = (String) arg;
         if ('0' <= s.charAt(0) && s.charAt(0) <= '9')
         {  if (start) display.setText(s);
            else display.setText(display.getText() + s);
            start = false;
         }
         else
         {  if (start)
            {  if (s.equals("-"))
               { display.setText(s); start = false; }
               else op = s;
            }
            else
            {  calculate(Format.atoi(display.getText()));
               op = s;
               start = true;
            }
         }
      }
```

```
        else return super.action(evt, arg);
        return true;
}

public void calculate(int n)
{   if (op == "+") arg += n;
    else if (op == "-") arg -= n;
    else if (op == "*") arg *= n;
    else if (op == "/") arg /= n;
    else if (op == "%") arg %= n;
    else if (op == "=") arg = n;
    display.setText("" + arg);
}

public static void main(String[] args)
{   Frame f = new Calculator();
    f.resize(300, 200);
    f.show();
}

private TextField display;
private int arg = 0;
private String op = "=";
private boolean start = true;
}
```

Of course, few applications have as rigid a layout as the face of a calculator. In practice, small grids (usually with just one or two columns) are useful to organize partial areas of a window.

Grid Bag Layout

This is the mother of all layout managers. You can think of a grid bag layout as a piece of graph paper—each component will be told to occupy one or more of the little boxes on the paper. The idea is that this layout manager lets you align components without requiring that they all be the same size—since you are only concerned with which cells they will occupy. (Many word processors have the same capability when editing tables: you start out with a grid, and then can merge adjacent cells if need be.)

Fair warning: using grid bag layouts can be incredibly complex. (The payoff is that they have the most flexibility and will work in the widest variety of situations.) Keep in mind that the purpose of layout managers is to keep the arrangement of the components reasonable under different font sizes and operating systems, so it is not surprising that you need to work somewhat harder than when you design a layout just for one environment.

Consider the font selection dialog of Figure 7-17. It consists of the following components:

- a list box to specify the font style
- two check boxes to select bold and italic
- a text field for the font size
- a label for that text box
- a text field at the bottom for the sample string.

Figure 7-17

Now chop up the dialog box into a four-by-three grid of cells, as shown in Figure 7-18. As you can see, the list box spans three columns; each check box spans two columns; and the text field at the bottom spans three fields.

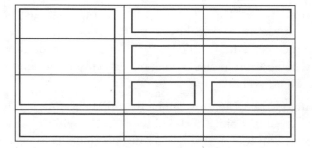

Figure 7-18

To describe the layout to the grid bag manager, you must go through the following convoluted procedure.

- Create an object of type GridBagLayout. (You don't tell it how many rows and columns the underlying grid has. Instead, Java will try to guess it from the information you give it later.)

- Set this GridBagLayout object to be the layout manager for the component.

- Create an object of type GridBagConstraints. (The GridBagConstraints object will specify how the components are laid out within the grid bag.)

- For *each component*, fill in the GridBagConstraints object and call the setConstraints object to pass this information to the GridBagLayout. Then (finally) add the component.

Here's an example of the code needed (we will go over the various constraints in more detail in the sections that follow—so don't worry if you don't know what some of the constraints do).

```
GridBagLayout layout = new GridBagLayout();
panel.setLayout(layout);
GridBagConstraints constraints = new GridBagConstraints();
constraints.weightx = 100;
constraints.weighty = 100;
constraints.gridx = 0;
constraints.gridy = 0;
constraints.gridwidth = 1;
constraints.gridheight = 3;
List style = new List(4);
layout.setConstraints(style, constraints);
panel.add(style);
```

(It is obviously best to write a small helper function for this kind of repetitive code—see the listing below for an example of one.)

The trick is knowing how to set the state of the GridBagConstraints object; this can be incredibly convoluted. We will go over the most important constraints for using this object in the sections that follow.

The gridx, gridy, gridwidth, *and* gridheight *Parameters*

These constraints define where the component is located in the grid. The gridx and gridy values specify the column and row positions of the upper left corner of the component to be added. The gridwidth and gridheight values determine how many columns and rows it occupies.

Weight Fields

You always need to set the *weight* fields (weightx and weighty) for each area in a grid bag layout. If you set the weight to 0, then the area never grows beyond its initial size in that direction. In the grid bag layout for the figure given above, we set the `weighty` field of the text field at the bottom to be 0. This allows the bottom field to remain a constant height when you resize the window. On the other hand, if you set the weights for all areas to 0, the container will huddle in the center of its allotted area, rather than stretching to fill it.

Note that the weights don't actually give the relative sizes of the columns. They tell what proportion of the "slack" space Java should allocate to each area. This isn't particularly intuitive. We recommend that you set the weights at 100. Then run the program and see how the layout looks. If you want to tweak the sizes of the columns or rows, adjust the weights. In our example, we set the weight of the first column to 20, to compress it somewhat relative to the rest of the dialog box.

The `fill` *and* `anchor` *Parameters*

If you don't want a component to stretch out and fill the entire area, you need to set the `fill` field for the layout manager. You have four possibilities for this parameter: the valid values are used in the forms `GridBagConstraints.NONE`, `GridBagConstraints.HORIZONTAL`, `GridBagConstraints.VERTICAL`, and `GridBagConstraints.BOTH`.

If the component does not fill the entire area, you can specify where in the area you want it by setting the `anchor` field. The valid values are: `GridBagConstraints.CENTER` (the default), `GridBagConstraints.NORTH`, `GridBagConstraints.NORTHEAST`, `GridBagConstraints.EAST`, and so on.

An Alternative Method to Specify the `gridx`, `gridy`, `gridwidth`, *and* `gridheight` *Parameters*

The AWT documentation recommends that, instead of setting the `gridx` and `gridy` values to absolute positions, you set them to the constant `GridBagConstraints.RELATIVE`. Then add the components to the grid bag layout in a standardized order, going from left to right in the first row, then moving along the next row, and so on.

You still specify the number of columns and rows spanned in the `gridwidth` and `gridheight` fields. Except, if the component extends to the *last* row or column, you aren't supposed to specify the actual number, but the constant `GridBagConstraints.REMAINDER`. This tells the layout manager that the component is the last one in its row. And if it is the *next-to-last* component in the current row or column, you are supposed to specify the constant RELATIVE.

This scheme does seem to work. But it sounds really goofy to hide the actual placement information from the layout manager and hope that it will rediscover it.

The Code for the Font Layout Dialog Box Example

Here is the complete code to implement the font dialog.

```java
import java.awt.*;

public class FontDialog extends Frame
{  private void add(Component c, GridBagLayout gbl,
      GridBagConstraints gbc,
      int x, int y, int w, int h)
   {  gbc.gridx = x;
      gbc.gridy = y;
      gbc.gridwidth = w;
      gbc.gridheight = h;
      gbl.setConstraints(c, gbc);
      add(c);
   }
   public FontDialog()
   {  setTitle("FontDialog");
      GridBagLayout gbl = new GridBagLayout();
      setLayout(gbl);

      style = new List(4, false);
      style.addItem("Times Roman");
      style.addItem("Helvetica");
      style.addItem("Courier");
      style.addItem("Zapf Dingbats");
      style.addItem("Dialog");
      style.addItem("DialogInput");

      Checkbox bold = new Checkbox("Bold");
      Checkbox italic = new Checkbox("Italic");
      Label label = new Label("Size: ");
      TextField size = new TextField();
      TextField sample = new TextField();

      GridBagConstraints gbc = new GridBagConstraints();
      gbc.fill = GridBagConstraints.BOTH;
      gbc.weightx = 20;
      gbc.weighty = 100;
      add(style, gbl, gbc, 0, 0, 1, 3);
      gbc.weightx = 100;
      gbc.fill = GridBagConstraints.NONE;
      gbc.anchor = GridBagConstraints.CENTER;
      add(bold, gbl, gbc, 1, 0, 2, 1);
      add(italic, gbl, gbc, 1, 1, 2, 1);
      add(label, gbl, gbc, 1, 2, 1, 1);
      gbc.fill = GridBagConstraints.HORIZONTAL;
      add(size, gbl, gbc, 2, 2, 1, 1);
      gbc.anchor = GridBagConstraints.SOUTH;
```

```
        gbc.weighty = 0;
        add(sample, gbl, gbc, 0, 3, 4, 1);
    }

    public boolean handleEvent(Event evt)
    {   if (evt.id == Event.WINDOW_DESTROY) System.exit(0);
        return super.handleEvent(evt);
    }


    public boolean action(Event evt, Object arg)
    {   if (evt.target.equals(bold)
            || evt.target.equals(italic))
        {   int m = (bold.getState() ? Font.BOLD : 0)
            + (italic.getState() ?
                Font.ITALIC : 0);

        }

        else return super.action(evt, arg);
        return true;
    }

    public static void main(String[] args)
    {   Frame f = new FontDialog();
        f.resize(250, 150);
        f.show();
    }

    private List style;
    private Checkbox bold;
    private Checkbox italic;
    private TextField size;
    private TextField sample;
}
```

`java.awt.GridBagConstraints`

• `int gridx, gridy`

indicates starting column and row of cell

• `int gridwidth, gridheight`

indicates column and row extent of cell

• `int weightx, weighty`

indicates capacity of cell to grow

- `int anchor`

indicates alignment of component inside cell, one of CENTER, NORTH, NORTHEAST, EAST, SOUTHEAST, SOUTH, SOUTHWEST, WEST, and NORTHWEST

- `int fill`

indicates the fill behavior of component inside cell, one of NONE, BOTH, HORIZONTAL, and VERTICAL

- `int ipadx, ipady`

indicates the "internal" padding around the component

- `Insets insets`

indicates the "external" padding along the cell boundaries

`java.awt.GridBagLayout`

- `void setConstraints(Component comp, GridBagConstraints constraints)`

sets the constraints for a component.

Parameters:

`comp`	the component for which constraint information is to be supplied
`constraints`	the constraints to be applied

Using No Layout Manager

There will be times when you don't want to bother with layout managers, but just want to drop a component at a fixed location. This is not a great idea for platform-independent applications, but there is nothing wrong with it for a quick prototype.

Here is what you do to place a component at a fixed location:

- Don't select a layout manager at all.

- Add the component you want to the container.

- Then specify the position and size that you want.
  ```
  panel.setLayout(null);
  Button ok = new Button("Ok");
  ok.reshape(10, 10, 30, 15);
  ```

java.awt.Component

• void reshape(int x, int y, int width, int height)

moves and resizes a component.

Parameters:

x, y	the new top left corner of the component
width, height	the new size of the component

Custom Layout Managers

In principle, it is possible to design your own LayoutManager class that manages components in a special way. For example, you could arrange all components in a container to form a circle (see Figure 7-19). This will almost always be a major effort and a real time sink, but as Figure 7-19 shows, the results can be quite dramatic.

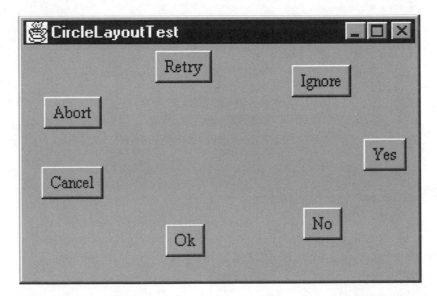

Figure 7-19

If you do feel you can't live without your own layout manager, here is what you do. Your own layout manager must implement the LayoutManager interface. You need to override the following five functions.

```
void addLayoutComponent(String s, Component c);
void removeLayoutComponent(Component c);
Dimension preferredLayoutSize(Container parent);
```

```
    Dimension minimumLayoutSize(Container parent);
    void layoutContainer(Container parent);
```

The first two functions are called when a component is added or removed. If you don't keep any additional information about the components, you can make them do nothing. The next two functions compute the space required for the minimum and the preferred layout of the components. These are usually the same quantity. The fifth function does the actual work and invokes reshape on all components.

Here is a simple implementation of the CircleLayout manager, which, amazingly and uselessly enough, lays out the components along an ellipse inside the parent.

```java
import java.awt.*;

public class CircleLayoutTest extends Frame
{   public CircleLayoutTest()
    {   setTitle("CircleLayoutTest");
        setLayout(new CircleLayout());
        add(new Button("Yes"));
        add(new Button("No"));
        add(new Button("Ok"));
        add(new Button("Cancel"));
        add(new Button("Abort"));
        add(new Button("Retry"));
        add(new Button("Ignore"));
    }

    public boolean handleEvent(Event evt)
    {   if (evt.id == Event.WINDOW_DESTROY) System.exit(0);
        return super.handleEvent(evt);
    }

    public static void main(String args[])
    {   Frame f = new CircleLayoutTest();
        f.resize(300, 200);
        f.show();
    }
}

class CircleLayout implements LayoutManager
{   public void addLayoutComponent(String name,
        Component comp)
    {}

    public void removeLayoutComponent(Component comp)
    {}
```

```java
    public void setSizes(Container parent)
    {   if (sizesSet) return;
        int n = parent.countComponents();

        preferredWidth = 0;
        preferredHeight = 0;
        minWidth = 0;
        minHeight = 0;
        maxComponentWidth = 0;
        maxComponentHeight = 0;

        for (int i = 0; i < n;  i++)
        {   Component c = parent.getComponent(i);
            if (c.isVisible()) {
            Dimension d = c.preferredSize();
            maxComponentWidth = Math.max(maxComponentWidth,
                d.width);
            maxComponentHeight = Math.max(maxComponentWidth,
                d.height);
            preferredHeight += d.height;
            }
        }
        preferredHeight += maxComponentHeight;
        preferredWidth = 2 * maxComponentWidth;
        minHeight = preferredHeight;
        minWidth = preferredWidth;
        sizesSet = true;
    }

    public Dimension preferredLayoutSize(Container parent)
    {   Dimension dim = new Dimension(0, 0);
        setSizes(parent);
        Insets insets = parent.insets();
        dim.width = preferredWidth + insets.left
            + insets.right;
        dim.height = preferredHeight + insets.top
            + insets.bottom;
        return dim;
    }

    public Dimension minimumLayoutSize(Container parent)
    {   Dimension dim = new Dimension(0, 0);
        setSizes(parent);
        Insets insets = parent.insets();
        dim.width = minWidth + insets.left + insets.right;
        dim.height = minHeight + insets.top + insets.bottom;
        return dim;
    }
```

```java
public void layoutContainer(Container parent)
{   Insets insets = parent.insets();
    int containerWidth = parent.size().width
        - insets.left - insets.right;
    int containerHeight = parent.size().height
        - insets.top - insets.bottom;
    int xradius = (containerWidth - maxComponentWidth)
        / 2;
    int yradius = (containerHeight - maxComponentHeight)
        / 2;

    setSizes(parent);
    int xcenter = insets.left + containerWidth / 2;
    int ycenter = insets.top + containerHeight / 2;

    int n = parent.countComponents();
    if (n == 0) return;
    for (int i = 0 ; i < n ; i++)
    {   Component c = parent.getComponent(i);
        if (c.isVisible())
        {   Dimension d = c.preferredSize();
            double angle = 2 * Math.PI * i / n;
            int x = xcenter
                + (int)(Math.cos(angle) * xradius);
            int y = ycenter
                + (int)(Math.sin(angle) * yradius);

            c.reshape(x - d.width / 2, y - d.width / 2,
                d.width, d.height);
        }
    }

}

private int minWidth = 0;
private int minHeight = 0;
private int preferredWidth = 0, preferredHeight = 0;
private boolean sizesSet = false;
private int maxComponentWidth = 0;
private int maxComponentHeight = 0;
}
```

java.awt.LayoutManager

• void addLayoutComponent(String name, Component comp)

adds a component to the layout.

Parameters:

> name   an identifier for the component placement
>
> comp   the component to be added

• void removeLayoutComponent(Component comp)

removes a component from the layout.

Parameters:

> comp   the component to be removed

• Dimension preferredLayoutSize(Container parent)

returns the preferred size dimensions for the container under this layout.

Parameters:

> parent   the container whose components are being laid out

• Dimension minimumLayoutSize(Container parent)

returns the minimum size dimensions for the container under this layout.

Parameters:

> parent   the container whose components are being laid out

• void layoutContainer(Container parent)

lays out the components in a container.

Parameters:

> parent   the container whose components are being laid out

Dialog Boxes

So far, all of our user interface components have appeared inside a frame window that was created in the application. This is the most common situation if you write *applets* that run inside a Web browser. But if you write applications, you usually want separate dialogs to pop up to get information from the user.

Just as with most windowing systems, AWT distinguishes between *modal* and *modeless* dialogs. A modal dialog won't let the user interact with the remaining windows of the application until he or she deals with it. You use a modal dialog when you need information from the user before you can proceed with execution. For example, when the user wants to read a file, a modal file dialog is the one to pop up. The user must specify a file name before beginning to the read operation. Only when the modal dialog is closed can the application proceed.

A modeless dialog lets the user enter information in both the dialog and the remainder of the application. One example of a modeless dialog is for a tool bar. The tool bar can stay in place as long as needed, and the user can interact with both the application window and the tool bar.

Figure 7-20 shows a typical modal dialog, a program information box that is displayed when the user selects the About button.

To implement a dialog box, you derive a class from `Dialog`. This is essentially the same process as deriving the main window for the application from `Frame`.

More precisely:

1. In the constructor of your dialog box, call the constructor of the base class `Dialog`. You will need to tell it the name of the parent window, the title of the window, and a boolean flag to indicate if the dialog is modal or modeless.

2. Add the controls of the dialog box.

3. Set the size for the dialog box.

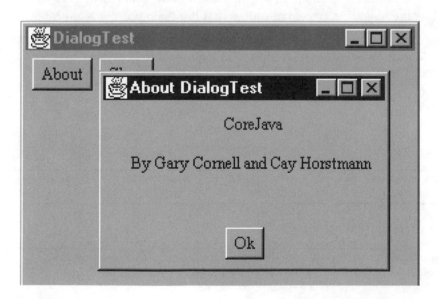

Figure 7-20

Here's an example of how the code will start:

```
class AboutDialog extends Dialog
{  public AboutDialog(Frame parent)
   {  super(parent, "About this program", true /* modal */);
      . . .
      Panel p = new Panel();
      p.add(new Button("Ok"));
      add("South", p);
      resize(220, 150);
   }
}
```

To display the dialog box, you create a new dialog object and invoke the show method.

```
Dialog d = new AboutDialog(this);
d.show();
```

When the user clicks on the OK button, the dialog should close. This is handled in the action procedure.

```
public boolean action(Event evt, Object arg)
{  if (arg.equals("OK")) dispose();
   else return false;
   return true;
}
```

Notice the call to dispose() here. This removes the dialog from the screen and reclaims the operating system resources that the dialog box was allocated.

If you want your user to be able to cancel a dialog by closing it (for example, by a click on the Exit button in Windows 95), you need to provide a handler for the WINDOW_DESTROY event.

```
public boolean handleEvent(Event evt)
{  if (evt.id == WINDOW_DESTROY) dispose();
   else return super.handleEvent(evt);
   return true;
}
```

If you don't supply this handler, the user can only close the dialog by clicking on the OK button.

If your application spawns child windows (such as dialogs), you must be careful about the WINDOW_DESTROY handler of the frame window. Suppose you use the following event handler for the frame component:

```
class MyFrame extends Frame
{    .  .  .
    public boolean handleEvent(Event evt)
    {   if (evt.id == WINDOW_DESTROY) System.exit(0);
        else .  .  .
        else return super.handleEvent(evt);
        return true;
    }
    .  .  .
}
```

Suppose you don't override the event handler in the dialog box to handle the WINDOW_DESTROY event for the dialog box. Since no event handler was provided for the derived class, that event will be transmitted to the parent—the frame window of the application. Closing the dialog box would then have the unfortunate side effect of closing the entire application!

To remedy this, find out where the WINDOW_DESTROY event originated. In particular, did it originate from the frame or the dialog box?

```
class MyFrame extends Frame
{    .  .  .
    public boolean handleEvent(Event evt)
    {   if (evt.id == WINDOW_DESTROY && evt.target == this)
            System.exit(0);
        else .  .  .
        else return super.handleEvent(evt);
        return true;
    }
    .  .  .
}
```

Similarly, one would have a handle-event procedure in the Dialog class.

Here is the code for the "About" dialog box test program.

```
import java.awt.*;

public class DialogTest extends Frame
{   public DialogTest()
    {   setTitle("DialogTest");

        Panel p = new Panel();
        p.setLayout(new FlowLayout(FlowLayout.LEFT));
        p.add(new Button("About"));
        p.add(new Button("Close"));
        add("North", p);
    }

    public boolean action(Event evt, Object arg)
    {   if(arg.equals("About"))
        {   AboutDialog ab = new AboutDialog(this);
            ab.show();
```

```
      }
      else if(arg.equals("Close"))
      { System.exit(0);
      }
      else return super.action(evt, arg);
      return true;
   }

   public boolean handleEvent(Event evt)
   { if (evt.id == Event.WINDOW_DESTROY
        && evt.target == this)
        System.exit(0);
      return super.handleEvent(evt);
   }

   public static void main(String args[])
   { Frame f = new DialogTest();
      f.resize(300, 200);
      f.show();
   }
}

class AboutDialog extends Dialog
{  public AboutDialog(Frame parent)
   { super(parent, "About DialogTest", true);
      Panel p1 = new Panel();
      p1.add(new Label("CoreJava"));
      p1.add(new Label("By Gary Cornell and Cay Horstmann"));
      add("Center", p1);

      Panel p2 = new Panel();
      p2.add(new Button("Ok"));
      add("South", p2);
      resize(220, 150);
   }

   public boolean action(Event evt, Object arg)
   { if(arg.equals("Ok"))
      { dispose();
        return true;
      }
      return false;
   }

   public boolean handleEvent(Event evt)
   { if (evt.id == Event.WINDOW_DESTROY
        && evt.target == this)
        System.exit(0);
      return super.handleEvent(evt);
   }
}
```

```
java.awt.Dialog
```

• public Dialog(Frame parent, String title, boolean modal)

constructs a dialog. The dialog is not visible until it is explicitly shown.

Parameters:

parent	the owner of the dialog
title	the title of the dialog
modal	true for modal dialogs (a modal dialog blocks input to other windows)

Data Exchange

The most common reason to put up a dialog box is to get information from the user. You have already seen how easy it is to make a dialog box object: give it initial data and then call show() in order to have Java display the dialog box on the screen. Unfortunately, in AWT it is hard to get the user-supplied data out of a dialog box.

Consider the dialog box in Figure 7-21 that could be used to obtain a user name and a password to connect to some on-line service.

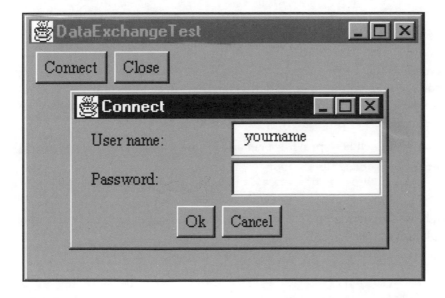

Figure 7-21

```
ConnectInfo defaults = new UserInfo(defaultName, "");
ConnectDialog d = new ConnectDialog(this, defaults);
d.show();
```

Unfortunately, the call to show() returns immediately, *even though the dialog is modal*. That means the following code will not work.

```
d.show();
name = d.getName();
ConnectInfo result = d.getResult(); // NO
```

This is—to say the least—annoying. There are two methods for getting results back from the dialog box. The first is to have the "OK" handler call a procedure of the frame class to tell it that the answer is ready. For example, the following code uses a ConnectInfo object to gather this information. The ConnectInfo object has instance fields for the needed information. Then you must provide a method called processConnect() in your frame class to deal with the information. Here's one way to write the event handler for a dialog box to reclaim the information.

```
public boolean action(Event evt, Object arg)
{   if (arg.equals("OK")
    {   dispose();//clear resources
        ConnectInfo result = new ConnectInfo(username.getText(),
            password.getText());
        ((MyFrame)getParent()).processConnect(result);
    }
    else return false;
    return true;
}
```

This method has a major drawback—it tightly couples the dialog box code with the code in your frame class. In particular, this affects reusability: if you want to reuse the dialog box code in another program, you have to rename the (MyFrame) cast appropriately.

A better approach is to provide a generic interface:

```
interface ResultProcessor
{   public void processResult(Dialog source, Object obj);
}
```

Then have the dialog box call its implementation of processResult upon completion by casting to the interface.

```
public boolean action(Event evt, Object arg)
{   if (arg.equals("Ok"))
    {   dispose();
        ConnectInfo result = new ConnectInfo(username.getText(),
            password.getText());
```

```
        ((ResultProcessor)getParent()).processResult
            (this, result);
    }
    else return false;
    return true;
}
```

For this to work, the frame you create in the application must implement the `ResultProcessor` interface. It can then get all the data stored in the dialog box in the `processResults` method.

```
class MyFrame extends Frame implements ResultProcessor
{   . . .
    public void processResult(Dialog source, Object obj)
    {   if (source instanceof ConnectDialog)
        {   ConnectInfo result = (ConnectInfo)obj;
            // process connect information
        }
    }
    . . .
}
```

Both methods have another major drawback: the handling of an action is chopped up into two pieces of code—from the pre-dialog phase and the post-dialog phase—but this is inevitable in Java.

Here is the complete code that illustrates the data flow into and out of a dialog box.

```
import java.awt.*;

public class DataExchangeTest extends Frame
    implements ResultProcessor
{   public DataExchangeTest()
    {   setTitle("DataExchangeTest");

        Panel p = new Panel();
        p.setLayout(new FlowLayout(FlowLayout.LEFT));
        p.add(new Button("Connect"));
        p.add(new Button("Close"));
        add("North", p);
    }

    public boolean action(Event evt, Object arg)
    {   if (arg.equals("Connect"))
        {   ConnectInfo in = new ConnectInfo("yourname", "");
            ConnectDialog pd = new ConnectDialog(this, in);
            pd.show();
        }
        else if(arg.equals("Close"))
```

```
            System.exit(0);
        else return super.action(evt, arg);
        return true;
    }

    public boolean handleEvent(Event evt)
    {   if (evt.id == Event.WINDOW_DESTROY
            && evt.target == this)
            System.exit(0);
        else
            return super.handleEvent(evt);
        return true;
    }

    public void processResult(Dialog source, Object result)
    {   if (source instanceof ConnectDialog)
        {   ConnectInfo info = (ConnectInfo)result;
            System.out.println(info.username + " "
                + info.password);
        }
    }

    public static void main(String args[])
    {   Frame f = new DataExchangeTest();
        f.resize(300, 200);
        f.show();
    }
}

interface ResultProcessor
{   public void processResult(Dialog source, Object obj);
}

class ConnectInfo
{   String username;
    String password;
    ConnectInfo(String u, String p)
        { username = u; password = p; }
}

class ConnectDialog extends Dialog
{   public ConnectDialog(DataExchangeTest parent,
        ConnectInfo u)
    {   super(parent, "Connect", true);
        Panel p1 = new Panel();
        p1.setLayout(new GridLayout(2, 2));
        p1.add(new Label("User name:"));
        p1.add(username = new TextField(u.username, 8));
        p1.add(new Label("Password:"));
```

```
        p1.add(password = new TextField(u.password, 8));
        add("Center", p1);

        Panel p2 = new Panel();
        p2.add(new Button("Ok"));
        p2.add(new Button("Cancel"));
        add("South", p2);
        resize(240, 120);
    }

    public boolean action(Event evt, Object arg)
    {   if(arg.equals("Ok"))
        {   dispose();
            ((ResultProcessor)getParent()).processResult(this,
                new ConnectInfo(username.getText(),
                    password.getText()));
        }
        else if (arg.equals("Cancel"))
            dispose();
        else return super.action(evt, arg);
        return true;
    }

    public boolean handleEvent(Event evt)
    {   if (evt.id == Event.WINDOW_DESTROY)
            dispose();
        else return super.handleEvent(evt);
        return true;
    }

    private TextField username;
    private TextField password;
}
```

File Dialogs

When you write an applet, you cannot access files on the remote user's
machine, so this topic won't be of great interest to you. However, when you
write an application, you usually want to be able to open and save files. A good
file dialog that shows files and directories and lets the user navigate the file system is hard to write, and you definitely don't want to reinvent that wheel.
Fortunately, AWT provides a file dialog class that displays the same file dialog
that most native applications use. Figures 7-22 and 7-23 show the file dialog
under Windows 95 and Solaris.

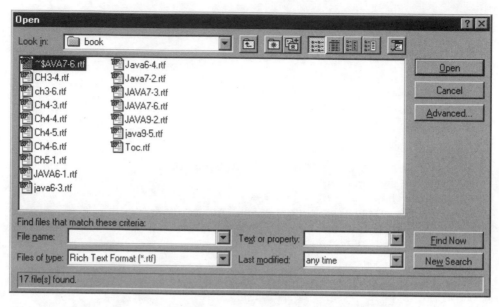

Figure 7-22

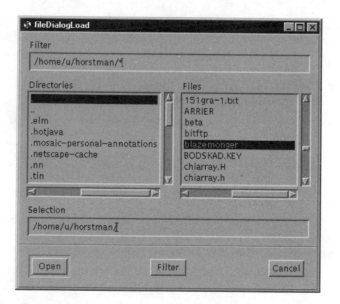

Figure 7-23

Here are the steps needed to put up a file dialog box and get what the user chooses from the box:

1. Make a file dialog object.

```
FileDialog d = new FileDialog(parent, "Save note file",
    FileDialog.SAVE);
```

The third argument is either LOAD or SAVE. Set the file name filter and directory.

```
d.setFileNameFilter("*.txt");
d.setDirectory(".");
```

If you have a default file name that you expect the user to choose, supply it here.

2. Then show the dialog box.

```
d.setFile(filename);
d.show();
```

Unlike the show() call for a regular dialog box, this call does not return until the user has filled in the file dialog box. You get the selected file back with the getFile() method. If the user cancels the dialog, getFile() returns null.

```
filename = d.getFile();
if (d != 0) . . .
```

java.awt.FileDialog

• FileDialog(Frame parent, String title, int mode)

creates a file dialog for loading or saving a file.

Parameters:

parent	the owner of the dialog
title	the title of the dialog
mode	the mode of the dialog, one of LOAD or SAVE

• setFilenameFilter(FilenameFilter filter)

sets the initial file mask for the file dialog.

• setDirectory(String dir)

sets the initial directory for the file dialog.

• setFile(String file)

sets the default file choice for the file dialog.

• String getFile()

gets the file that the user selected (or returns null if the user didn't select any file).

More on Event-Handling

In AWT, events can come from the following sources:

- the keyboard

- the mouse

- window creation, destruction, and movement

- scroll bar activities

- list box item selection and deselection

- change of input focus

- component and menu actions

 Windows has a more sophisticated event structure than AWT. There are hundreds of Windows events, compared to fewer than two dozen events in AWT. For example, Windows routes all paint notifications through the event queue. That is smart since it lets the queue sort and aggregate the paint events. In AWT, a window is instructed to paint itself by a method call to update, not by receiving an event. AWT does not have timer events either. We will discuss how to implement timers in Chapter 12.

Each event is described by an object of the Event class. The class has the following fields (all of which are public—you don't need to use accessor functions).

id an identifier for this event (one of ACTION_EVENT, GOT_FOCUS, KEY_ACTION, KEY_ACTION_RELEASE, KEY_PRESS, KEY_RELEASE, LIST_DESELECT, LIST_SELECT, LOAD_FILE, LOST_FOCUS, MOUSE_DOWN, MOUSE_DRAG, MOUSE_ENTER, MOUSE_EXIT, MOUSE_MOVE, MOUSE_UP, SAVE_FILE, SCROLL_ABSOLUTE, SCROLL_LINE_DOWN, SCROLL_LINE_UP, SCROLL_PAGE_DOWN, SCROLL_PAGE_UP, WINDOW_DEICONIFY, WINDOW_DESTROY, WINDOW_EXPOSE, WINDOW_ICONIFY, and WINDOW_MOVED)

target the component originating the event

when a time stamp (not present with action events, and not usually interesting)

x, y the x and y coordinates of mouse events

clickCount the number of clicks in a MOUSE_DOWN event. Used to detect double clicks

key the character or function key in a keyboard event. This is either a byte representing a printable character (> 32), space (32), or control character (between 0 and 32), or one of LEFT, RIGHT, UP, DOWN, HOME, END, PGUP, PGDN, F1, ... and F12 `modifier`   this is a set of four bits describing the states of the SHIFT, CTRL, ALT and meta keys. (The meta key is present on some workstation keyboards. It has a purpose similar to the ALT key on a PC keyboard.) You use bitwise masking techniques to analyze the state of the modifier. For example, if the bitwise AND of the modifier field and the flag SHIFT_MASK, CTRL_MASK, ALT_MASK, or META_MASK are non-zero, then the corresponding key was depressed. This is useful to detect SHIFT + a function key or CTRL + a mouse click, for example.

AWT does not distinguish between the mouse buttons because it is intended to be useable on platforms for which mice have only one button, such as the Macintosh.

Event-Handler Procedures

Every time an event is generated, it is passed to a `handleEvent` procedure. The object whose `handleEvent` procedure is initially called is the one that is "closest" to the event. For example, when the user types a keystroke into a component, the component that processes the keystroke gets first crack at it. If that component does not process the event, it is passed to the parent component.

Parent here refers to the parent in the *window* hierarchy, not in the inheritance hierarchy. For example, the parent of a text field is the panel that contains the text field. Its parent is the frame containing the panel.

If you put only standard components into your window, you don't care about this part of the event-routing. You just wait for the event to reach the frame window. However, if you design your own components, you can achieve special effects by grabbing events in the event-handler for your component. For example, consider the `IntTextField` that we introduced earlier in this chapter. We could trap keyboard events in that class and erase any character text that the user entered when the user hit a key other than a number.

When you write your own `handleEvent` procedure, remember that there are *three* possible exits from the procedure:

> `return true:` the event is handled—don't propagate

> `return false:` the event is not handled—propagate to parent in the *window* hierarchy (don't do it)

> `return super.handleEvent(evt):` the event is not handled—propagate to the parent in the *inheritance* hierarchy

You should never use the second option, returning `false`. *Always* handle an event or pass it to its parent *class*, not its parent *window*, if you won't handle it in the current class. The predefined handler in the AWT base class will eventually route the message to the parent window, but if you skip a base class, then some actions that you may be relying on may be skipped as well.

If an action, mouse, keyboard, or focus event was not handled in a `handleEvent` procedure, then Java calls a *convenience function* to give the window a second chance to process the event. The convenience functions are `action`, `mouseEnter`, `mouseExit`, `mouseMove`, `mouseUp`, `mouseDown`, `mouseDrag`, `keyDown`, `keyUp`, `lostFocus`, and `gotFocus`, and the names are self-explanatory.

Strictly speaking, these convenience events are not needed, but using them can make your code clearer. For example, we have used the `action` function in many examples in the previous sections. There is actually no need to process action events in the `action` function. You can process them in the `handleEvent` function when `evt.id` equals `Event.ACTION_EVENT`. But processing them separately makes the code a little less cluttered.

What is wrong with the following handler?

```java
class MyFrame extends Frame
{   . . .
    public boolean handleEvent(Event evt) // won't work
    {  if (evt.id == Event.WINDOW_DESTROY) System.exit(0);
       return false; // all other events handled in action
          method
    }

    public boolean action(Event evt, Object arg)
    {   if (arg.equals("Ok") . . .
    }
}
```

The answer is that `action` is never called. Here is why. The `handleEvent` function returns `false`. When an action event occurs, it is first passed to `MyFrame.handleEvent`, which returns `false`. It is then passed to the parent of `MyFrame` in the *window* hierarchy. But the `MyFrame` object is a top-level window, so it has no parent. The `Frame.handleEvent` function is never executed, and it is that function that calls `action`. The remedy is simple and is worth repeating: don't return `false`, return `super.handleEvent(evt)`.

`java.awt.Component`

• `boolean action(Event evt, Object obj)`

is called if a user interface action (button click, menu select,...) occurs.

Parameters:

evt	the event
obj	additional information on the event (usually the label of the originating component)

Menus

AWT supports the same kind of pull-down menus with which you are familiar from all Windows and Motif applications. A *menu bar* on top of the window contains the names of the pull-down menus. Clicking on a name opens up the menu containing *menu items* and *submenus*. When the user clicks on a menu item, all menus are closed and a message is sent to the program. Figure 7-24 shows a typical menu with a submenu.

Adding menus is straightforward. You create a menu bar.

```
MenuBar mb = new MenuBar();
```

For each menu, you create a menu object.

```
Menu editMenu = new Menu("Edit");
```

You add menu items, separators, and submenus to the menu object.

```
editMenu.add(new MenuItem("Paste"));
editMenu.addSeparator();
editMenu.add(optionsMenu);
...
```

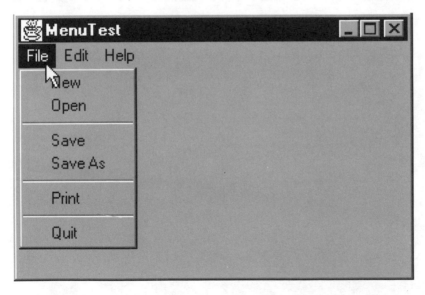

Figure 7-24

When the user selects a menu, Java triggers an action event. You catch the event in the `action` procedure. Menu events are distinguished by the fact that the event target is a menu item. The `arg` string contains the menu item name.

```
public boolean action(Event evt, Object arg)
{   if (evt.target instanceof MenuItem)
    {   if (arg.equals("Open")) . . .
        else if (arg.equals("Save")) . . .
        . . .
    }
}
```

A check box menu item is one that can display a check box next to the name (see Figure 7-25). When the user selects the menu, the state of the item automatically toggles between checked and unchecked. Use the getState method of the CheckboxMenuItem class to test the current state and the setState method to set the state.

In Windows programs, menus are generally defined in an external resource file and tied to the application with resource identifiers. It is possible to build menus in the menu bar used by Java, but it is not commonly done. In Java, menus must be built inside the program, because Java applications have no external resources. It is a common Windows programming error to have a mismatch of the resource numbers. In Java, you must, likewise, make sure that the string of the menu name matches the string in the action procedure.

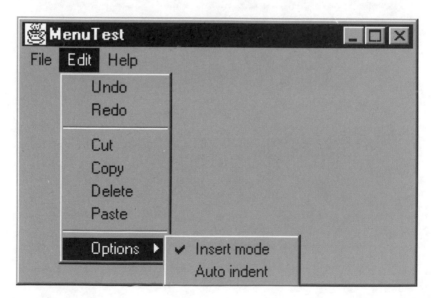

Figure 7-25

Here is a sample program that generates a set of menus.

```java
import java.awt.*;

public class MenuTest extends Frame
{   public MenuTest()
    {   setTitle("MenuTest");

        MenuBar mbar = new MenuBar();
        Menu m = new Menu("File");
        m.add(new MenuItem("New"));
        m.add(new MenuItem("Open"));
        m.addSeparator();
        m.add(new MenuItem("Save"));
        m.add(new MenuItem("Save As"));
        m.addSeparator();
        m.add(new MenuItem("Print"));
        m.addSeparator();
        m.add(new MenuItem("Quit"));
        mbar.add(m);

        m = new Menu("Edit");
        m.add(new MenuItem("Undo"));
        m.add(new MenuItem("Redo"));
        m.addSeparator();
        m.add(new MenuItem("Cut"));
        m.add(new MenuItem("Copy"));
        m.add(new MenuItem("Delete"));
        m.add(new MenuItem("Paste"));
        m.addSeparator();

        Menu f = new Menu("Options");
        f.add(new CheckboxMenuItem("Insert mode"));
        f.add(new CheckboxMenuItem("Auto indent"));
        m.add(f);

        mbar.add(m);

        m = new Menu("Help");
        m.add(new MenuItem("Index"));
        m.add(new MenuItem("About"));
        mbar.add(m);

        setMenuBar(mbar);
    }

    public boolean action(Event evt, Object arg)
    {   if (evt.target instanceof MenuItem)
        {   if(arg.equals("Quit"))
```

```
                    System.exit(0);
            }
        else return false;
        return true;
    }

    public boolean handleEvent(Event evt)
    {   if (evt.id == Event.WINDOW_DESTROY
            && evt.target == this)
            System.exit(0);
        return super.handleEvent(evt);
    }

    public static void main(String args[])
    {   Frame f = new MenuTest();
        f.resize(300, 200);
        f.show();
    }
}
```

java.awt.Menu

• Menu(String label)

Parameters:

>   label   the menu description in the menu bar or parent menu

• void add(MenuItem item)

adds a menu item (or a menu).

Parameters:

>   item   the item or menu to add

• void addSeparator()

adds a separator line to the menu.

java.awt.MenuItem

• MenuItem(String label)

Parameters:

>   label   the label for this menu item (the label "-" is reserved for a
>   separator between menu items)

```
java.awt.CheckboxMenuItem
```
• CheckboxMenuItem(String label)

Parameters:

    label   the label for this menu item

• boolean getState()

returns the check state of this item.

• void setState(boolean t)

sets the check state of this item.

Parameters:

    t   the new check state

Keyboard Events

When a key is pressed, a "key down" event is generated. When the key is released, there is a corresponding "key up" event. The most convenient place to trap these events are in the keyDown and keyUp procedures.

The key code is either the ASCII code of the key or a special code for a function key (LEFT, RIGHT, UP, DOWN, HOME, END, PGUP, PGDN, F1, ... F12). You get the state of the SHIFT, CONTROL, ALT, and meta keys by bit masking using the AND operator. For example, the following code tests whether or not the user hits SHIFT + RIGHT ARROW:

```
public boolean keyDown(Event evt, int key)
{   if (key == Event.RIGHT &&
        (evt.modifiers & Event.SHIFT_MASK) != 0)
    {   . . .
    }
}
```

In general, you use one of the following flags: Event.SHIFT_MASK, Event.CTRL_MASK, Event.ALT_MASK, and Event.META_MASK.

The following application shows how to handle keystrokes. The program is a simple implementation of the Etch-A-Sketch toy. You move a pen up, down, left, and right with the cursor keys. If you hold down the SHIFT key, the pen moves by a larger increment.

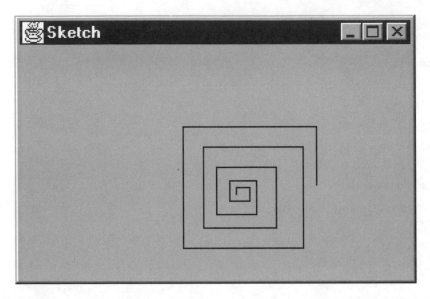

Figure 7-26

```java
import java.awt.*;

public class Sketch extends Frame
{  public Sketch()
   {  setTitle("Sketch");
   }

   public boolean handleEvent(Event evt)
   {  if (evt.id == Event.WINDOW_DESTROY) System.exit(0);
      return super.handleEvent(evt);
   }

   public boolean keyDown(Event evt, int key)
   {  int d = ((evt.modifiers & Event.SHIFT_MASK) == 0) ?
      1 : 5;
      if (key == Event.LEFT) add(-d, 0);
      else if (key == Event.RIGHT) add(d, 0);
      else if (key == Event.UP) add(0, -d);
      else if (key == Event.DOWN) add(0, d);
      else return false;
      return true;
   }

   public void update(Graphics g)
   {  paint(g);
      requestFocus();
   }
```

```
public void paint(Graphics g)
{  g.drawLine(start.x, start.y, end.x, end.y);
   start.x = end.x;
   start.y = end.y;
}

public void add(int dx, int dy)
{  end.x += dx;
   end.y += dy;
   repaint();
}

public static void main(String[] args)
{  Frame f = new Sketch();
   f.resize(300, 200);
   f.show();
}

private Point start = new Point(0, 0);
private Point end = new Point(0, 0);

}
```

`java.awt.Component`

• `boolean keyDown(Event evt, int key)`

is called when a key is pressed.

Parameters:

evt	the event
key	the key that is pressed

• `boolean keyUp(Event evt, int key)`

is called when a key is released.

Parameters:

evt	the event
key	the key that is pressed

Mouse Events

Users can use a mouse for three separate purposes: for selection, for navigation between components of a frame, and for drawing. The AWT mechanism recognizes when the user selects menu items or clicks on a button. It then notifies you of what happened in the appropriate action event.

If you want to enable the user to draw with the mouse, you will need to trap the `mouseMove`, `mouseUp`, `mouseDown`, and `mouseDrag` functions. (How often a `mouseMove` event is checked for and then reported is operating system dependent. It will be checked frequently but you cannot rely on it to be continuous.)

Java is also supposed to trigger an event in an application when the mouse has entered or exited a subwindow, or when a subwindow has gained or lost the keyboard focus. You trap these events with the `mouseEnter`, `mouseExit`, `gotFocus`, and `lostFocus` methods. At the time of this writing, these events are generated inconsistently on different platforms, and we cannot yet recommend that you rely on them. Nonetheless, at some point, these events should be more consistently generated, so it is worth learning how to handle them in preparation for that happy moment.

In this section, we will consider a simple graphics editor application that allows the user to place, move and erase squares on a canvas (see Figure 7-27).

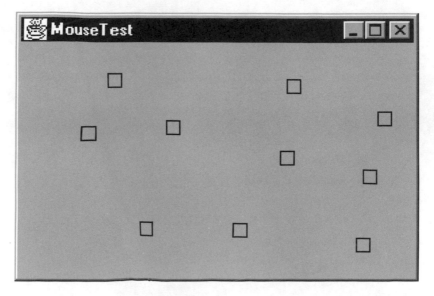

Figure 7-27

When the user clicks a mouse button, Java calls the `mouseDown` function of the active window. Its arguments include the event and the *x*- and *y*-coordinates of the pointer when the mouse was clicked. If you want to distinguish between single and double clicks, look at the `clickCount` field of the event structure. (You can even get triple clicks, but your users will hate you if you force them to exercise their fingers too much.) You *cannot*, however, distinguish between the mouse buttons, assuming the user has more than one.

Here is the mouseDown function for our sample program. When you click onto a pixel that is not inside any of the squares that have been drawn, a new square is added. When you double-click inside an existing square, it is erased.

```
public boolean mouseDown(Event evt, int x, int y)
{   current = find(x, y);
    if (current < 0) // no square under the cursor
        add(x, y);
    else if (evt.clickCount >= 2)
        remove(current);
    return true;
}
```

As the mouse moves over a window, the window receives a steady stream of mouseMove calls. These are ignored by most applications. However, our test application traps the events to change the cursor to a different shape when it is under a square.

```
public boolean mouseMove(Event evt, int x, int y)
{   if (find(x, y)) setCursor(Frame.CROSSHAIR_CURSOR);
    else setCursor(Frame.DEFAULT_CURSOR);
}
```

If a mouse button is depressed while the mouse is in motion, mouseDrag calls are generated instead. Our test application lets you drag the square under the cursor. Before the square is moved, we erase the old location by drawing it over itself in XOR mode. (A bug under Windows 95 seems to leave the four pixels at the corners of the square intact.) Then we set the new location for the square and draw it again.

```
public boolean mouseDrag(Event evt, int x, int y)
{   if (current >= 0)
    {   Graphics g = getGraphics();
        g.setXORMode(getBackground());
        draw(current);
        squares[current].x = x;
        squares[current].y = y;
        draw(current);
        g.dispose();
    }
}
```

Here is the program listing.

```
import java.awt.*;

public class MouseTest extends Frame
{   public MouseTest()
    {   setTitle("MouseTest");
    }
```

```java
public boolean handleEvent(Event evt)
{   if (evt.id == Event.WINDOW_DESTROY) System.exit(0);
    return super.handleEvent(evt);
}

public void paint(Graphics g)
{   for (int i = 0; i < nsquares; i++)
        draw(g, i);
}

public int find(int x, int y)
{   for (int i = 0; i < nsquares; i++)
        if (squares[i].x <= x && x <= squares[i].x
            + SQUARELENGTH && squares[i].y <= y
            && y <= squares[i].y + SQUARELENGTH)
            return i;
    return -1;
}

public void draw(Graphics g, int i)
{   g.drawRect(squares[i].x, squares[i].y, SQUARELENGTH,
    SQUARELENGTH);
}

public void add(int x, int y)
{   if (nsquares < MAXNSQUARES)
    {   squares[nsquares] = new Point(x, y);
        nsquares++;
        repaint();
    }
}

public void remove(int n)
{   nsquares--;
    squares[n] = squares[nsquares];
    if (current == n) current = -1;
    repaint();
}

public boolean mouseDown(Event evt, int x, int y)
{   current = find(x, y);
    if (current < 0) // not inside a square
    {   add(x, y);
    }
    else if (evt.clickCount >= 2)
    {   remove(current);
    }
    return true;
}
```

```java
public boolean mouseMove(Event evt, int x, int y)
{   if (find(x, y) >= 0)
        setCursor(Frame.CROSSHAIR_CURSOR);
    else
        setCursor(Frame.DEFAULT_CURSOR);
    return true;
}

public boolean mouseDrag(Event evt, int x, int y)
{   if (current >= 0)
    {   Graphics g = getGraphics();
        g.setXORMode(getBackground());
        draw(g, current);
        squares[current].x = x;
        squares[current].y = y;
        draw(g, current);
        g.dispose();
    }
    return true;
}

public static void main(String args[])
{   Frame f = new MouseTest();
    f.resize(300, 200);
    f.show();
}
private static final int SQUARELENGTH = 10;
private static final int MAXNSQUARES = 100;
private Point[] squares = new Point[MAXNSQUARES];
private int nsquares = 0;
private int current = -1;

}
```

`java.awt.Component`

• `boolean mouseMove(Event evt, int x, int y)`

is called when the mouse moves with no mouse button depressed.

Parameters:

evt   the event

x, y   the mouse location

- `boolean mouseUp(Event evt, int x, int y)`

is called when a mouse button is released.

Parameters:

      evt   the event

      x, y   the mouse location

- `boolean mouseDown(Event evt, int x, int y)`

is called when a mouse button is clicked.

Parameters:

      evt   the event

      x, y   the mouse location

- `boolean mouseDrag(Event evt, int x, int y)`

is called when the mouse moves with a mouse button depressed.

Parameters:

      evt   the event

      x, y   the mouse location

- `boolean mouseEnter(Event evt, int x, int y)`

is called when the mouse enters this component.

Parameters:

      evt   the event

      x, y   the mouse location

- `boolean mouseExit(Event evt, int x, int y)`

is called when the mouse exits the component.

Parameters:

      evt   the event

      x, y   the mouse location

- `boolean lostFocus(Event evt, Object other)`

is called when this component has lost the input focus.

Parameters:

      evt   the event

      other   the object that gained the input focus

- `boolean gotFocus(Event evt, Object other)`

is called when this component has gained the input focus.

Parameters:

`evt`	the event
`other`	the object that lost the input focus

Scroll Bars

The two most common uses for scroll bars in a Java application are as follows:

- You can use a scroll bar in a control as a slider.

- You can place scroll bars at the right and at the bottom of a window, to scroll through its contents.

We will look briefly at both of these uses in this section.

You create a scroll bar by specifying its direction (`HORIZONTAL` or `VERTICAL`). The default range of the scroll bar is 0–100. If you want to change the range, use the `setValues` method. It takes four arguments: the value of the scroll position, the size of the "visible area," and the minimum and maximum values of the scroll bar positions. If you use scroll bars to scroll the contents of a window, the visible area is the size of the window. A positive visible area value limits scrolling so that the *right* (or bottom) edge of the window scrolls up to the right (or bottom) edge of the logical area. If you just use a scroll bar as a slider control, set the visible area to zero.

When the user clicks on a scroll bar, the scroll bar value changes. The scroll bar sends messages to the parent window. When the user clicks on the arrow on either end of the scroll bar, Java changes the value by the *line increment*. When the user clicks on the area between the arrow and the slider, the value is changed by the *page increment*. The default values for these quantities are 1 and 10. You can change these quantities with the `setLineIncrement` and `setPageIncrement` methods.

In our first example, we use scroll bars to pick red, green, and blue values to mix and display a color value. (See Figure 7-28.) Each scroll bar is initialized like this.

```
red = new Scrollbar(Scrollbar.HORIZONTAL);
red.setValues(0, 0, 0, 255);
red.setPageIncrement(16);
```

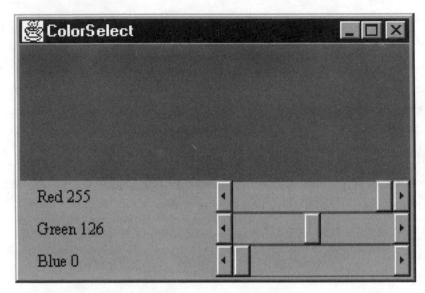

Figure 7-28

When the user clicks on a scroll bar or moves the scroll bar slider to a new position, the scroll bar sends messages to the parent window. When the user clicks on the arrow on either end of the scroll bar, SCROLL_LINE_DOWN and SCROLL_LINE_UP events are generated. When the user clicks between the arrow and the slider, SCROLL_PAGE_DOWN and SCROLL_PAGE_UP events are generated. When the slider is moved and dropped to a new position, a SCROLL_ABSOLUTE event is generated.

AWT does not support continuous tracking of the slider.

There are no convenience functions to trap scroll bar events. You need to catch them in the handleEvent procedure for the class you derive from Frame. When processing a scroll bar event, you use the getValue() method to obtain the current position of the scroll bar. As an example of this, here is the event-handler for the color mixer application.

```java
public boolean handleEvent(Event e)
{   if (evt.id == Event.SCROLL_ABSOLUTE
        || evt.id == Event.SCROLL_LINE_DOWN
        || evt.id == Event.SCROLL_LINE_UP
        || evt.id == Event.SCROLL_PAGE_DOWN
        || evt.id == Event.SCROLL_PAGE_UP)
    {   Color nc = new Color(red.getValue(), green.getValue(),
            blue.getValue());
        . . .
    }
    . . .
}
```

Here is the complete source code for the color selection application.

```java
import java.awt.*;

public class ColorSelect extends Frame
{   public ColorSelect()
    {   setTitle("ColorSelect");
        Panel p = new Panel();
        p.setLayout(new GridLayout(3, 2));
        p.add(redLabel = new Label("Red 0"));
        p.add(red = new Scrollbar(Scrollbar.HORIZONTAL, 0, 0,
            0, 255));
        red.setPageIncrement(16);
        p.add(greenLabel = new Label("Green 0"));
        p.add(green = new Scrollbar(Scrollbar.HORIZONTAL, 0,
            0, 0, 255));
        green.setPageIncrement(16);
        p.add(blueLabel = new Label("Blue 0"));
        p.add(blue = new Scrollbar(Scrollbar.HORIZONTAL, 0, 0,
            0, 255));
        blue.setPageIncrement(16);
        add("South", p);

        c = new Canvas();
        c.setBackground(new Color(0, 0, 0));
        add("Center", c);
    }

    public boolean handleEvent(Event evt)
    {   if (evt.id == Event.WINDOW_DESTROY) System.exit(0);
        else if (evt.id == Event.SCROLL_ABSOLUTE
            || evt.id == Event.SCROLL_LINE_DOWN
            || evt.id == Event.SCROLL_LINE_UP
            || evt.id == Event.SCROLL_PAGE_DOWN
            || evt.id == Event.SCROLL_PAGE_UP)
        {   redLabel.setText("Red " + red.getValue());
            greenLabel.setText("Green " + green.getValue());
            blueLabel.setText("Blue " + blue.getValue());
            c.setBackground(new Color(red.getValue(),
                green.getValue(), blue.getValue()));

            c.repaint();
            return true;
        }
        return super.handleEvent(evt);
    }

    public static void main(String[] args)
```

```
      {   Frame f = new ColorSelect();
          f.resize(300, 200);
          f.show();
      }

      private Label redLabel;
      private Label greenLabel;
      private Label blueLabel;

      private Scrollbar red;
      private Scrollbar green;
      private Scrollbar blue;

      private Canvas c;
  }
```

`java.awt.Scrollbar`

• `Scrollbar(int orientation)`

Parameters:

     `orientation`   either `HORIZONTAL` or `VERTICAL`

• `void setValue(int value)`

Parameters:

     `value`   the new scroll position. Set to the current minimum or maximum if it is outside the scroll range

• `setPageIncrement(int 1)`

sets the page increment, the amount by which the scroll position changes when the user clicks between the arrows and the slider.

• `void setLineIncrement(int 1)`

sets the line increment, the amount by which the scroll position changes when the user clicks on the arrows at the ends of the scroll bar.

• `int getValue()`

returns the current scroll position.

• void setValues(int value, int visible, int minimum, int maximum)

Parameters:

value	the scroll position
visible	the visible area of the window, or 0 for a slider control
minimum	the minimum position value of the scroll bar
maximum	the maximum position value of the scroll bar

Scrolling a Window

In this section, we add scroll bars to the drawing application in the section on mouse events. Suppose we want to allow an area of 600 by 400 pixels to be filled with squares. Our window has an area of only 300 by 200 pixels, so we want the user to be able to scroll over the total area.

The basic idea is simple. Whenever we draw the window, we translate the graphics coordinates by the negatives of the scroll values. For example, if the values of the horizontal and vertical scroll bars are 200 and 100, then we want to draw the area starting at (200, 100). We move the origin to (–200, –100) and repaint the entire 600-by-400-pixel image. Much of the image is clipped, but the part of the underlying image that we want to see is then shown in the window (see Figure 7-29).

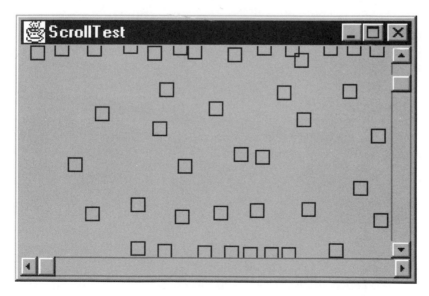

Figure 7-29

Thus what we need to do is:

- trap all scroll events and

- force a redraw when an event occurs.

Here's an example of the code to do this:

```
public boolean handleEvent(Event evt)
{   if (evt.id == Event.SCROLL_ABSOLUTE
        || evt.id == Event.SCROLL_LINE_DOWN
        || evt.id == Event.SCROLL_LINE_UP
        || evt.id == Event.SCROLL_PAGE_DOWN
        || evt.id == Event.SCROLL_PAGE_UP)
    {   canvas.translate(horiz.getValue(), vert.getValue())
    }
    . . .
}
```

The `translate` method of our canvas class stores the scroll offset and calls `repaint`.

```
public void translate(int x, int y)
{   dx = x;
    dy = y;
    repaint();
}
```

The data structure that stores the list of rectangles keeps them in *absolute coordinates*. That is not a problem in the `paint` procedure because we can translate the origin of the graphics context.

```
public void paint(Graphics g)
{   g.translate(-dx, -dy);
    for (int i = 0; i < nsquares; i++) draw(g, i);
}
```

But the mouse functions report the mouse locations in window coordinates. To test that a mouse click falls inside a square, we must add the scroll offset to all mouse coordinates.

```
public boolean mouseDown(Event evt, int x, int y)
{   x += dx;
    y += dy;
    current = find(x, y);
    . . .
}
```

The exact dimensioning of the scroll bars is a bit tricky. The visible area of the window is somewhat less than 300 by 200, because the scroll bars take some amount of space. We override the `show` procedure of the frame class as a convenient spot to initialize the scroll bars.

```
   public void show()
{   super.show();
    Dimension d = canvas.size();
    horiz.setValues(0, d.width, 0, 600);
    vert.setValue(0, d.height, 0, 400);
}
```

If the window is resized, we have to redo the entire computation. Resizing the window results in a WINDOW_MOVE (!) event. We trap it in the handleEvent function.

```
   public boolean handleEvent(Event evt)
{   if (evt.id == Event.MOVE_EVENT)
    {   Dimension d = canvas.size();
        horiz.setValues(horiz.getValue(), d.width, 0, 600);
        vert.setValue(horiz.getValue(), d.height, 0, 400);
    }
    else . . .
}
```

Here is the listing of the program.

```
import java.awt.*;

public class ScrollTest extends Frame
{   public ScrollTest()
    {   setTitle("ScrollTest");
        add("East", vert = new Scrollbar(Scrollbar.VERTICAL));
        add("South", horiz =
            new Scrollbar(Scrollbar.HORIZONTAL));
        add("Center", canvas = new SquareCanvas());
    }

    public boolean handleEvent(Event evt)
    {   if (evt.id == Event.WINDOW_DESTROY) System.exit(0);
        else if (evt.id == Event.WINDOW_MOVED)
        {   Dimension d = canvas.size();
            horiz.setValues(horiz.getValue(), d.width, 0, 600);
            vert.setValues(vert.getValue(), d.height, 0, 400);
        }
        else if (evt.id == Event.SCROLL_ABSOLUTE
            || evt.id == Event.SCROLL_LINE_DOWN
            || evt.id == Event.SCROLL_LINE_UP
            || evt.id == Event.SCROLL_PAGE_DOWN
            || evt.id == Event.SCROLL_PAGE_UP)
        {   canvas.translate(horiz.getValue(), vert.getValue());
            return true;
        }
        return super.handleEvent(evt);
    }
```

```java
    public void show()
    {   super.show();
        Dimension d = canvas.size();
        horiz.setValues(0, d.width, 0, 600);
        vert.setValues(0, d.height, 0, 400);
    }

    public static void main(String args[])
    {   Frame f = new ScrollTest();
        f.resize(300, 200);
        f.show();
    }

    private Scrollbar horiz;
    private Scrollbar vert;
    private SquareCanvas canvas;
}

class SquareCanvas extends Canvas
{   public void translate(int x, int y)
    {   dx = x;
        dy = y;
        repaint();
    }

    public void paint(Graphics g)
    {   g.translate(-dx, -dy);
        for (int i = 0; i < nsquares; i++)
            draw(g, i);
    }

    public int find(int x, int y)
    {   for (int i = 0; i < nsquares; i++)
            if (squares[i].x <= x
                    && x <= squares[i].x + SQUARELENGTH
                    && squares[i].y <= y
                    && y <= squares[i].y + SQUARELENGTH)
                return i;
        return -1;
    }

    public void draw(Graphics g, int i)
    {   g.drawRect(squares[i].x, squares[i].y, SQUARELENGTH,
        SQUARELENGTH);
    }

    public void add(int x, int y)
    {   if (nsquares < MAXNSQUARES)
        {   squares[nsquares] = new Point(x, y);
```

```
            nsquares++;
            repaint();
        }
    }

    public void remove(int n)
    {   nsquares--;
        squares[n] = squares[nsquares];
        if (current == n) current = -1;
        repaint();
    }

    public boolean mouseDown(Event evt, int x, int y)
    {   x += dx; y += dy;
        current = find(x, y);
        if (current < 0) // not inside a square
        {   add(x, y);
        }
        else if (evt.clickCount >= 2)
        {   remove(current);
        }
        return true;
    }

    public boolean mouseDrag(Event evt, int x, int y)
    {   x += dx; y += dy;
        if (current >= 0)
        {   Graphics g = getGraphics();
            g.translate(-dx, -dy);
            g.setXORMode(getBackground());
            draw(g, current);
            squares[current].x = x;
            squares[current].y = y;
            draw(g, current);
            g.dispose();
        }
        return true;
    }

    private static final int SQUARELENGTH = 10;

    private static final int MAXNSQUARES = 100;
    private Point[] squares = new Point[MAXNSQUARES];
    private int nsquares = 0;
    private int current = -1;
    private int dx = 0;
    private int dy = 0;
}
```

`java.awt.Graphics`

- `void translate(int x,  int y)`

changes the origin of the coordinate system used for drawing. All subsequent drawing operations are shifted left and up by the translation amount.

Parameters:

    `x, y`   the coordinates of the top left corner of the screen

CHAPTER

8

- Applet Basics

- Converting Applications to Applets

- The Applet HTML Tags

- Passing Information to Applets

- Dialog Boxes in Applets

- Multimedia

- The Applet Context

- The Life Cycle of an Applet

- It's an Applet. It's an Application. It's Both!

Applets

At this point, you should be comfortable with most of Java's language elements. We hope that you agree that Java is a nice (if not perfect), general purpose OOP language. The class libraries need improvements—but that will certainly come with time. Of course, being a simplified dialect of C++ is not enough to justify the hype surrounding Java. The unbelievable hype (as was mentioned in Chapters 1 and 2) stems from Java's ability to create programs ("applets") that can be downloaded from the Net and run in any Java-enabled WWW browser. Since you know the basics of the Java language, it is now time to learn the few extra details needed to write applets.

Applets work best when combined with Java's networking abilities and its ability to handle multiple threads. Please see Chapter 12 for information about threads and Chapter 13 for more on networking than we cover here.

Applet Basics

Java Applets and HTML Files

You run Java applications from the command line by having the Java interpreter interpret the bytecode contained in a class file. Applets, on the other hand, usually run within a Web page via a Java-enabled browser such as Netscape 2.0 or above. The JDK does come with a stand-alone applet viewer program that allows you to test your applets more easily—see the section "Viewing Applets" for more on the applet viewer. (For Windows 95, this program is called `appletviewer.exe` and may be found in the bin directory below the java directory if you use the normal installation defaults.)

To load applets into your Web browser, you must create a separate file that contains HTML tags to tell the browser which applets to load and where to put each applet on the Web page. Before the development of Java, HTML was simply a vehicle to indicate elements of a hypertext page. For example, <TITLE> indicates the title of the page, and any text that follows this tag becomes the title of the page. You indicate the end of the title with the </TITLE> tag. (This is one of the general rules for tags: a slash followed by the name of the element indicates the end of the element.)

The Java extensions to HTML tell any Java-enabled browser the following:

1. the name of the class file,

2. the location of the class file,

3. how the applet sits on the Web page.

The browser then retrieves the class file from the Net (or from a directory on the user's machine) and automatically runs the applet.

In addition to the applet itself, the Web page can contain all the other HTML elements you have seen in use on Web pages: multiple fonts, bulleted lists, graphics, links, and so on. Applets are just one part of the hypertext page. It is always worth keeping in mind that Java is *not* a tool for designing HTML pages; it is a tool for *bringing them to life*. This is not to say that the GUI design elements in a Java applet are not important, but they must work with (and, in fact, are subservient to) the underlying HTML design of the Web page.

 We do not cover general HTML tags at all; we assume that you know—or are working with someone who knows—the basics of HTML. There are only a few special HTML tags needed for Java applets. We do, of course, cover those later in this chapter. As for learning HTML, there are probably dozens of HTML books at your local bookstore. One that covers what you need and will not insult your intelligence (in spite of the title) is Mary Morris's *HTML Authoring for Fun and Profit* (SunSoft Press, 1995).

A Simple Applet

From a programmer's point of view, an applet is simply a Java class that extends the Applet class. Applet is part of the java.applet package. The Applet class is closely related to the AWT classes that you saw in the previous two chapters. For example, the event-handling and the buffering techniques you learned in Chapter 6 to avoid a flicker when loading images are useful for building applets as well.

Here is an example of one of the simplest Java applets:

```
import java.awt.*;
import java.applet.*;

public class NotHelloAgain extends Applet
{ Font f = new Font("System", Font.BOLD, 18);
    public void paint(Graphics g)
    {  g.setFont(f);
        g.drawString("We won't use 'hello world.'", 25, 50);
    }
}
```

Notice, as usual, that we are overriding the `paint` method in order to actually display something.

In addition to this Java file, which needs to be compiled into a class file, we need, at the minimum, a trivial HTML file. It is customary (but not necessary) to give it the same name as that of the major applet inside. Let us call it `NotHelloAgain.html`. Here is what you need in this file:

```
<APPLET CODE="NotHelloAgain.class" WIDTH=100 HEIGHT=100>
</APPLET>
```

We will explain the options for the APPLET tag later in this chapter.

If you are using our customized version of WinEdit, then you can get a first glimpse at your applet by compiling the program from within WinEdit and choosing Execute from the Project menu.

This invokes a (rather weird) batch file that:

1. creates a file and puts in the minimum number of HTML tags needed to be able to run your code as an applet (the size of the applet is fixed at 300 by 200 pixels),

2. saves the file with an HTM extension (so it will not overwrite any of your .html files),

3. invokes Sun's applet viewer on this file.

Close the applet viewer when you have finished testing your applet.

This method gives you a quick and dirty way to test your applets without creating a full-blown HTML page.

Viewing Applets

More generally, there are three ways for you to see your applet at work.

1. You can use Sun's applet viewer directly.

   Enter

   ```
   appletviewer NotHelloAgain.html
   ```

The command line for the applet viewer program is the name of the HTML file, not the class file.

2. In Netscape, you can load a local file by choosing File | Open File from the File menu and entering the file name or by selecting the file name from the dialog box. This tells Netscape to load the HTML file.

3. You can give Netscape the URL for the HTML page that contains the applet and tell it to open this URL. Do this by selecting File | Open Location (or click the Open button, of course) and typing in a file URL. For example, something like:

```
file:///C|/CoreJavaBook/ch8/NotHelloAgain/NotHelloAgain.html
```

or, you can open the file through a bookmark that you previously saved.

Netscape saves bookmarks to local files as file URLs and not as file names. For security purposes, Netscape considers a local file location saved as a bookmark just as alien as a Net URL. (See below for more on security restrictions on applets.)

Instead of Netscape, you can use another Java-enabled browser. We have used Netscape in our examples because no other Java-enabled browsers for the 1.0 release of Java were available to us.

At this time, the HotJava browser that Sun created *cannot* run applets created with the 1.0 release of Java. Sun has announced plans to update HotJava, but no date has been given.

There are pros and cons to all three approaches.

- The applet viewer program is simple and it starts up quickly. However, it only shows you the applet, not the surrounding HTML text. (If an HTML file contains multiple applets, the applet viewer pops up multiple windows.)

- Netscape shows you the text and graphics of the Web page together with the applet, exactly as the user of your page would see it. Also, if you load the file as a URL (either directly or via a bookmark), Netscape enforces its security restrictions for downloaded applets. This is the most realistic test you can give your applets: your applet will behave exactly as it would on your users' Web pages. The applet viewer does not enforce security restrictions, and Netscape does not enforce them on applets opened inside a local file.

For debugging applets, you will find Netscape maddening. If you load your applet into Netscape, do not like the result, fix up the applet, and reload the Web page containing it, Netscape will continue to use your old applet code. You need to quit and restart Netscape to reload the new version of the applet. When you are still debugging the applet code, the applet viewer is a better choice than Netscape. Use Netscape to test the look of the final Web page and to test the security aspects.

The key point is that when you run the applet inside the applet viewer, all of the text in the HTML file is ignored. The applet viewer only shows the applet. But when you view the applet with Netscape, it sits inside a Web page filled with text. You should use the surrounding text to your advantage. Explain what the applet is good for, and make clear how to use it. We have seen far too many applets that require double-clicking to activate them, or users must type in unadvertised keystrokes. You have plenty of space on the Web page to explain every aspect of the applet.

Getting Your Computer Ready for Java Networking

Several of the applets in this chapter require Internet access so that the applets can retrieve Web pages from the Internet. There are many ways to connect to the Net; unfortunately, not all of them are compatible with Java. For example, a connection through CompuServe or America Online does not yet work. Merely being connected to the Net is not enough; Java expects that your network supports the TCP/IP protocol. (TCP/IP stands for Transmission Control Protocol/Internet Protocol.)

If your computer has a network card and is currently connected to a network running the TCP/IP protocol, then you are all set. That is certainly the case when you are running Unix or Linux and are connected to a local network that, in turn, is connected to the Internet. If you have a PC running Windows 95 or NT and are using an Internet browser such as Netscape through a network connection, then you are also almost certainly ready.

The problems arise if you are browsing the Net through a telephone connection. This is done through the intermediary of a program, usually called a "stack." The stack program implements the TCP/IP protocol for communicating with the Internet. (Some services, such as CompuServe, do not use a standard stack at all.) Unfortunately, there are various possible stacks that you can use for your Internet connection. Many third-party Internet providers have their own version of a TCP/IP stack (or WinSock driver, as it is often called in the Windows world). On Windows-based machines, the applet viewer in Java 1.0 *requires* that you use the Microsoft TCP/IP stack.

This means that if you are using a dialup connection with a third-party WinSock driver such as Trumpet WinSock, you will need to replace that driver with the Windows Dial-up Networking package that uses the Microsoft TCP/IP stack. This software comes free with both Windows 95 and Windows NT. Of course, actually removing your old stack and telling the operating system that you are using a new stack may require pulling out a manual—we will leave those details to you.

Security Basics

Because applets are designed to be loaded from a remote site and then executed locally, security becomes important. For this reason, applets (unlike applications) are restricted in what they can do. In particular,

1. applets can *never* run any local executable program;

2. applets cannot communicate with any host other than the server from which they were downloaded (that server is called the *originating host*);

3. applets cannot read or write to the local computer's file system (this is true only of Netscape. It is possible that other browsers will implement less stringent security restrictions because Sun has not made this part of the Java specification);

4. applets cannot find any information about the local computer, except for the Java version used; the name and version of the operating system; and the characters used to separate files (for instance, / or \), paths (such as : or ;), and lines (such as \n or \r\n). In particular, applets cannot find out the user's name, e-mail address, and so on.

The following table shows what Java programs can do in the following four scenarios:

NL = Netscape loading a URL

NF = Netscape loading a local file

AV = Applet viewer

JA = Java running an application (not an applet)

Table 8-1	NL	NF	AV	JA
read local file	no	no	yes	yes
write local file	no	no	yes	yes
get file information	no	no	yes	yes
delete file	no	no	no	yes
run another program	no	no	yes	yes
read the user.name property	no	yes	yes	yes
connect to network port on server	yes	yes	yes	yes
connect to network port on other host	no	yes	yes	yes
load Java library	no	yes	yes	yes
call exit	no	no	yes	yes
create a pop-up window	with warning	yes	yes	yes

Converting Applications to Applets

It is easy to convert a graphical Java application (that is, one you can start with the `java` command line interpreter) into an applet that you can embed in a Web page. Essentially, all of the user-interface code is completely unchanged. To understand why, look at Figure 8-1.

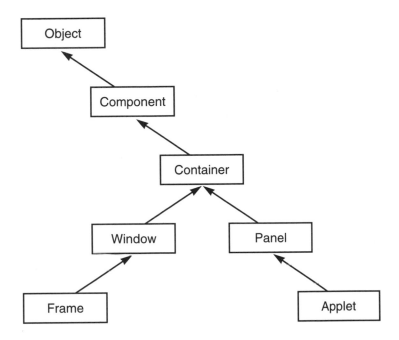

Figure 8-1

Notice that the `Applet` and the `Frame` class both descend from `Container`. Therefore, you can continue to use the same methods to add user-interface components. For example, you add a button to an applet with a call to

```
add(new Button("Start"));
```

or a canvas with a call to

```
add(new Canvas());
```

On the other hand, there are a few subtle points that can trip you up. Probably the most common is that the default layout managers are different. Recall that, for frames (used in applications), the default layout manager is `BorderLayout`. For panels (and, hence, applets), it is the `FlowLayout` manager. This means that, if you have not set a specific layout manager for your application, you will have implicitly used the `BorderLayout` manager. In that case, you will need to change the layout manager in the applet to `BorderLayout`.

Here are the specific steps for converting an application to an applet.

1. Make an HTML page with an APPLET tag.

2. Eliminate the `main` method in the application. Usually `main` contains code to make a new frame object. With applets, that is automatically taken care of by the browser, since it makes an object of the class specified in the APPLET tag. Also, `main` usually sets the frame size. For applets, this is done with the WIDTH and HEIGHT fields of the APPLET tag in the actual HTML file.

3. Derive the class from `Applet`, not from `Frame`.

4. Replace the constructor with a method called `init`. When the browser creates an object of the applet class, it calls the `init()` method.

5. If the application's frame implicitly uses a border layout, you must set the layout manager for the applet in the `init` function. For example, compare the following code with the constructor for the calculator program in Chapter 7:

```
public class CalculatorApplet extends Applet
{   public void init()
    {   setLayout(new BorderLayout());

        // required in applet, not in frame
        display = new TextField("0");
        display.setEditable(false);
        add("North", display);
        . . .

    }

}
```

6. If the application calls `setTitle`, eliminate the call to the method. Applets do not have title bars. (You can, of course, title the Web page itself, using the <TITLE> HTML tag.) If the application uses menus, eliminate them and replace them with buttons or some other user-interface component. Applets cannot have menu bars.

As an example of this transformation, we will change the calculator application from Chapter 7 into an applet. Here is how it looks, sitting inside a Web page:

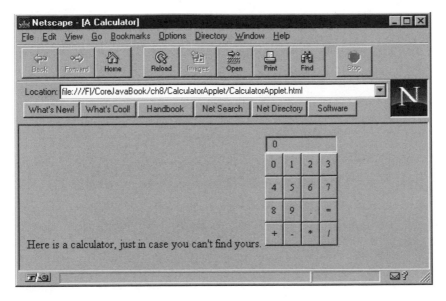

Figure 8-2

Here is the HTML page:

```
<HTML>
<TITLE>A Calculator</TITLE>
<BODY>
Here is a calculator, just in case you can't find yours.
<APPLET CODE="CalculatorApplet.class" WIDTH=100 HEIGHT=150>
</APPLET>
</BODY>
</HTML>
```

And here is the code for the applet.

```
public class CalculatorApplet extends Applet
{  public void init()
   {  setLayout(new BorderLayout());

      display = new TextField("0");
      display.setEditable(false);
      add("North", display);

      Panel p = new Panel();
      p.setLayout(new GridLayout(4, 4));
      for (int i = 0; i <= 9; i++)
      p.add(new Button("" + (char)('0' + i)));
```

```java
        p.add(new Button("."));
        p.add(new Button("="));
        p.add(new Button("+"));
        p.add(new Button("-"));
        p.add(new Button("*"));
        p.add(new Button("/"));
        add("Center", p);
    }

    public boolean handleEvent(Event evt)
    {   if (evt.id == Event.WINDOW_DESTROY) System.exit(0);
        return super.handleEvent(evt);
    }

    public boolean action(Event evt, Object arg)
    {   if (arg instanceof String)
        {   String s = (String) arg;
            char ch = s.charAt(0);
            if ('0' <= ch && ch <= '9' || ch == '.')
            {   if (start) display.setText(s);
                else display.setText(display.getText() + s);
                start = false;
            }
            else
            {   if (start)
                {   if (s.equals("-"))
                    { display.setText(s); start = false; }
                    else op = s;
                }
                else
                {   calculate(Format.atof(display.getText()));
                    op = s;
                    start = true;
                }
            }
        }
        else return super.action(evt, arg);
        return true;
    }

    public void calculate(double n)
    {   if (op == "+") arg += n;
        else if (op == "-") arg -= n;
        else if (op == "*") arg *= n;
        else if (op == "/") arg /= n;
        else if (op == "%") arg %= n;
        else if (op == "=") arg = n;
        display.setText("" + arg);
    }
```

```
    private TextField display;
    private double arg = 0;
    private String op = "=";
    private boolean start = true;
}
```

java.applet.Applet

• void init()

This method is called when the applet is first loaded. You must override this method and place all intialization code here.

• void resize(int width, int height)

This method requests that the applet be resized. This would be a great method if it worked on Web pages; unfortunately, it does not usually work in browsers because it interferes with their page-layout mechanisms. This method does nothing in Netscape 2.0, but it does work in the applet viewer.

The Applet HTML Tags

The Required Tags

We have already seen the APPLET tag in action. In its most basic form, it looks like this:

```
<APPLET CODE="NotHelloAgain.class" WIDTH=100 HEIGHT=100>
```

As you have seen, the CODE tag gives the name of the class file and must include the .class extension; the WIDTH and HEIGHT tags size the window that will hold the applet. Both are measured in pixels. You also need a matching </APPLET> tag that marks the end of the HTML tagging needed for an applet. These tags are required. If any are missing, the browser cannot load your applet.

All of this would usually be embedded in an HTML page that, at the very least, might look like this:

```
<HTML>
<HEAD>
<TITLE>NotHelloAgain</TITLE>
</HEAD>
<BODY>
The next line of text is displayed through
  the auspices of Java:
```

```
<APPLET CODE= "NotHelloAgain.class" WIDTH=100 HEIGHT= 100>
Any text here appears in non-Java enabled browsers only.
</APPLET>
</BODY>
</HTML>
```

 Whether or not case is relevant in the various applet tags such as <APPLET> depends on your system. Windows 95 and Solaris ignore case in HTML tags. The beta version of the applet viewer on the Macintosh only likes lowercase for all applet related HTML tags. (Case is relevant in identifying the name of the applet class.)

What follows are short discussions of the various attributes you can (or must) use following the <APPLET> tag in order to position your applet. (For those familiar with HTML, these tags are similar to those used with the <IMG> tag for image placement on a Web page.)

Applet Tags for Positioning

WIDTH, HEIGHT

These attributes are required and give the width and height of the applet, as measured in pixels. In the applet viewer, this is the initial size of the applet. You can resize any window that the applet viewer creates. In Netscape, you *cannot* resize the applet. You will need to make a good guess about how much space your applet requires to show up well for all users.

ALIGN

This attribute specifies the alignment of the applet. There are two basic choices. The applet can be a block, with text flowing around it. Or the applet can be *inline*, floating inside a line of text as if it were an oversized text character. The first two values (LEFT and RIGHT) make the text flow around the applet. The others make the applet flow with the text.

The choices are described as follows:

Attribute	What It does
LEFT	Places the applet at the left margin of the page. Text that follows on the page goes in the space to the right of the applet.
RIGHT	Places the applet at the right margin of the page. Text that follows on the page goes in the space to the left of the applet.
BOTTOM	Places the bottom of the applet at the bottom of the text in the current line.
TOP	Places the top of the applet with the top of the current line.

TEXTTOP	Places the top of the applet with the top of the current line.
MIDDLE	Places the middle of the applet with the baseline of the current line.
ABSMIDDLE	Places the middle of the applet with the middle of the current line.
BASELINE	Places the bottom of the applet with the baseline of the current line.
ABSBOTTOM	Places the bottom of the applet with the bottom of the current line.

VSPACE, HSPACE

These optional attributes specify the number of pixels above and below the applet (VSPACE) and on each side of the applet (HSPACE).

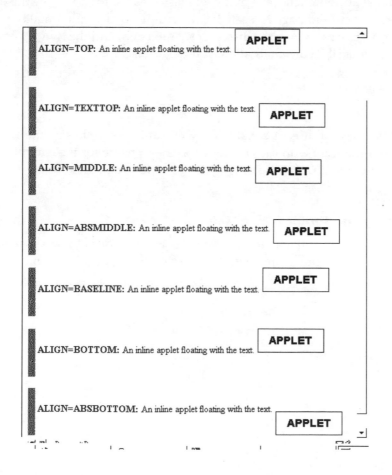

The Applet Tags for Coding

There are four applet tags that work directly with the code you write; here are short descriptions of the first three. (The last one is for passing parameters to your applets; we take that up in the next section.)

CODE

This required tag gives the name of the applet's class (or compiled) file. This name is taken relative to where the current page was located. This could be either a local directory or a Net URL. You cannot use absolute path names here. For example, if you are reading a page in a directory called C:\applets, you can only use class files in this directory. (See the CODEBASE tag that we discuss next for how to get at the subdirectories of this directory.)

CODEBASE

This optional attribute tells Java that your class files are found below the directory where the current page is located. For example, if an applet called FirstApplet.class is in the directory MyApplets, and the MyApplets directory is *below* the current location, you would use:

```
<APPLET CODE="FirstApplet.class" CODEBASE="MyApplets" WIDTH=100
    HEIGHT=100>
```

Name

This is a rare tag, but it is essential when you want two applets on the same page to communicate with each other. It specifies a name for the current applet instance. You would pass this string to the getApplet method of the AppletContext class.

Embedding an Applet into a Web Page

Here is a fun and useful applet that calculates whether or not you are saving enough money for your retirement. You enter your age, how much money you save every month, and so on.

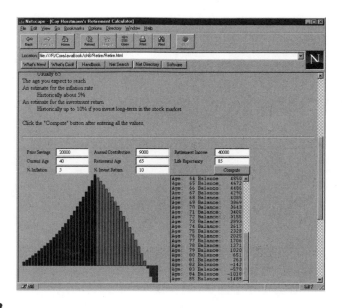

Figure 8-3

The text box and the graph show the balance of the retirement account for every year. If the numbers turn negative towards the later part of your life, and the bars in the graph turn red, you need to do something, for example, save more money or postpone your retirement. The surrounding Web page tells how to enter the information and how to interpret the outcome.

When you look at the code for the applet, you will find that it is almost identical to the code for the graphical applications that we discussed in the last two chapters. There are two differences. We derive from `Applet`, not `Frame`. And we move the code from the `main` function and the constructor into the `init` method.

```
import java.awt.*;
import java.applet.*;
import java.io.*;
import corejava.*;

public class Retire extends Applet
{  public void init()
   {  GridBagLayout gbl = new GridBagLayout();
      setLayout(gbl);

      GridBagConstraints gbc = new GridBagConstraints();
      gbc.fill = GridBagConstraints.BOTH;
      gbc.weightx = 100;
      gbc.weighty = 100;
```

```
        add(new Label("Prior Savings"), gbl, gbc, 0, 0, 1, 1);
        add(savingsField, gbl, gbc, 1, 0, 1, 1);
        add(new Label("Annual Contribution"),
            gbl, gbc, 2, 0, 1, 1);
        add(contribField, gbl, gbc, 3, 0, 1, 1);
        add(new Label("Retirement Income"),
            gbl, gbc, 4, 0, 1, 1);
        add(incomeField, gbl, gbc, 5, 0, 1, 1);
        add(new Label("Current Age"), gbl, gbc, 0, 1, 1, 1);
        add(currentAgeField, gbl, gbc, 1, 1, 1, 1);
        add(new Label("Retirement Age"), gbl, gbc, 2, 1, 1, 1);
        add(retireAgeField, gbl, gbc, 3, 1, 1, 1);
        add(new Label("Life Expectancy"), gbl, gbc, 4, 1, 1, 1);
        add(deathAgeField, gbl, gbc, 5, 1, 1, 1);
        add(new Label("% Inflation"), gbl, gbc, 0, 2, 1, 1);
        add(inflationPercentField, gbl, gbc, 1, 2, 1, 1);
        add(new Label("% Invest Return"), gbl, gbc, 2, 2, 1, 1);
        add(investPercentField, gbl, gbc, 3, 2, 1, 1);
        add(new Button("Compute"), gbl, gbc, 5, 2, 1, 1);
        add(retireCanvas, gbl, gbc, 0, 3, 4, 1);
        add(retireText, gbl, gbc, 4, 3, 2, 1);
        retireText.setEditable(false);
        retireText.setFont(new Font("Courier", Font.PLAIN, 10));
    }

    private void add(Component c, GridBagLayout gbl,
        GridBagConstraints gbc, int x, int y, int w, int h)
    {   gbc.gridx = x;
        gbc.gridy = y;
        gbc.gridwidth = w;
        gbc.gridheight = h;
        gbl.setConstraints(c, gbc);
        add(c);
    }

    public boolean action(Event evt, Object arg)
    {   if (arg.equals("Compute"))
        {   if (savingsField.isValid()
                && contribField.isValid()
                && incomeField.isValid()
                && currentAgeField.isValid()
                && retireAgeField.isValid()
                && deathAgeField.isValid()
                && inflationPercentField.isValid()
                && investPercentField.isValid())
            {   RetireInfo info = new RetireInfo();
                info.savings = savingsField.getValue();
                info.contrib = contribField.getValue();
                info.income = incomeField.getValue();
```

```
            info.currentAge = currentAgeField.getValue();
            info.retireAge = retireAgeField.getValue();
            info.deathAge = deathAgeField.getValue();
            info.inflationPercent
                = inflationPercentField.getValue();
            info.investPercent
                = investPercentField.getValue();
            retireCanvas.redraw(info);
            int i;
            retireText.setText("");
            for (i = info.currentAge; i <= info.deathAge; i++)
            {  retireText.appendText(
                  new Format("Age: %3d").form(i)
                     + new Format(" Balance: %8d\n")
                     .form(info.getBalance(i)));
            }
         }
      }
      else return super.action(evt, arg);
      return true;
   }

   private IntTextField savingsField
      = new IntTextField(0, 0, 10000000, 10);
   private IntTextField contribField
      = new IntTextField(9000, 0, 1000000, 10);
   private IntTextField incomeField
      = new IntTextField(0, 0, 1000000, 10);
   private IntTextField currentAgeField
      = new IntTextField(0, 0, 150, 4);
   private IntTextField retireAgeField
      = new IntTextField(65, 0, 150, 4);
   private IntTextField deathAgeField
      = new IntTextField(85, 0, 150, 4);
   private IntTextField inflationPercentField
      = new IntTextField(5, 0, 1000, 4);
   private IntTextField investPercentField
      = new IntTextField(10, 0, 1000, 4);
   private RetireCanvas retireCanvas = new RetireCanvas();
   private TextArea retireText = new TextArea(10, 25);
}

class RetireInfo
{  int getBalance(int year)
   {  if (year < currentAge) return 0;
      else if (year == currentAge)
      {  age = year;
         balance = savings;
         return balance;
```

```
        }
        else if (year == age)
            return balance;
        if (year != age + 1)
            getBalance(year - 1);
        age = year;
        if (age < retireAge)
            balance += contrib;
        else
            balance -= income;
        balance = (int)(balance
            * (1 + (investPercent - inflationPercent) / 100.0));
        return balance;
    }

    int savings;
    int contrib;
    int income;
    int currentAge;
    int retireAge;
    int deathAge;
    int inflationPercent;
    int investPercent;

    private int age;
    private int balance;
}

class RetireCanvas extends Canvas
{   RetireCanvas()
    {   resize(400, 200);
    }
    void redraw(RetireInfo newInfo)
    {   info = newInfo;
        repaint();
    }

    public void paint(Graphics g)
    {   if (info == null) return;

        int minValue = 0;
        int maxValue = 0;
        int i;
        for (i = info.currentAge; i <= info.deathAge; i++)
        {   int v = info.getBalance(i);
            if (minValue > v) minValue = v;
            if (maxValue < v) maxValue = v;
        }
```

```
    if (maxValue == minValue) return;

    Dimension d = size();
    int barWidth = d.width / (info.deathAge
        - info.currentAge + 1);
    double scale = (double)d.height
        / (maxValue - minValue);

    for (i = info.currentAge; i <= info.deathAge; i++)
    {   int x1 = (i - info.currentAge) * barWidth + 1;
        int y1;
        int v = info.getBalance(i);
        int height;
        int yOrigin = (int)(maxValue * scale);

        if (v >= 0)
        {   y1 = (int)((maxValue - v) * scale);
            height = yOrigin - y1;
        }
        else
        {   y1 = yOrigin;
            height = (int)(-v * scale);
        }

        if (i < info.retireAge)
            g.setColor(Color.blue);
        else if (v >= 0)
            g.setColor(Color.green);
        else
            g.setColor(Color.red);
        g.fillRect(x1, y1, barWidth - 2, height);
        g.setColor(Color.black);
        g.drawRect(x1, y1, barWidth - 2, height);
    }
}

private RetireInfo info = null;
}
```

Passing Information to Applets

Just as applications have the ability to use command line information, applets have the ability to use parameters that are embedded in the HTML file. This is done via the HTML tag PARAM. For example, suppose you want to let the Web page determine the size of the font to use in your applet. You could use the following HTML tags:

```
<APPLET CODE="FontTestApplet.class" WIDTH = 200, HEIGHT = 200>
<PARAM NAME=font VALUE="Helvetica">
</APPLET>
```

You then pick up the value of the parameter using the `getParameter` method of the `Applet` class, as in the following example of a `paint` procedure:

```
import java.awt.*;
import java.awt.*;

public class FontTestApplet extends Applet
{   public void paint(Graphics g)
    {   String fontName = getParameter("font");
        Font f = new Font(fontName, Font.BOLD, 18);
        g.setFont(f);
        g.drawString("We won't use 'hello world.'", 25, 50);
    }
}
```

Parameters are always returned as strings. You need to convert the string to a numeric type if that is what is called for. You do this in the standard ways: either by using the appropriate method, such as `parseInt` of the `Integer` class, or by using methods such as `atof` in our `Format` class.

For example, if we wanted to add a size parameter for the font, then the HTML code might look like this:

```
<APPLET CODE="FontTestApplet.class WIDTH = 200 HEIGHT = 200>
<PARAM NAME=font VALUE="Helvetica">
<PARAM NAME=size VALUE="24">
</APPLET>
```

The following source code shows how to read the integer parameter.

```
import java.awt.*;
import java.awt.*;

 public class FontTestApplet extends Applet
{   public void paint(Graphics g)
    {   String fontName = getParameter("font");
        int fontSize = Integer.parseInt(getParameter("size"));
        Font f = new Font(fontName, Font.BOLD, fontSize);
        g.setFont(f);
        g.drawString("We won't use 'hello world.'", 25, 50);
    }
}
```

The strings used when you define the parameters via the PARAM tag and those used in the `getParameter` method must match exactly. In particular, both are case sensitive.

In addition to assuring that the parameters match in your code, you should find out whether or not the `sizeString` parameter was left out. You do this with a simple test for `null`. For example:

```
int fontsize;
String sizeString = getParameter("size");
if (sizeString ==null) fontSize = 12;
else fontSize = Integer.parseInt(sizeString);
```

Here is a useful applet that uses parameters extensively. The applet draws a bar chart.

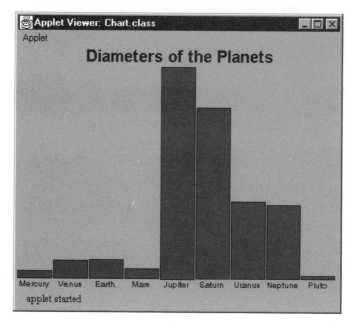

Figure 8-4

The applet takes the labels and the heights of the bars from the PARAM values in the HTML file. Here is what the HTML file for Figure 8-4 looks like:

```
<APPLET CODE="Chart.class" WIDTH=400 HEIGHT=300>
<PARAM NAME="title" VALUE="Diameters of the Planets">
<PARAM NAME="values" VALUE="9">
<PARAM NAME="name_1" VALUE="Mercury">
<PARAM NAME="name_2" VALUE="Venus">
<PARAM NAME="name_3" VALUE="Earth">
<PARAM NAME="name_4" VALUE="Mars">
<PARAM NAME="name_5" VALUE="Jupiter">
<PARAM NAME="name_6" VALUE="Saturn">
<PARAM NAME="name_7" VALUE="Uranus">
```

```
<PARAM NAME="name_8"  VALUE="Neptune">
<PARAM NAME="name_9"  VALUE="Pluto">
<PARAM NAME="value_1"  VALUE="3100">
<PARAM NAME="value_2"  VALUE="7500">
<PARAM NAME="value_3"  VALUE="8000">
<PARAM NAME="value_4"  VALUE="4200">
<PARAM NAME="value_5"  VALUE="88000">
<PARAM NAME="value_6"  VALUE="71000">
<PARAM NAME="value_7"  VALUE="32000">
<PARAM NAME="value_8"  VALUE="30600">
<PARAM NAME="value_9"  VALUE="1430">
</APPLET>
```

You could have set up an array of strings and an array of numbers in the applet. But there are two advantages to using the PARAM mechanism instead. You can have multiple copies of the same applet on your Web page, showing different graphs: just put two APPLET tags with different sets of parameters on the page. And you can change the data that you want to chart. Admittedly, the diameters of the planets will stay the same for quite some time, but suppose your Web page contains a chart of weekly sales data. It is easy to update the Web page, because it is plain text. Editing and recompiling a Java file on a weekly basis is more tedious.

In fact, someone has probably figured out how to do fancier graphs than the one in our chart applet. If you find one, you can drop it into your Web page and feed it parameters without ever needing to know how the applet renders the graphs.

Here is the source code of our chart applet. Note that the init method reads the parameters, and the paint method draws the chart.

```
import java.awt.*;
import java.applet.*;
import java.io.*;
import corejava.*;

public class Chart extends Applet
{  double values[];
   String names[];
   String title;

   public void init()
   {  int n = Format.atoi(getParameter("values"));
      values = new double[n];
      names = new String[n];
      title = getParameter("title");
```

```
      int i;
      for (i = 0; i < n; i++)
      {   values[i]
              = Format.atof(getParameter("value_" + (i + 1)));
          names[i] = getParameter("name_" + (i + 1));
      }
   }

   public void paint(Graphics g)
   {   int i;
       int n = Format.atoi(getParameter("values"));
       double minValue = 0;
       double maxValue = 0;
       for (i = 0; i < values.length; i++)
       {   if (minValue > values[i]) minValue = values[i];
           if (maxValue < values[i]) maxValue = values[i];
       }

       Dimension d = size();
       Insets in = insets();
       int clientWidth = d.width - in.right - in.left;
       int clientHeight = d.height - in.bottom - in.top;
       int barWidth = clientWidth / n;

       Font titleFont = new Font("Helvetica", Font.BOLD, 20);
       FontMetrics titleFontMetrics
          = g.getFontMetrics(titleFont);
       Font labelFont = new Font("Helvetica", Font.PLAIN, 10);
       FontMetrics labelFontMetrics
          = g.getFontMetrics(labelFont);

       int titleWidth = titleFontMetrics.stringWidth(title);
       int y = titleFontMetrics.getAscent();
       int x = (clientWidth - titleWidth) / 2;
       g.setFont(titleFont);
       g.drawString(title, x, y);

       int top = titleFontMetrics.getHeight();
       int bottom = labelFontMetrics.getHeight();
       if (maxValue == minValue) return;
       double scale = (clientHeight - top - bottom)
          / (maxValue - minValue);
       y = clientHeight - labelFontMetrics.getDescent();
       g.setFont(labelFont);

       for (i = 0; i < n; i++)
       {   int x1 = i * barWidth + 1;
           int y1 = top;
           int height = (int)(values[i] * scale);
```

```
        if (values[i] >= 0)
            y1 += (int)((maxValue - values[i]) * scale);
        else
        {   y1 += (int)(maxValue * scale);
            height = -height;
        }

        g.setColor(Color.red);
        g.fillRect(x1, y1, barWidth - 2, height);
        g.setColor(Color.black);
        g.drawRect(x1, y1, barWidth - 2, height);
        int labelWidth
            = labelFontMetrics.stringWidth(names[i]);
        x = i * barWidth + (barWidth - labelWidth) / 2;
        g.drawString(names[i], x, y);
        }
    }
}
```

`java.applet.Applet`

• `public String getParameter(String name)`

This gets a parameter defined with a PARAM directive in the Web page loading the applet. The string is case sensitive.

• `public String getAppletInfo()`

This is a method that many applet authors override to return a string that contains information about the author, version, and copyright of the current applet. You need to create this information by overriding this method in your applet class.

• `public String[][] getParameterInfo()`

This is a method that many applet authors override to return an array of PARAM tag options that this applet supports. Each row contains three entries: the name, the type, and a description of the parameter. Here is an example:

```
"fps", "1-10", "frames per second"
"repeat", "boolean", "repeat image loop?"
"images", "url", "directory containing images"
```

Dialog Boxes in Applets

An applet sits embedded in a Web page, in a frame of a size that is fixed by the WIDTH and HEIGHT values in the APPLET tag of the HTML page. This can be quite limiting. Many programmers wonder whether or not they can have a pop-up dialog box or menus to make better use of the available space. It is, indeed, possible to create a pop-up dialog box. Here is a simple applet with a single button labeled "Calculator." When you click on the button, a calculator pops up in a separate window.

This is easy to do. We simply use the `Calculator` class from Chapter 7. Recall that it is derived from `Frame`, so we add the necessary code to create a new calculator object as indicated by the bold line of the following code.

```
class CalculatorApplet extends Applet
{   public void init()
    {   add(new Button("Calculator"));
    }

    public boolean action(Event evt, Object arg)
    {   if (arg.equals("Calculator"))
        {   if (calc.isShowing()) calc.hide();
            else calc.show();
        }
        else return super.action(evt, arg);
        return true;
    }

    Frame calc = new Calculator();
}
```

When you click on the calculator button, the dialog box pops up and floats over the Web page. When you click on the button again, the calculator goes away.

There is, however, a catch that you need to know about before you put this applet on your Web page. To see how the calculator looks to a potential user, load the Web page from a file URL (for example, by making a bookmark to it, exiting and restarting Netscape, and then opening the bookmark). The calculator will be surrounded by a yellow border with an ominous warning message (see Figure 8-5).

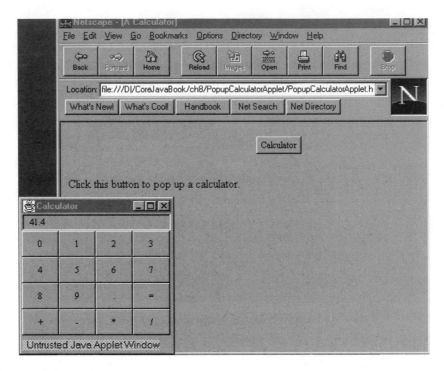

Figure 8-5

This is a security feature of Netscape. Netscape wants to make sure that your applet does not launch a window that the user might mistake for a local application. It does this regardless of the fact that it would take a super-human effort to write AWT code that even remotely resembles a professional Windows program. The fear is that if such a feat could be done, an unsuspecting user could visit a Web page, which automatically launches the applets on it, and mistakenly type in a password or credit card number, which the applet would send back to its host.

To avoid any possibility of shenanigans like this, all pop-up windows launched by an applet bear the "Untrusted Java Applet" label. That label is likely to be so scary to most users that you may want to avoid launching any external frames from your applet.

By the way, an applet inside a Web page cannot have menus. But a frame spawned by the Web page can have a menu bar. Of course, such a frame still has a warning border.

The yellow frame and warning label are only applied if the Web page is loaded through a URL, not if you load it through the File | Open File dialog.

Multimedia

URLs

A URL is really nothing more than a description of a resource on the Internet. For example, `"http://java.sun.com"` tells the browser to use the hypertext transfer protocol on the file located at `java.sun.com`. Java has the class `URL` that encapsulates URLs. The simplest way to make a URL is to give a string to the URL constructor:

```
URL u = new URL("http://java.sun.com");
```

This is called an *absolute* URL because we specify the entire resource name. Another useful URL constructor is a *relative* URL.

```
URL data = new URL(u, "data/planets.dat");
```

This specifies the file `planets.dat`, located in the data subdirectory of the URL `u`.

Both constructors make sure that you have used the correct syntax for a URL. If you haven't, they cause a run time error, a so-called `MalformedURLException`. Up to now, you have been able to ignore most run time errors, but this error is one the compiler will not let you ignore. You must tell the compiler that you are prepared for the error condition. The relevant code is as follows:

```
try
{   String s = "http://java.sun.com";
    URL u = new URL(s);
    . . .
}
catch(MalformedURLException e)
{   // deal with error
    System.out.println("Error " + e);
}
```

We will discuss this syntax for dealing with exceptions in detail in Chapter 10. For now, if you see code like this in one of our code samples, just gloss over the `try` and `catch` keywords.

A common way of obtaining a URL is to ask an applet where it came from, in particular,

- What is the URL of the page that is calling it?

- What is the URL of the applet itself?

To find the former, use the `getDocumentBase` method; to find the latter, use `getCodeBase`. You do not need to place these calls in a `try` block.

Obtaining Multimedia Files

You can retrieve images and audio files with the `getImage` and `getAudioClip` methods.

```
Image cat = getImage(getDocumentBase(), "images/cat.gif");
AudioClip meow = getAudioClip(getDocumentBase(),
    "audio/meow.au");
```

Here we use the `getDocumentBase` method that returns the URL from which your applet is loaded. The second argument to the `URL` constructor specifies where the image or audio clip is located, relative to the base document.

Once you have the images and audio clips, what can you do with them? You saw in Chapter 6 how to display a single image. In Chapter 12, you will see how to play an animation sequence composed of multiple images. To play an audio clip, simply invoke its `play` method.

You can also call `play` without first loading the audio clip.

```
play(getDocumentBase(), "audio/meow.au");
```

But, to show an image, you must first load it.

`java.net.URL`

• `URL(String name)`

creates a URL object from a string describing an absolute URL.

• `URL(URL base, String name)`

creates a relative URL object. If the string `name` describes an absolute URL, then the `base` URL is ignored. Otherwise, it is interpreted as a relative directory from the base URL.

`java.applet.Applet`

• `public URL getDocumentBase()`

gets the URL for the page that contains the applet.

• `public URL getCodeBase()`

gets the URL of the applet code itself.

• `void play(URL url)`
• `void play(URL url, String name)`

The first form plays an audio file specified by the URL. The second form uses the string to provide a path relative to the URL in the first argument. Nothing happens if the audio clip cannot be found.

- `AudioClip getAudioClip(URL url)`
- `AudioClip getAudioClip(URL url, String name)`

gets an audio clip, given a URL. The second form uses the string to provide a path relative to the URL in the first argument. The function returns `null` if the audio clip cannot be found.

- `Image getImage(URL url)`
- `Image getImage(URL url, String name)`

gets an image, given a URL. This method always returns an image object immediately, even if the image does not exist. The actual image data are loaded when the image is first displayed. See Chapter 6 for details on image acquisition.

The Applet Context

Locating the Ambient Browser

An applet runs inside a browser such as Netscape or the applet viewer. An applet can ask the browser to do things for it, for example, to fetch an audio clip, show a short message in the status line, or show a different Web page. The ambient browser can carry out these requests, or it can ignore them. For example, if an applet running inside the applet viewer asks the applet viewer program to show a Web page, nothing happens.

To communicate with the browser, an applet calls the `getAppletContext` method. That method returns an object of type `AppletContext`.

Inter-Applet Communication

A Web page can contain more than one applet. If a Web page contains multiple applets, they can communicate with each other. Naturally, this is an advanced technique that you probably will not need very often.

If you give `NAME` tags to each applet in the HTML file, you can use the `getApplet(String)` method of the `AppletContext` class to get a reference to the applet. For example, if your HTML file contains the tag

```
<APPLET CODE="Chart.class" WIDTH=100 HEIGHT=100 NAME="Chart1">
```

then the call

```
Applet chart1 = getAppletContext().getApplet("Chart1");
```

gives you a reference to the applet. What can you do with the reference? Provided you give the `Chart` class a method to accept new data and redraw the chart, you can call it by making the appropriate cast.

```
((Chart)chart1).setData(3, "Earth", 9000);
```

You can also list all applets on a Web page, whether or not they have a NAME tag. The getApplets method returns a so-called *enumeration object.* (You will learn more about enumeration objects in Chapter 9.) Here is a loop that prints the class names of all applets on the current page.

```
Enumeration e = getAppletContext().getApplets();
while (e.hasMoreElements())
{   Object a = e.nextElement();
    System.out.println(e.getClass().getName());
}
```

An applet cannot communicate with an applet on a different Web page.

Displaying Items in the Browser

You have access to two areas of the ambient browsers: the status line and the Web page display area. Both use methods of the AppletContext class.

You can display a string in the status line at the bottom of the browser with the showStatus message, for example

```
getAppletContext().showStatus("Loading data . . . please wait");
```

In our experience, showStatus is of limited use. The browser is also using the status line, and more often than not it will overwrite your precious message with chatter like "Applet running". Use the status line for fluff messages like "loading data . . . please wait", but not for something that the user cannot afford to miss.

You can tell the browser to show a different Web page with the showDocument method. There are several ways to do this. The simplest is with a call to showDocument with one argument, the URL you want to show.

```
URL u = new URL("http://java.sun.com");
getAppletContext().showDocument(u);
```

The problem with this call is that it opens the new Web page in the same window as your current page, thereby displacing your applet. To return to your applet, the user must select Back.

You can tell the browser to show the applet in another window by giving a second parameter in the call to showDocument. The second argument is a string. If it is the special string "_blank", the browser opens a new window with the document, instead of displacing the current document. More importantly, if you take advantage of the Netscape frame feature, you can split a browser window into multiple frames, each of which has a name. You can put your applet into one frame and have it show documents in other frames. We will discuss this in detail in the next section.

The following table shows all possible arguments to `showDocument`.

Table 8-2

Second Parameter to showDocument	Location
"_self" or none	Show the document in the current frame.
"_parent"	Show the document in the parent container.
"_top"	Show the document in the topmost frame.
"_blank"	Show in new, unnamed top-level window.
any other string	Show in the frame with that name.

A Bookmark Applet

This applet takes advantage of the frames feature in Netscape. The screen is tiled into two frames. The left frame contains a Java applet that shows a list of bookmarks. When you double-click on any of the bookmarks in the list, the corresponding Web page is displayed in the frame on the right.

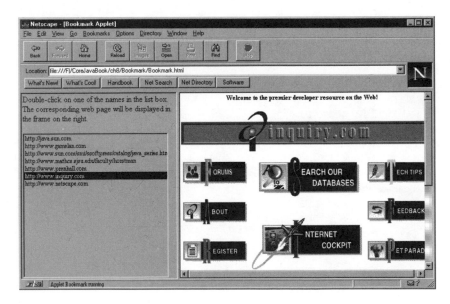

Figure 8-6

Frames are a new HTML feature, and you many not have seen the relevant tags. Here is the HTML file that defines the frames.

```
<HTML>
<HEAD>
<TITLE>Bookmark Applet</TITLE>
</HEAD>
<FRAMESET COLS="320,*">
<FRAME NAME="left" SRC="Left.html" MARGINHEIGHT=2 MARGINWIDTH=2
    SCROLLING = "no" NORESIZE>
<FRAME NAME="right" SRC="Right.html" MARGINHEIGHT=2 MARGINWIDTH=2
    SCROLLING = "yes" NORESIZE>
</FRAMESET>
</HTML>
```

We will not go over the exact syntax elements. What is important is that each frame has two essential features: a name (given by the NAME tag) and a URL (given by the SRC tag). We could not think of any good names for the frames, so we simply named them "left" and "right".

The left frame loads a file that we called Left.html, which loads the applet into the left frame. It simply specifies the applets and the bookmarks. You can customize this file for your own Web page by changing the bookmarks.

```
<HTML>
<TITLE>A Bookmark Applet</TITLE>
<BODY>
Double-click on one of the names in the list box. The correspond-
ing web page will be displayed in the frame on the right.
<P>
<APPLET CODE="Bookmark.class" WIDTH=290 HEIGHT=300>
<PARAM NAME=link_1 VALUE="http://java.sun.com">
<PARAM NAME=link_2 VALUE="http://www.gamelan.com">
<PARAM NAME=link_3 VALUE
    ="http://www.sun.com/smi/ssoftpress/catalog/java_series.html">
<PARAM NAME=link_4
VALUE="http://www.mathcs.sjsu.edu/faculty/horstman">
<PARAM NAME=link_5 VALUE="http://www.prenhall.com">
<PARAM NAME=link_6 VALUE="http://www.inquiry.com">
<PARAM NAME=link_7 VALUE="http://www.netscape.com">
</APPLET>
</BODY>
</HTML>
```

The right frame loads a dummy file that we called Right.html. (Netscape did not approve when we left the right frame blank, so we gave it a dummy file for starters.)

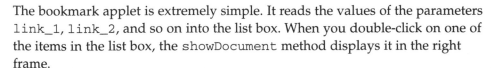

```
<HTML>
<TITLE>
Web pages will be displayed here.
</TITLE>
<BODY>
Double-click on one of the names in the list box to the left. The
web page will be displayed here.
</BODY>
</HTML>
```

The bookmark applet is extremely simple. It reads the values of the parameters
`link_1`, `link_2`, and so on into the list box. When you double-click on one of
the items in the list box, the `showDocument` method displays it in the right
frame.

```
import java.awt.*;
import java.applet.*;
import java.net.*;
import java.io.*;

public class Bookmark extends Applet
{   public void init()
    {   setLayout(new BorderLayout());
        add("Center", links);
        int i = 1;
        String s;
        while ((s = getParameter("link_" + i)) != null)
        {   links.addItem(s);
            i++;
        }
    }

    public boolean action(Event evt, Object arg)
    {   if (evt.target == links)
        {   try
            {   AppletContext context = getAppletContext();
                URL u = new URL((String)arg);
                context.showDocument(u, "right");
            } catch(Exception e)
            {   showStatus("Error " + e);
            }
        }
        else return super.action(evt, arg);
        return true;
    }

    private List links = new List(10, false);
}
```

`java.applet.Applet`

• `public AppletContext getAppletContext()`

This gives you a handle on the applet's browser environment. On most browsers, you can use this information to control the browser in which the applet is running.

`java.applet.AppletContext`

• `void showStatus(String msg)`

shows the string specified in the status line of the browser.

• `Enumeration getApplets()`

returns an enumeration (see Chapter 9) of all the applets in the same context, that is, the same Web page.

• `Applet getApplet(String name)`

returns the applet in the current context with the given name; returns `null` if none exists. Only the current Web page is searched.

• `void showDocument(URL url)`
• `void showDocument(URL url, String target)`

These calls show a new Web page in a frame in the browser. In the first form, the new page displaces the current page. The second form uses the string to identify the target frame. The target string can be one of the following: `"_self"` (show in current frame, equivalent to the first form of the method), `"_parent"` (show in parent frame), `"_top"` (show in topmost frame), and `"_blank"` (show in new, unnamed top-level window). Or it can be the name of a frame.

> Not every browser will accept these commands. For example, Sun's applet viewer does not show Web pages. The second form of the method requires that the browser support Netscape 2.0–style frames.

• `Image getImage(URL url)`

returns an image object that encapsulates the image specified by the URL. If the image does not exist, this immediately returns `null`. Otherwise, a separate thread is launched to load the image. See Chapter 6 for details on image acquisition.

• `AudioClip getAudioClip(URL url)`

returns an `AudioClip` object, which stores the sound file specified by the URL. Use the `play` method to actually play the file.

The Life Cycle of an Applet

There are four methods in the `Applet` class that give you the framework on which you build any serious applet: `init()`, `start()`, `stop()`, `destroy()`. We want to show you when these methods are called and what code you should place into them.

init

This method is used for whatever initializations are needed for your applet. This works much like a constructor—it is automatically called by the system when Java launches the applet for the first time. Common actions in an applet include processing `PARAM` values and adding user-interface components.

Applets can have a default constructor, but it is customary to perform all initialization in the `init` method, instead of the default constructor.

---

start

This method is automatically called *after* Java calls the `init` method. It is also called whenever the user returns to the page containing the applet after having gone off to other pages. This means that the `start` method can be called repeatedly, unlike the `init` method. For this reason, put the code that you want executed only once in the `init` method, rather than in the `start` method. For example, the `start` method is where you usually restart a thread for your applet, for example, to resume an animation. We will look at an example of this later in this section.

If your applet does nothing that needs to be suspended when the user leaves the current Web page, you do not need to implement this method (or the `stop` method described next).

stop

This method is automatically called when the user moves off the page on which the applet sits. It can, therefore, be called repeatedly in the same applet. The purpose is to give you a chance to stop a time-consuming activity from slowing down the system when the user is not paying attention to the applet. You should not call this method directly. If your applet does not perform animation, play audio files, or perform calculations in a thread, you do not usually need to use this method.

destroy

Unlike the `finalize` method for objects, Java is guaranteed to call this method when the browser shuts down normally. Since applets are meant to live on an HTML page, you do not need to worry about destroying the panel. This will happen automatically when the browser shuts down. What you *do* need to put in the `destroy` method is the code for reclaiming any non-memory dependent resources such as window handles that you may have consumed. (Of course, Java calls the `stop` method before calling the `destroy` method if the applet is still active.)

A Web-Crawler Applet

You do not yet know how to write a program that works with threads, but because threads are so common in sophisticated applets, we want to give you one example in this chapter. We will simply explain the general mechanism here, and you should turn to Chapter 12 for the details.

This example is similar to the bookmark example, except that the applet does something useful while you are admiring the Web page on the right-hand side.

1. It opens the Web pages whose URLs are in the list box in the left-hand side, one by one, without displaying them.

2. It then searches through the HTML tags for links to other Web pages.

3. Whenever it finds a link, it adds it to the list box.

    (Such a program is usually called a *Web crawler*.)

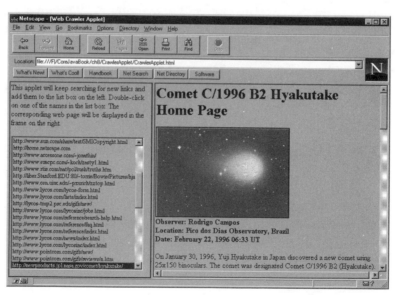

Figure 8-7

The Web crawler relentlessly fills the list box with more and more URLs until you go to another Web page; then it temporarily stops. That is as it should be—the applet should not occupy machine and network resources if you are not